# 19



# *a year in*
# Psychedelic Rock

## The bands and the sounds of the Summer of Love

Kevan Furbank

SONICBOND

sonicbondpublishing.com

Sonicbond Publishing Limited
www.sonicbondpublishing.co.uk
Email: info@sonicbondpublishing.co.uk

First Published in the United Kingdom 2021
First Published in the United States 2021

British Library Cataloguing in Publication Data:
A Catalogue record for this book is available from the British Library



ISBN 978-1-78952-155-9



Typeset in ITC Garamond & ITC Avant Garde
Printed and bound in England

Graphic design and typesetting: Full Moon Media

# 1967
## *a year in*
# Psychedelic Rock

The bands and the sounds of the Summer of Love

Kevan Furbank

SONICBOND

sonicbondpublishing.com

# 1967: a year in
# Psychedelic Rock

## Contents

# Introduction

I was six in 1967. Some may say I'm too young to be writing this book. But I'm a musical throwback – someone who loves the jazz of Duke Ellington, the smart, sassy show songs of Gershwin, Porter and Sondheim, the swing of Frank Sinatra, the sublime pop of The Beatles, the satirical snark of Frank Zappa, and the progressive pomp of King Crimson.

If I were to choose a year that, for me, encapsulates the joy of musical invention and creativity, it would be those twelve months between 1 January and 31 December 1967, when the rule book was ripped apart and folded into origami butterflies, when 'You can't do that', became 'I wonder what it would sound like if we did this'.

Before 1967, the world was mostly dull and monochrome. Sure, there were a few shards of light twinkling in the gloom. The Fab Four were shining their musical torches in the right direction with *Rubber Soul* and *Revolver*, The Beach Boys introduced us to *Pet Sounds*, and Frank Zappa was encouraging us to *Freak Out!*.

But they were like fireflies in the dark compared to the 100,000-watt beams that were suddenly switched on when 1967 burst into view. And it wasn't just our eyes that were dazzled – our ears were treated to new, exciting sounds that throbbed and parped and vibrated and clanged. It was the year of psychedelic music, when the boundaries between pop, rock, jazz, folk and the classics were smashed to pieces by precocious young men and women with their heads full of strange sounds and their veins full of LSD.

Spearheading this musical revolution was psychedelic rock – the mind-altering genre that reached its peak in 1967, dominating rock music and resulting in albums that – more than 50 years later – are still venerated as supreme examples of their art. Of course, not every song released that year was psychedelic. There was still plenty of dull, grey, middle-of-the-road sludge around, particularly in the singles charts. Look at the year's number ones, and you'll still find the likes of Engelbert Humperdinck, Sandie Shaw, and Petula Clark.

It was the album market that was the arrow point of change, where artists were exploring new sonic landscapes. Consider the timeless classics released in 1967: *Days of Future Passed* by The Moody Blues, Love's *Forever Changes*, two great Jimi Hendrix albums, *Disraeli Gears* by Cream, *Mr Fantasy* by Traffic, Jefferson Airplane's *Surrealistic Pillow* and *After Bathing at Baxter's*, and debuts from The Doors, Pink Floyd, Procol Harum and The Grateful Dead.

And standing head and shoulders above them like a multicoloured colossus is *Sgt. Pepper's Lonely Hearts Club Band*, which even today will top many a list of the Greatest Albums of All Time, Ever. It may not be, but listen to it and you'll realise that it still thinks it is.

This book is a celebration of the psychedelic music of 1967. I'll be looking at where it came from, how it became the dominant rock music of the year, and where it went next. So join me on this magical mystery tour through the psychedelic rock music of 1967.

## Turn On Your Mind

John Lennon wanted the song to sound like it was being chanted by a thousand Tibetan monks on a mountain. George Martin was an inventive producer – he had cut his teeth on comedy records rather than Elgar symphonies – but even that was beyond him. Instead, he and The Beatles created tape loops involving orchestral chords, Mellotron strings, a sitar and a cawing seagull. It didn't sound like chanting Tibetan monks – but it didn't sound like anything else, either.

Music critics are divided on what was the first psychedelic record – but, in my view, 'Tomorrow Never Knows' on the August 1966 Beatles album *Revolver* was the first song that screamed 'I'm psychedelic!' at the shocked and surprised record-buying public.

There are, of course, other contenders for the title. The Byrds' 'Eight Miles High' came out in March 1966 and contains many of the elements that define the genre – the Indian influence of raga rock; a somewhat fumbling lead break inspired by the saxophone-playing of John Coltrane, over a single, pounding chord; ethereal, otherworldly harmonies and cheeky suggestions of drug use in the title and lyrics (although the band insisted it was actually about their transatlantic flight to the UK for a tour).

Some critics go back even further and cite The Yardbirds' 'Heart Full of Soul', released nearly a year earlier in April 1965. They point to the fact that, again, there were Indian stylings in Jeff Beck's fuzz-toned guitar work – indeed, there was an early version with the riff played on sitar – and drums were augmented with tabla percussion. Or perhaps it was The Kinks' 'See My Friend', released in July that year, with its drone-like guitar and vocals drawing on the sound of the Indian tambura.

In fact, psychedelic rock didn't just pop into existence like Doctor Who's Tardis – it evolved out of other genres and drew on influences from folk, jazz, classical and what we now call *world* music. And its name goes back even further than the 1960s. The word 'psychedelic' was coined by British psychiatrist Humphry Osmond – from the Greek 'psyche', goddess of the soul, and 'deloun', to reveal. He wasn't talking about music. He was trying to find a term to describe the effects of a substance created in 1943 by Swiss chemist Albert Hoffmann, who was investigating the medicinal properties of ergot: a fungus that grows on rye bread.

Nobody really knew what to do with lysergic acid diethylamide, or LSD, as it was immediately abbreviated by Hoffmann. He thought it could cure headaches, while some believed it might be a suitable treatment for a number of unfortunate psychological conditions, such as sexual perversion and alcoholism. The CIA even tested it out on volunteers and unwitting victims as a mind-control drug.

But they knew what it *did*, which was put the user into a powerful hallucinogenic state – that later became known as a 'trip' – sometimes followed by a feeling of immense well-being. Its use spread to writers and then to

Hollywood, where movie stars such as Cary Grant became enthusiastic users. He claimed the drug made him 'truly, deeply and honestly happy' for the first time in his life.

Inevitably, LSD – also known as acid – spread through the artistic community, particularly after 1963, when the original patent ran out and anyone could have a go at making it. It didn't become illegal until 1968. US psychologist and writer Timothy Leary was an enthusiastic promoter of hallucinogenic drugs (at one stage claiming they could 'cure' homosexuality), and famously called on the 1960s counterculture to 'turn on, tune in, drop out'. Meanwhile, in 1964, a group calling itself The Merry Pranksters staged public events near San Francisco, during which LSD was taken to the accompaniment of light shows and discordant music from the newly-formed Grateful Dead.

We don't know who the very first musician to take LSD was because they're not telling. But we do know that – according to producer Paul Rothchild – Bob Dylan dropped acid in April 1964, and the effects started leaking into his lyrics, such as the 'magic swirling ship' in 'Mr. Tambourine Man' and Johnny 'in the basement, mixing up the medicine' from 'Subterranean Homesick Blues'.

In fact, it was US folk singers who performed the earliest experiments with sound, content and form that helped usher in psychedelic rock. John Fahey used odd guitar tunings, backwards tapes and Eastern instruments, recording songs inspired by Gregorian chants and classical composer Vaughan Williams: one – 'The Great San Bernadino Birthday Party' – was nineteen minutes long. Another US folk multi-instrumentalist, Sandy Bull, is seen as a precursor of the psychedelic sound – his 1963 album *Fantasias for Guitar and Banjo*, with its 22-minute opening track 'Blend', is an early example of raga rock: music built on a single-note drone typical of Indian instruments.

As the use of LSD and other drugs became more widespread, they also made themselves felt in the recorded music of the early to mid-1960s. That's not to say everyone taking LSD could make a great album, or that all great psychedelic music was inspired by hallucinogens. Frank Zappa was famously anti-drugs, and that didn't stop him from creating some seriously weird music. But it is probably true that being high made everything in the studio seem like a great idea – and, sometimes, it was.

## Light My Fire

But it wasn't just drugs that created a new genre of rock. Society was to blame, too – LSD needed a *counterculture* to embrace it. But what was this counterculture and what or who was it countering?

After World War II, the US experienced what's been described as the greatest economic expansion in world history. Despite occasional recessions, incomes soared and the middle class swelled – the white middle class, that is. At the same time, this exposed glaring inequalities and discrimination – the lid had been kept tightly sealed during the 1950s, but by the 1960s, tensions erupted.

Teenagers were not a 1960s invention. Some commentators suggest the first time adolescence became a recognisable stage in the growth and maturity of the western human being was during the 1920s, thanks to stricter child-labour laws in the West and delayed marriage. In the late 1940s, the bobby soxers – enthusiastic teenage girls named after their footwear – screamed at Frank Sinatra some 20 years before their daughters did the same to The Beatles.

But from the mid-1950s onwards, young people began turning their backs on many of their parents' moral standards and the injustices they believed the older generation supported, such as racial segregation, the subjugation of women, the Vietnam War, and the nuclear arms race. America's teenagers had the money and time to devote to social issues, having access to a changing media landscape keen to document the growing unrest and conflict. They had cars, which gave them mobility and the opportunity for more sexual experimentation, and also allowed them to travel to large, central high schools where a solely-teen culture rapidly grew. They had their own slang, their own way of dressing, their own movie heroes in James Dean and Marlon Brando, and their own music in rock 'n' roll. When Elvis wiggled his hips, parents saw the Devil in blue suede shoes. But their children saw the future.

The media industry responded by creating products it thought young people would buy. Music that was once safe, smooth and sensible, suddenly became angry and anarchic, matching the mood of its listeners. Beginning with Presley, continuing through the protest folk of Bob Dylan and the sex appeal of The Beatles, right up to the turned-on, tuned-in psychedelic sounds of the mid-1960s, modern popular music was designed for, and marketed to, young consumers. If it made their parents write angry letters to *The Times* about the corruption of modern society and the length and cleanliness of musical performers' hair, then so much the better.

By 1967, the counterculture was in full swing, with rave-ups and happenings, riots and protests. The first countries to see in the new year are usually the Pacific Island nations of Tonga, Samoa and Kiribati. But 1967 really started on the west coast of America, particularly in Los Angeles and San Francisco. They were two very different places. L.A. was where the record labels were based and the businessmen did their deals. L.A. had the money. Frisco, on the other hand, was where the hippies hung out and all the wild things happened. Frisco had most of the bands, the happenings, the festivals and the historic music venue that was Bill Graham's Fillmore West. But they were bankrolled by L.A.

Given that 1967 was supposed to be a year of love and light, it's ironic that it was bookended by albums from L.A. band The Doors, fronted by the dark, moody and threatening Jim Morrison. The Doors seemed to presage the breakdown of the Swinging Sixties, not its zenith. When Jim Morrison invited listeners to light his fire, you weren't sure if he wasn't actually asking you to join him on some destructive arson spree, and it's no surprise he became the first rock star to be arrested onstage after telling a police officer to 'Eat it'.

But for most people, the year started on a more positive, upbeat note, with exciting new albums and singles from Jefferson Airplane, Donovan, The Rolling Stones, The Byrds, and The Beatles. Given that they were all recorded at the end of 1966, it's clear something was in the air even before the new year had gotten under way. In fact, 1967 hit the ground running on 14 January with a Human Be-In at San Francisco's Golden Gate Park that drew up to 30,000 people to listen to words of trippy wisdom from speakers such as LSD guru Timothy Leary, and poetry from Allen Ginsberg. Musical accompaniment came from bands including Jefferson Airplane, Grateful Dead and Quicksilver Messenger Service. It was the first of many happenings up and down America's west coast, including what's seen as the very first pop music festival – the KFRC Fantasy Fair and Magic Mountain Music Festival on 10 and 11 June at Mt Tamalpais State Park in Marin County, California. This was followed just a few days later by the Monterey International Pop Festival: a three-day event that featured a who's-who of the US rock fraternity, The Who from the UK, Indian classical music maestro Ravi Shankar, and sealed the reputations of Janis Joplin and Jimi Hendrix.

The Summer of Love had truly arrived, as an estimated 100,000 hippies descended on San Francisco's Haight-Ashbury neighbourhood – an area that had attracted freethinkers and nonconformists since the 1950s – to put flowers in their hair and listen to psychedelic music. There was even a song about them – 'San Francisco (Be Sure To Wear Flowers in Your Hair)' – penned by John Phillips of The Mamas & the Papas and sung by his friend Scott McKenzie. It reached number 4 in the US hit parade – number 1 in the UK – and became the soundtrack to the Summer of Love, at least until *Sgt. Pepper* marched in.

But there were other gatherings that year, not all of them full of love and peace. Some ended in death and horror. The Vietnam War was still raging, and protests against the conflict gathered pace during 1967. In April, 10,000 people marched in San Francisco, culminating in demonstrations on both US coasts, and in October, a student protest at the University of Wisconsin-Madison ended in a riot injuring 76 people.

On October 21, some 70,000 Vietnam War veterans protested in Washington DC, leading President Lyndon B. Johnson to decide what the public really needed were more positive war reports. The following month, he lied to the nation: 'We are inflicting greater losses than we're taking ... We are making progress.' The nineteen-year conflict didn't end for the US until its troops were withdrawn in 1973, after at least 966,000 Vietnamese soldiers and civilians were killed, and more than 58,000 American soldiers lost their lives. The country was also rocked by violently suppressed race riots – 159 of them swept the US during the long hot summer of 1967, leaving 43 dead in Detroit and forcing a ten-day shutdown of Milwaukee. They persuaded the president to form a commission to investigate issues affecting black people, while Miami police chief Walter Headley demanded tougher action with his infamous remark, 'When the looting starts, the shooting starts': repeated by President Donald Trump in 2020.

In case you thought the only news worth mentioning was in the US, things were happening in the rest of the world that have a bearing on psychedelic rock and the movements associated with it. The UK had to wait until 1968 for its first proper music festival, but it *did* see Jimi Hendrix set fire to his guitar for the first time – at the Astoria in London in March – and the first-ever quadraphonic concert by Pink Floyd in May.

Rioting wasn't a very British thing, so it was the musicians rather than students who were at the front line of the culture clash as police targeted long-haired menaces such as Keith Richards and Mick Jagger of The Rolling Stones over their drug use. Support came not from grassroots street activism, but from the usually toffee-nosed *Times* newspaper, with its now-famous editorial, 'Who breaks a butterfly upon a wheel?', and from musicians such as The Who, who recorded two Stones songs as a fundraising single. The Stones responded with 'We Love You', which featured the sound of a cell door clanging shut.

The Beatles were national treasures, so they generally escaped the attention of P.C. Plod, despite their drug use apparently being on open display in songs such as 'Lucy in the Sky With Diamonds' and 'A Day in the Life': both banned by the BBC. But 1967 was the last year the fab four would be treated as rock royalty – it was all downhill after the death of their manager Brian Epstein in August that year.

Across the world, there were wars, coups, tragedies, disasters and triumphs, as there are in every year in human history. But the musical soundtrack of 1967 remained mostly upbeat and out of this world, as young bands and their fans attempted to make some sense of the chaos.

## Embryonic Journey

But this is *still* only part of the story. The music industry itself was on a strange trip, as power shifted from record labels and studios to the artists themselves. Previously, pop stars were mostly puppets, told what to sing, what to wear and what to say, as portly, balding, cigar-smoking managers pulled the strings and counted the money. Studios decided how recordings would sound – some, such as EMI at Abbey Road, insisted their producers wore shirts and ties, and their engineers, white lab coats, and famously had strict rules about what could or could not be done on a recording. Artists either shaped up or shipped out.

But along came The Beatles, who, right from the start, insisted on writing most of their own songs – they point-blank refused to release Mitch Murray's 'How Do You Do It?' as their second single, recording their own 'Please Please Me' instead. Luckily, they wrote great songs, and their combination of catchy melodies and cheeky Scouse personalities was catnip for the record-buying public.

Soon, The Beatles were so successful and making so much money for EMI that they gradually took control of the studio, with the help and encouragement of George Martin, who was 20 years older than his charges but still younger than many of his colleagues in the former townhouse in St John's Wood, London. The Beatles began to say, 'Can you make it sound like it's being chanted by a thousand Tibetan monks?' or 'I wonder what it would sound like if we had a solo on a French horn'.

Inspired by the fab four, other artists began throwing their weight around in the studio, experimenting with new ideas, some of which actually worked. Yes, it was self-indulgent, all about pleasing the artists rather than the consumers, but I would contend that's what all great art is. And it turned out that, in a surprisingly large number of instances, what pleased the artists, pleased the listeners too, because they were all the same age with the same interests.

In this internet age, it's difficult to imagine not being able to hear new releases at the click of a mouse. But there was a time – before recorded sound – when you might hear your favourite tune just two or three times in your life. In the 1960s, there was AM radio, but it was dominated by easy listening and the classics. In the UK, the BBC seemed to make a point of ignoring anything mildly interesting, to steer its audience towards big bands and crooners.

But there was also FM – a better-quality but more expensive system that nobody really bothered about until the US passed a law insisting that radio stations use it for something more than just repeating their AM output. Some stations let younger, renegade DJs take control of it and do what they wanted, which frequently included playing the latest rock albums all the way through without interrupting them with mindless chatter. Young people who could afford an FM receiving set suddenly found a new world of music open to them.

At the same time, there was the growth of pirate radio – unlicensed stations on land or sea, playing a diet of modern popular music. The BBC eventually responded by succeeding the old Light Programme with Radio 1, making its debut in September 1967 with The Move's 'Flowers in the Rain'.

While we're on the subject of technological advances, it should also be mentioned that 1967 saw a boom in sales of headphones, and was the year eight-track tape players could be installed in cars, so one could hear music on the move.

There is one last social change that affected music, and that was education. Most of the 1950s rock 'n' rollers did little more than graduate from high school. But in the 1960s, particularly in the UK, bands were being formed by art school students with an interest in design or literature. Some were even musically trained. Mick Ratledge, one of the founders of Soft Machine (who had a 1967 hit with 'Love Makes Sweet Music'), played classical piano and clarinet. Jim Morrison of The Doors majored in film at UCLA. Ray Manzarek, also a Door, got an undergraduate degree in Chicago. Tom Rapp of psychedelic folksters Pearls Before Swine practised civil rights law. Even two of The Beatles got into grammar school – the *clever kids*' route – after the age of eleven.

When the songwriters of the 1960s sat down to pen a tune, they had more cultural and literary references to draw from. Buddy Holly, for all his melodic genius, never wrote a song inspired by *The Tibetan Book of the Dead*. But John Lennon did, even though he was thrown out of art school. In the 1960s, eyes, ears and minds were more open. And what went in came out again, in the form of psychedelic rock.

## Strange Brew

'Tomorrow Never Knows' divided critics when it was first released. What is this noise?', the unimpressed faction asked, praising Ringo Starr's stuttering drum rhythm as the only thing that was good about it. Clearly, those critics hadn't been listening. Popular music was changing rapidly, becoming more complicated, challenging, questioning and provoking. Old ideas about how songs should sound, how they were constructed, what they were about and what instruments should be used to create them, were being swept away by the new breed of young rock experimenters.

But what makes a song psychedelic? If you search online for examples of psychedelic rock albums, you will find a bewildering selection. Most of us would agree that Pink Floyd's remarkable debut, *Piper at the Gates of Dawn*, fits the bill. Look at the title for a start. But The Monkees? The Who? Jimi Hendrix? The Beach Boys? Pearls Before Swine? Donovan?

The genre was dominated by artists from the US and UK – yes, there were psychedelic bands in other countries (including, surprisingly, Cambodia), and these will be looked at in a later chapter. But none had the same influence or the same commercial clout as the groups and albums that came out of Britain and America.

There are also distinct differences between the psychedelia of the US and the UK. In America, it was strongly influenced by the protest culture of folk music (US folk was singer/songwriters excoriating society on acoustic guitars; British folk was chartered accountants in chunky sweaters singing 36-verse a cappella sea shanties in the back rooms of pubs where they couldn't be heard by the general public), and when it went electric, spawned angry young bands with abrasive guitar sounds.

UK psychedelia was more whimsical and surreal, inspired by the post-war humour of The Goons and the nonsense poetry of Edward Lear. It also wallowed in idyllic childhood nostalgia, drawing particularly on a rose-tinted view of the Edwardian and Victorian eras.

But they all had something about them for so many people to slot them into the same pigeonhole. Perhaps we can identify a set of basic ingredients, a recipe that marks them out, that enables us to say with confidence that, yes, The 13th Floor Elevators were psychedelic, and Herb Alpert and the Tijuana Brass definitely were not.

Here then, is my psychedelic checklist for you. Not all the songs and albums we will discuss, contain *all* these ingredients. But some of them at least must be present to earn the right to be labelled psychedelic.

## Thoughts and Words

For most of the history of popular song, lyrics were about love. To paraphrase Earl Okin (who released the unsuccessful single 'Yellow Petals' in 1967 before, many years later, carving out a career as a musical comedian), most songs said 'I love her and I've got her', 'I love her, but he's got her', and, very occasionally,

'I love her, but he's welcome to her'. When they strayed from talking about love, it was for novelty songs, music hall and stage-and-screen musicals.

But the early 1960s saw US folk singers turn away from love, to sing about society and its failings. Bob Dylan said 'The Times They Are A-Changin', Phil Ochs insisted 'I Ain't Marching Anymore' and even Sam Cooke thought 'A Change Is Gonna Come'. By 1967, Country Joe and the Fish felt like they were 'fixin' to die', with a vaudeville number that included the couplet, 'Ain't no time to wonder why / Whoopee, we're all gonna die.' In fact, black humour seemed to be the best way to deal with the mind-numbing tragedy of the Vietnam War, with Arlo Guthrie telling a whimsical tale of how his conviction for littering made him morally unsuitable for murdering Vietnamese children, in the 18-minute 'Alice's Restaurant Massacree'.

But it wasn't all about Vietnam. LSD either unhinged minds or opened them – the result was a flood of fantasy themes and stream-of-consciousness lyrics that sometimes made no attempt to make any sense whatsoever. Again, we can probably point a finger at Bob Dylan and his 1965 song 'Subterranean Homesick Blues', consisting of a seemingly disjointed stream of phrases and images – and we have already pointed out how his drug experiments seeped into his songs. By 1967, bands were being pretty blatant about their acid trips, with Jefferson Airplane singing, 'Here in crystal chandelier I'm home / Too many days I've left unstoned', Jimi Hendrix saying the frequently hilariously misheard 'Excuse me while I kiss the sky', and The Velvet Underground on their debut album recording a song that was simply called 'Heroin'.

When it came to stringing together apparent stream-of-consciousness lyrics, you would be hard-pressed to beat The Beatles in 1967. In songs such as 'Strawberry Fields Forever', 'Lucy in the Sky With Diamonds' and 'I Am the Walrus', John Lennon let his mind relax and float downstream, conjuring up lines that seemed to exist purely for the sounds they made. Lennon's inspirations were the Goon-ish fun of surreal British comedy and poetry – he even published books that were lauded for their inventive, psychedelic imagery. And he spent most of the mid-1960s stoned – if it wasn't for Paul McCartney pushing him to compose and record, I doubt the fab four would've made any more albums after 1965's *Rubber Soul*.

The fantasy themes – that frequently harked back to childhood and nursery rhymes – were mostly a British preoccupation: it seemed many psychedelic artists couldn't wait to get back to a more innocent time. So 'Yellow Submarine' combined trippy colours with a childish ditty (sung by future *Thomas the Tank Engine* narrator Ringo Starr), the Small Faces' 'Itchycoo Park' took us over a 'bridge of sighs' to get high in fields of green, and the Airplane followed the 'White Rabbit' from Alice in Wonderland.

So we can see that, lyrically, practically anything goes in psychedelic music, even love – bands still sang about the four-letter word, but it was rarely a boy-meets-girl romance, more a universal love that would unite the world. Again, we look to Lennon for giving us the anthem to one-ness for 1967. 'All You Need Is Love', he sang. Sadly, he was wrong, but his heart was in the right place.

## Good Vibrations

From the mid-1950s, rock 'n' roll established the troika of guitar, bass and drums as the basis for popular music, with a bit of piano thrown in, and they continued to be the dominant instruments of the psychedelic era – indeed, they remain today the noise-makers of choice for all proper, bona fide rock bands.

But the guitar, in particular, changed its sound – it became buzzy and fuzzy thanks to distortion boxes first made commercially available in 1962. The sound reflected the distorting effect of drugs and also helped some of those angry US garage bands sound even meaner. Sometimes the bass got fuzzy too – such as on 'Think for Yourself' on The Beatles *Rubber Soul* – but it never really caught on, despite the efforts of Canterbury musician Hugh Hopper a few years later.

There was also the wah-wah effect, available commercially as a guitar pedal from 1966 onwards and embraced by Eric Clapton of Cream on 'Tales of Brave Ulysses' and Jimi Hendrix on, well, practically everything. And sometimes the guitar was recorded and then played backwards (originally on The Beatles' 1966 B-side 'Rain', but used frequently thereafter).

The piano made a bit of a comeback, frequently played with ham-fisted amateurism by guitarists translating their knowledge of chords to the keyboard as they messed about in the studio. The Hammond organ – originally intended for churches but embraced by the jazz fraternity – became a rock instrument particularly favoured by Ray Manzarek of The Doors, Alan Price of The Animals, Mark Stein of Vanilla Fudge and, of course, Procol Harum on their 1967 smash-hit 'A Whiter Shade of Pale'.

Another keyboard instrument became popular at this time – the mighty Mellotron. Designed and built in Birmingham, it was an early sound sampler that played eight-second tapes of instruments when the keys were depressed, and was originally intended for home use. But bands who wanted to have that full, orchestral sound without paying for a full orchestra, seized upon it as a useful psychedelic studio tool.

Graham Bond was the first to use it, in 1965, followed by Manfred Mann in 1966. Mike Pinder of The Moody Blues had actually worked in the Mellotron factory and persuaded The Beatles to buy one, which they used on 'Strawberry Fields Forever'. Pinder himself reworked his Mellotron for a fuller classical sound for his band's 1967 masterpiece *Days of Future Passed*, and Brian Jones of The Rolling Stones used it during their brief psychedelic period. Later, it would become a ubiquitous part of progressive rock.

Another new keyboard instrument made available to psychedelic bands was the Moog synthesizer, debuted by US engineer Robert Moog in 1964 (pronounced 'Moge' to rhyme with 'vogue'). With its huge board of modulators, oscillators and other electronic gizmos, users could obtain practically any sound they wanted – not necessarily a musical one but certainly something out of this world. Early users included The Monkees, The Doors, Grateful Dead, The Beatles and The Stones, but it took a few more years to become established as a rock instrument.

Bands that could afford a proper orchestra, frequently used one, as psychedelic music drew inspiration from the classical world. There were trumpets, French horns, even full string orchestras – sometimes just tuning up, as at the start of *Sgt. Pepper* or linking rock songs in an album-length suite, such as on *Days of Future Passed*. Flutes, piccolos and recorders decorated songs from the folk end of psychedelia, while tuned percussion such as marimbas leaked over from the jazz world, particularly in Frank Zappa's band from 1967 onwards.

As we've already seen, Indian instruments began to make their presence felt in western music, thanks to Ravi Shankar making a deliberate effort to spread the popularity of the sitar by touring Europe and the US. In 1965, George Harrison picked one up on the set of The Beatles second film *Help!* – the plot involved a spoof on the Indian thuggee cult, and the sitar was used on the soundtrack. He played it on John Lennon's composition 'Norwegian Wood', and from that moment on, there was no stopping the instrument's ubiquitous use in psychedelic music. Notoriously difficult to play – the high action would shred your fingers to bits – the sitar nonetheless insinuated its way onto many albums and singles in the mid-1960s – embellishing Traffic's 'Paper Sun', The Rolling Stones' 'Paint It Black', and eventually taking over entire songs with other Indian instruments, as on the Harrison compositions, 'Love You To', 'Within You Without You', and 'The Inner Light'.

The introduction of Indian and Middle Eastern instruments helped shape some of the melodies bands were creating. So-called 'raga rock' came from the scales used in Indian classical music. The western diatonic scale in C major would move to D, E, F, G, A, B and end on C again. But eastern scales could throw in a D flat, A flat and B flat, creating mysterious, sinuous melodies that instantly define themselves to western ears. Add the drone of the tambura or Indian harmonium, plus the intricate rhythms produced by eastern percussion instruments, and you had a whole new soundscape for western bands to explore.

## Stop, Hey, What's That Sound?

Audience laughter, animal noises, bells ringing, strange backward voices or just a mélange of odd noises meant to signify... well, something trippy. Many psychedelic rock bands plundered their studio's sound effects libraries to add something mysterious and entertaining to their songs. Donovan sang about a magpie, and opened with the bird's distinctive, clattering call. The Beatles put a high-pitched tone only audible to dogs on the run-out groove of *Sgt. Pepper*, and Pink Floyd devoted nearly half the length of their song 'Bike' to random bangings, boingings and twangings. If a song mentioned a fire engine, you put on the sound of a fire engine. It was frequently as simple and straightforward as that.

## Changes

The first songs were just verses sung to the same repetitive melody – you'll see what I mean if you listen to early British folk music. 'Matty Groves' – a ballad from the early 17th century that was later rocked up by Fairport Convention – is a typical example: nineteen or twenty verses consisting of two lines each, repeated until the end when the titular Matty has been murdered by a cuckolded lord.

Then choruses were added, particularly if you wanted everyone to sing along at the same time, perhaps while doing boring, repetitive work onboard a ship. So sea shanties (originally *chants*) will commonly have a verse by a single voice, before a sing-along chorus as salty sea dogs spliced the mainbrace or turned the capstan.

As popular songs became more sophisticated and composed, rather than being built up and handed down through the oral tradition, writers introduced the middle eight or bridge, so-called because it tended to be in the middle of the song and lasted for about eight bars. This created a bit of a melodic change, a small diversion from the main tune that created a bridge between the first half and the second. Originally a simple adaptation of the original melody and chord sequence, the middle eight assumed more importance as composers attempted to find ways to make it more interesting.

One could say that popular song reached its zenith in terms of composition from the 1920s to the 1950s, when the musical masters of Tin Pan Alley – Jerome Kern, George Gershwin, Irving Berlin, Cole Porter and many others – used their skills to create almost mini-symphonies that played clever games with structure. Then rock 'n' roll came along and dumbed the form down to verse/chorus/verse/chorus, sometimes a verse instrumental, then a repeat of the chorus to the end. If you were lucky, you got a rudimentary middle eight.

But psychedelic rock brought back the idea of playing with structure, sometimes going back to primitive forms such as on 'Tomorrow Never Knows', or going the other way, creating songs that twist and turn in surprising ways, such as with The Beach Boys' 'Good Vibrations', or practically anything by the early Pink Floyd. In the past, structure dictated the song – by the mid-1960s, the song dictated structure. There were no longer any boundaries – your composition could have as many chord changes in it as you liked, or the whole thing could be performed on one chord or even one note. And it could also be as long as you liked.

Most songs were three minutes or less, so they could fit on one side of a 45 rpm single. This wasn't because it was the best length for a song, but because of the time restrictions of the recording medium, stretching back to the days of 78s. Adam Faith's 1959 single 'What Do You Want?' was just one minute and

38 seconds long: too short to even boil an egg. Anything that exceeded the time limits – such as classical music written in the days when recording wasn't even dreamt of – had to be stretched across several 78s and packaged like a photograph album (hence the use of the word to describe an LP).

The introduction of the commercially available long-playing record in 1948 allowed artists the opportunity to stretch out. We've seen that some folk instrumentalists as far back as 1963 were creating tracks that filled the whole side of a 33 rpm album – they were joined by jazzers, such as John Coltrane with *A Love Supreme* in 1964 and *Ascension* the following year.

In 1966, Frank Zappa filled one side of The Mothers of Invention's double-LP debut *Freak Out!* with one track, 'The Return of the Son of Monster Magnet', while The Who created a nine-minute mini-opera, 'A Quick One, While He's Away', in the same year. As the 1960s wore on, bands experimented further with the long-form, resulting eventually in the progressive rock excesses of Yes on *Tales From Topographic Oceans* – a double LP with just four songs on it, one per side.

A word here on improvisation. The early jazz bands took solos because that helped stretch out a song and keep people on the dance floor. Gradually, the ability to improvise effectively became a badge of honour, certainly in jazz where, by the 1940s, songs became little more than the basis on which to build improvised performances. Extensive improvisation in rock took longer to develop, partly because of the time restrictions of recording media but also because, well, many of the rock instrumentalists were not really good enough.

Listen, and grimace to some guitarists trying to play a lead break in the 1950s and early-1960s. Even George Harrison's early attempts sound ham-fisted and amateurish, and few rock musicians were any good at it even by 1967. The exceptions include guitarists Jimi Hendrix, Eric Clapton and Jeff Beck, and the keyboard-playing of Ray Manzarek of The Doors, Stevie Winwood of Traffic and Matthew Fisher of Procol Harum. Generally, there wasn't a lot of improvisation in psychedelic rock – the twenty-minute drum solos would come later.

## Sing This All Together (See What Happens)

The idea of an album having a unifying theme was nothing particularly new – Woody Guthrie did it with *Dust Bowl Ballads* in 1940, so did Frank Sinatra for Capitol in the 1950s, and jazz composers – notably Duke Ellington – did it frequently throughout their careers. But the idea of an album telling a story that had to be listened to from start to finish, now that was something new that perhaps drew more from symphonic classical composers than dusty old Woody. The Moody Blues' *Days of Future Passed* is a prime example – an album that presents a musical 'day', starting with 'Dawn Is a Feeling', and finishing with 'Nights in White Satin'.

Real, full-blown storytelling albums such as The Who's *Tommy* and *The Lamb Lies Down on Broadway* by Genesis, had to wait until the progressive rock years. But the seeds were planted in 1967 – with releases such as *The Who Sell Out*, which linked mostly unrelated songs with spoofs of radio advertisements and public service announcements, and Frank Zappa's *Absolutely Free*, which presented each LP side as suites of interconnected songs ripping into American politics and culture. More obscurely, *The Story of Simon Simopath* – by UK band Nirvana – was ostensibly a life-to-death narrative about a boy who dreams of having wings.

The concept went beyond the music and extended to the covers and packaging. Originally, album covers were just plain coloured paper, but in 1938, graphic designer Alex Steinweiss invented cover art for Columbia Records, and others soon followed suit. But for the next twenty years, album art usually consisted of a picture of the band or artist, sometimes caught in mid-performance, sometimes scowling or grinning inanely at the potential record buyer.

Slowly, cover art became, well, more arty. Look at how The Beatles' covers developed, from four fresh-faced lads looking down from a stairwell at EMI's London HQ on *Please Please Me* (1963), moody half-lit profiles on *With the Beatles* (1963), jokey film-strip larks on *A Hard Day's Night* (1964), distorted, rubbery faces on *Rubber Soul* (1965), to cartoon-like line drawing and cutouts on *Revolver* (1966). By the time we get to 1967, we are treated to the iconic montage of the fab four surrounded by their heroes and villains on *Sgt. Pepper's Lonely Heart Club Band*. Others eschewed showing the artistes at all, opting instead for swirls of trippy colours, the band names going under, over, sideways and down in big, bulbous text or drippy candle-wax letters. Very frequently, the covers were more psychedelic than the music. Imagine the disappointment of people buying the debut album by Big Brother and the Holding Company, with the band members' faces contained within the petals of a multi-coloured flower, only to find that in the grooves was a hurriedly-recorded, poorly-produced collection of weak songs and subdued performances.

But this was the year when the album was seen as a complete artistic product, when musicians took pains to ensure the packaging reflected and sometimes amplified the musical contents. It was also the year when the gatefold cover became ubiquitous. It wasn't a new idea at all – it was common for Broadway and Hollywood musical soundtrack albums, and in 1957, an Elvis Presley Christmas release was presented as a gatefold.

By 1967, the gatefold became standard practice for many major releases in the US and UK (although other countries were frequently short-changed with a single sleeve), and musicians and record companies took the opportunity to use that inner 24-inch spread to present dramatic and artistic images, employing some of the current top photographers and designers. Despite this, in 1967, the double album remained a rarity for anything other than compilations, even though both Bob Dylan and Frank Zappa indulged in the practice in 1966.

## Heroes and Villains

So who were the most popular and influential psychedelic rockers of 1967? Those two terms are not necessarily linked – some of the bands and albums now recognised as the genre's touchstones barely troubled the charts at the time of their release. And that leaves your humble author in a bit of a quandary. Should we concentrate on the recordings that fired the imagination and opened the wallets of the record-buying public of 1967? Or can we benefit from the wonders of hindsight and critical reassessment? In the event, what I have for you is a mixture of both – we cannot ignore the big sellers, but we must also pay tribute to the trailblazers and the ones with staying power who went on to even greater things.

The other puzzler is whether we concentrate on bands and musicians or albums. In later years, that would be a no-brainer because album releases slowed down to a point where most artists still rarely release more than one a year. But in 1967, the average psychedelic rock band could well release two albums in a year, along with three or four non-album singles that also deserve to be discussed. The Beatles did it. So did The Doors, Jefferson Airplane, The Rolling Stones, Donovan, and Jimi Hendrix, to name but a few.

Unlike the internet, a book can't have virtually unlimited space, so we have had to be selective here. Some of your favourite bands won't make the cut because there is no room for them or, even more unkindly, because I have decided they just ain't psychedelic enough. So farewell to The Monkees – the mere fact that 1967 was the year they gained control of their music and began actually playing on their own releases doesn't make them psychedelic rock. But The Beach Boys make it in, even though 1967 marked the start of their long slow decline, because how can one ignore such important tracks as 'Good Vibrations' and 'Heroes and Villains', and also dwell on the alleged lost masterpiece, the *Smile* album?

So put on your tie-dye shirts, slip into some moccasins, string your love beads around your necks, and let us delve deep into the psychedelic rock of 1967. A word of caution – tearing out the pages of this book, rolling them up and smoking them, will *not* give you a high. But the music most certainly will.

## The Beatles

Key personnel:
George Harrison: vocals, guitars, percussion, sitar, tambura, swarmandal
John Lennon: vocals, guitars, keyboards, percussion
Paul McCartney: vocals, bass, guitars, keyboards, percussion
Ringo Starr: drums, percussion

### History

Formed in Liverpool, England, in 1960, their name was inspired by Buddy Holly's backing group The Crickets, with a letter changed to emphasise 'beat'. Turned down by several record companies, they were eventually signed to EMI's novelty-record label Parlophone, run by producer George Martin. Original drummer Pete Best was replaced by Richard Starkey – alias Ringo Starr – during recording of their first single, 'Love Me Do', which reached a respectable number 17 in the UK. The follow-up, 'Please Please Me', hit number 2, while the third release 'From Me to You' started a string of eleven number 1s and the spread of Beatlemania across the world. Regarded as the most influential pop/rock band of all time, they are also the best selling music act ever, with estimated worldwide record sales of 600,000,000. They broke up in 1970.

### Key releases in 1967

**'Penny Lane' / 'Strawberry Fields Forever'** (Single)
Both songs by Lennon/McCartney
Double A-side single
Label: Parlophone (UK), Capitol (US)
Release date: 13 February 1967
Charts: UK: 2; US: 8; Australia: 1; Netherlands: 1; Norway: 1; Sweden: 1

**Sgt. Pepper's Lonely Hearts Club Band** (Album)
All songs by Lennon/McCartney except as noted.
Label: Parlophone (UK), Capitol (US)
Release date: 1 June 1967 (UK), 2 June 1967 (US)
Charts: UK: 1; US: 1 (and many, many other countries)
Side 1: 1.'Sgt. Pepper's Lonely Hearts Club Band' 2.'With a Little Help From My Friends' 3. 'Lucy in the Sky With Diamonds' 4. 'Getting Better' 5. 'Fixing a Hole' 6. 'She's Leaving Home' 7. 'Being for the Benefit of Mr Kite'. Side 2: 1. 'Within You Without You (George Harrison)' 2. 'When I'm Sixty-Four' 3. 'Lovely Rita' 4. 'Good Morning Good Morning' 5. 'Sgt. Pepper's Lonely Hearts Club Band (Reprise)' 6. 'A Day in the Life'.

**'All You Need Is Love' / 'Baby, You're a Rich Man'** (Single)
Both songs by Lennon/McCartney.
Label: Parlophone (UK), Capitol (US)

Release date: 7 July 1967
Charts: UK: 1; US: 1 (and many, many other countries)

**'Hello Goodbye' / 'I Am the Walrus'** (Single)
Both songs by Lennon/McCartney.
Label: Parlophone (UK), Capitol (US)
Release date: 24 November 1967
Charts: UK: 1; US: 1 (and many, many other countries)

**Magical Mystery Tour** (Album)
All songs by Lennon/McCartney except as noted.
Label: Capitol (US)
Release date: 27 November 1967 (Originally in US only)
Charts: US: 1
Side 1: 1. 'Magical Mystery Tour' 2. 'The Fool on the Hill' 3. 'Flying' (Lennon/McCartney/Harrison/Starr) 4. 'Blue Jay Way' (Harrison) 5. 'Your Mother Should Know' 6. 'I Am the Walrus' Side 2: 1. 'Hello Goodbye' 2. 'Strawberry Fields Forever' 3. 'Penny Lane' 4. Baby, You're a Rich Man' 5. 'All You Need Is Love'

**Magical Mystery Tour** (Double EP)
All songs by Lennon/McCartney except as noted.
Label: Parlophone (UK)
Release date: 8 December 1967 (UK)
Charts: UK: 2 (Held off the number 1 spot by 'Hello Goodbye'); Netherlands: 2; Australia: 2; New Zealand: 2; Sweden: 2
Record 1 – Side 1: 1. 'Magical Mystery Tour' 2. 'Your Mother Should Know'
Record 1 – Side 2: 1. 'I Am the Walrus'
Record 2 – Side 1: 1. 'The Fool on the Hill' 2. 'Flying' (Lennon/McCartney/Harrison/Starr). Record 2 – Side 2: 1. 'Blue Jay Way' (Harrison).

The Beatles had gone very quiet after *Revolver* was released in August 1966. Apart from the usual Christmas flexi disc to fan club members and a *Greatest Hits* in December, there was no peep from Messrs. Harrison, Lennon, McCartney and Starr, and no inkling of what they were up to behind the doors of EMI Studios in Abbey Road, London. In a *Melody Maker* interview from January 1967, The Who's guitarist and main songwriter Pete Townshend complained: 'I'm a bit disappointed they're not making records. If they are, then I wish they'd hurry up. They are basically my main source of inspiration – and everybody else's for that matter'.

They were not to disappoint. Six months after their last collection of wholly new material – and about the same length of time since they had given up touring – The Beatles released a double-A-side single that showed they were using their studio time to the full, and also making music that couldn't possibly be reproduced on stage by four lads with two guitars, bass and drums.

'Penny Lane' and 'Strawberry Fields Forever' are prime slices of British psychedelia, marrying cutting-edge music technology and studio effects with rose-tinted nostalgia and genre-busting instrumentation. Both songs are about geographical places in the band's home city of Liverpool – but there the resemblance ends. They reflect the personalities of the people who wrote them: Paul McCartney's 'Penny Lane' is clever, sophisticated, witty and carefully constructed; John Lennon's 'Strawberry Fields Forever' is a jumbled stream of consciousness that says more about the writer's mental state than the Salvation Army children's home it was named after. It had to be pieced together from two separate recordings, because characteristically, Lennon wasn't entirely sure what he wanted.

'Strawberry Fields…' came first, written by Lennon while he was filming *How I Won the War* in Spain in 1966. Feeling lonely and vulnerable and perhaps searching for some meaning in his life after the end of The Beatles as a touring entity, he began recording some ideas and lyrics, initially without any reference to the Strawberry Fields home in the title. 'Living is easy with eyes closed / Misunderstanding all you see' seems pretty obvious and straightforward. So are 'It's getting hard to be someone but it all works out / It doesn't matter much to me.' Then things get a bit obscure.

In an interview with *Playboy* in 1980, Lennon explained:

> The second verse goes, 'No one I think is in my tree'. Well, I was too shy and self-doubting. Nobody seems to be as hip as me, is what I was saying. Therefore, I must be crazy or a genius – 'I mean it must be high or low', the next line. There was something wrong with me, I thought, because I seemed to see things other people didn't see. I thought I was crazy or an egomaniac for claiming to see things other people didn't see. As a child, I would say, 'But this is going on!', and everybody would look at me as if I was crazy. I always was so psychic or intuitive or poetic or whatever you want to call it, that I was always seeing things in a hallucinatory way. It was scary as a child, because there was nobody to relate to.

The song had no identifiable chorus until early November when Lennon was inspired by memories of playing in the grounds of the Strawberry Field home near where he lived in Liverpool. The line 'nothing to get hung about' came from his Aunt Mimi's orders not to play there, and his response 'They can't hang you for it'. Later, he said he chose the name because it was groovy-sounding: '...because Strawberry Fields is anywhere you want to go.'

Recorded across November and December 1966, 'Strawberry Fields Forever' is famously constructed out of two different versions: one relatively gentle and dreamlike, the other more manic, with Ringo's drumming to the fore (the edit is dead-on the one-minute mark). The final version is 'Tomorrow Never Knows' with knobs on – the longest recording The Beatles had done so far and the first to feature a false ending.

It opens tentatively and mysteriously, with McCartney playing a Mellotron on the flute setting, and includes cello, flute, harpsichord and brass, along with a vast array of percussion devices, particularly in what has been described as the 'free-form coda' at the end (which apparently used to drive DJs nuts). Lennon's voice adds to the dream-like quality by slurring the lyrics together and slowing down the second section to match the tempo and take the recording from C major to B flat, gives the vocal a swirly, smoky quality.

Add George Harrison's swarmandal (a sort of Indian zither) and touches of slide guitar, plus George Martin's brass and string arrangement, and you have a mini-symphony that seems to encapsulate the entire psychedelic era in four mind-blowing minutes.

And, finally, 'Strawberry Fields Forever' ends with a mystery: as the free-form coda fades in and back out again, you can clearly hear Lennon say 'I buried Paul' – a statement that was later seized upon as proof that McCartney had died in 1966 and been replaced by a double. Except Lennon actually says 'cranberry sauce'. And why not.

The song exhibits all the psychedelic rock credentials: stream-of-consciousness lyrics, off-beat instrumentation, a wistful, ethereal atmosphere, a simple chorus/verse/chorus/verse/chorus/verse structure, the cacophony of noise at the end, the fake fade-out and, finally, a mystery phrase for listeners to puzzle over.

Paul McCartney composed 'Penny Lane' as an answer to 'Strawberry Fields…', almost as a lighthearted balance to the latter's dark soul. Where Lennon's song is about himself, McCartney's is about a made-up cast of characters. Where Lennon's is dense and messy, McCartney's is clean and precise. Where Lennon's nostalgia was hinted at, McCartney's was explicit.

Indeed, 'Penny Lane' takes on greater stature because of its proximity to 'Strawberry Fields…'. On its own, it comes across as clever but a bit lightweight, its psychedelic credentials less obvious. But coupled with its evil twin sibling, it seems a deliberate attempt to dampen down the menace: an 'upper' to Lennon's 'downer'. It's important to listen to them the right way around – Lennon's first, then McCartney's. Capitol Records in America frequently butchered The Beatles' albums but did the right thing when they packaged the *Magical Mystery Tour* EP and the year's singles into an album at the end of the year, putting the two songs in the right order on side two.

'Penny Lane' opens with McCartney's voice and simple, descending piano chords, as he sings about the barber with photographs of 'every head he's had the pleasure to have known', the fireman with his hourglass, and the nurse selling poppies from a tray for Remembrance Day. The barber really existed, as does Penny Lane as a district and also a street – in fact, Lennon was the only one of The Beatles who actually lived in the Penny Lane district.

The song heads into a different key for a sunny, optimistic chorus that ends with 'meanwhile back..', as if McCartney is narrating the plot of a TV soap opera. Lennon may be living with his eyes closed, misunderstanding all he sees, but McCartney has his eyes wide open and is recording everything in front of him. He made the following quote in *The Beatles Anthology* book:

> It's part fact, part nostalgia for a great place – blue suburban skies, as we remember it, and it's still there. And we put in a joke or two: 'Four of fish and finger pie.' The women would never dare say that, except to themselves. Most people wouldn't hear it, but 'finger pie' is just a nice little joke for the Liverpool lads who like a bit of smut.

For me, 'Penny Lane''s psychedelic credentials rest not so much on its unabashed optimistic nostalgia but on the unique lead break played not on guitar but on a piccolo trumpet. Here's George Martin from the same source:

> They were always asking me about classical instruments of the orchestra. I introduced them to a bassoon, bass clarinet, or whatever, but I had never introduced them to a Bach trumpet. But Paul, one evening, watched on television a Bach Brandenberg Concerto, and he came to me the following day and said: 'Great sound I heard last night, a tremendously high trumpet.' 'Yes,' I said, 'It's a Bach trumpet'. 'Can we use it,' he asked. 'Yes, of course we can,' I replied. It never occurred to me, but it occurred to him. So, we got the guy from the London Symphony Orchestra, David Mason, to play piccolo trumpet, and that was that.

David Mason did it in one take, and it's become the most famous piccolo trumpet piece in rock. It not only feeds into the nostalgia theme but lifts the song into the realms of something timeless and classic: Get Bach, if you will. Add Ringo playing a handbell at the reference 'the fireman rushes in', plus the slight feedback accompanying the final chord, and you have a bona fide psychedelia classic, but one whose credentials are enhanced by the song it mirrored.

There is one final psychedelic touch we should mention – before the single was released, The Beatles recorded a film to be shown on TV – a precursor to the modern-day music video – so they wouldn't have to appear anywhere in person. Filmed at Knole Park in Sevenoaks, Kent, it had little to do with either song, showing the foursome larking about, jumping from trees and pouring paint over a piano. But with close-ups, jump-cuts and some of the footage shot backwards, it was almost as disturbing as 'Strawberry Fields...' itself.

Both tracks were originally intended for The Beatles' next album, but the record company wanted a single, so it was rushed out (and kept off the number 1 in the UK slot by Engelbert Humperdinck's 'Release Me'). Luckily, they had a number of equally good tunes to work on – the band rarely put singles on albums – and the result was released at the start of the Summer of Love.

How to describe the impact made by *Sgt. Pepper's Lonely Hearts Club Band? Gramophone* magazine came closest when in 1967, it described the album as 'bizarre, wonderful, perverse, beautiful, exciting, provocative, exasperating, compassionate and mocking'. In the *Partisan Review*, Richard Poirier called it 'an astounding accomplishment for which no one could have been wholly prepared', while Kenneth Tynan in *The Times* loftily proclaimed it 'a decisive moment in Western civilization'.

Andrew Loog Oldham – manager of The Rolling Stones until later in the year – pronounced it 'The second coming of the audio Christ', while in September, *Time* magazine described The Beatles as 'messengers from beyond rock 'n' roll, they are creating the most original, expressive and musically interesting sounds being heard in pop music'.

Not everyone was charmed by the album, and it remains divisive today, with some believing it's a triumph of style and presentation over content. But here's the thing: in 1967, it was the right album at the right time and has come to define psychedelic rock and, in particular, the Summer of Love. 'A splendid time is guaranteed for all', it claimed, and the record-buying youth all over the world took that promise to their hearts. US radio stations cancelled their usual broadcasts to play the album, in its entirety, over and over again. Even other musicians were open-mouthed with awe, or paid tribute to it, as Jimi Hendrix did by performing the title track live on stage just three days after the album came out.

*Sgt. Pepper* wasn't just a collection of songs; it was a complete work of art, from the astounding and thought-provoking cover on which the band posed with cardboard effigies of various heroes and villains, through to the insert of cutouts, the lyrics printed on the back sleeve – the first time for a major pop release – and the presentation of the songs as a concert: not by The Beatles, but by the titular sergeant and his band. You didn't just play the record, you dove headlong into a new, colourful psychedelic world.

The creation of *Sgt. Peppe*r has been chronicled many, many times, and we shouldn't spend too much ink and paper on it here. Suffice to say, it was a deliberate attempt to get away from the image of the fab four moptops and create something more surreal and mischievous. The title came first, inspired by some of the lengthy names bands were using in the US, such as Country Joe and the Fish or Big Brother and the Holding Company, and Paul McCartney soon turned the name into a song.

The band's personal assistant Neil Aspinall claims to have come up with the idea of presenting the album as a concert. He explains in *The Beatles Anthology* book:

> I said to Paul, why don't you have Sgt. Pepper as the compere of the album? He comes on at the beginning of the show and introduces the band, and at the end, he closes it. A bit later, Paul told John about it in the studio, and John came up to me and said, 'Nobody likes a smart-arse, Neil'.

So there was a concept of sorts, although the band didn't extend it much beyond the first two songs and the reprise. But it worked because the band said it worked – as Lennon pointed out again in the *Anthology* book: 'Every other song could have been on any other album.'

Not everything on *Sgt. Pepper* is psychedelic. 'With a Little Help From My Friends' could have been Ringo's spot on any of the last three or four albums, while 'When I'm Sixty-Four' – one of Paul's 'granny songs' – ticks the nostalgia box, but little else. 'She's Leaving Home' is a beautiful, moving and surprisingly conservative song about the generation gap: notable for featuring a string nonet and harp, but no guitar, bass or drums. But their lack of psychedelic credentials is more than made up for by the rest of the album's weird and wonderful tracks, from the raga rock of 'Getting Better' (Lennon was experiencing an LSD trip when he recorded the backing vocals), to the slightly perverse traffic-warden tribute in 'Lovely Rita' (complete with an orgasmic coda) and the drug reference in 'Fixing a Hole'.

Then there was the bizarre mixture of horns, jagged electric lead guitar, and animal noises on 'Good Morning Good Morning' (inspired by the coda on The Beach Boys' 'Caroline, No'), and George Harrison's exquisite 'Within You Without You', performed entirely with Indian musicians.

The songs that really tick so many of the psychedelic boxes are John's 'Lucy in the Sky With Diamonds' – another of his nonsense lyrics songs with a suspiciously druggy title – his 'Being for the Benefit of Mr Kite', that, like 'Tomorrow Never Knows', used cut-up recorded noises to replace the steam organ Lennon really wanted, and the final number, 'A Day in the Life', which ends with the famous long, drawn-out piano chord on E major.

First, let's look at 'Lucy...'. Lennon said it was inspired by his son Julian's drawing of classmate Lucy O'Donnell – it was actually a teacher who had written the title above the picture. John thought it was so beautiful that he decided to write a song about it. In *The Beatles Anthology* book, Paul says, 'We went up to his music room and wrote the song, swapping psychedelic suggestions as we went. I remember coming up with 'cellophane flowers' and 'newspaper taxis', and John answered with things like 'kaleidoscope eyes' and 'looking-glass eyes'. They claimed they never noticed the initials LSD in the title until someone pointed them out – and if you believe that, you're a fool on the hill.

The instrumental backing emphasises the song's dream-like nature. McCartney played organ on a setting that produced bell-like notes, while Harrison added tambura – a long-necked, plucked string instrument from India – and doubled Lennon's vocal on lead guitar. Structurally, it's simply alternating verses and choruses, except the former are in waltz time and the latter in straight 4/4, resulting in a childlike music-box effect that suddenly bursts into life.

'Being for the Benefit of Mr Kite' is a prime example of psychedelic rock's ability to take inspiration from anywhere, but particularly from the past. In this case, it was a 19th-century poster for Pablo Fanque's circus (he was a black equestrian performer whose real name was William Darby) that Lennon had bought in an antiques shop. Practically every line in the song is there on the poster, except for Henry the Horse – the performing ungulate was actually named Zanthus. Comprised of a simple four-verse structure with no chorus, it was backed by sliced-up recordings of fairground organs – Lennon told producer George Martin he wanted to 'smell the sawdust'. Martin also plays three different types of organ, including a mighty Wurlitzer.

The album's final song – and arguably the pinnacle of their musical achievement – was also penned by John, who seemed to have the monopoly on psychedelic Beatles songs at the time, and was inspired by genuine news items that he propped up on his piano as he wrote. So there was the story about a council survey finding 4,000 potholes in Blackburn, Lancashire, and one about a car crash that killed Tara Browne, a friend of the band. Lennon's line 'The English army had just won the war' came from his experiences filming *How I Won the War* in Spain, while his repeated requests to 'turn you on' echo the words of Timothy Leary.

At first, 'A Day in the Life' had a beginning and an end, but no middle – McCartney supplied that with a nostalgic ditty about getting up and catching the bus to school, where he has a smoke and falls into a dream. But the two elements were so different in style and feeling that they needed something to link them. It was Paul who suggested having an orchestral 'freak-out'. George Martin then wrote a score for a 41-piece orchestra in which he marked down the lowest and highest notes for each instrument and instructed them to go from one to the other at a gentle slide.

There are two orchestral freak-outs in the song, and the second one was originally intended to end on a long, drawn-out 'hummmmm' sung by the band and various celebrity friends. But that didn't sound powerful enough, so twelve days later the band recorded three pianos and a harmonium playing a single chord that reverberates for 42 seconds – a kind of final musical 'Ommmmm' (though that wasn't the end of the fun – the run-out groove featured a high-pitched tone that only dogs can hear).

The album hit number 1 in the UK and stayed there for an astonishing 23-week run. In the US, it topped the *Billboard* charts for fifteen weeks from July 1 and also became the number 1 album in Australia, Canada, Norway, Sweden and West Germany. It also topped the charts in several countries – including the UK – when it was re-released 50 years later and has sold an estimated 32,000,000 copies worldwide.

But, if anything, the youth of America seemed more enthusiastic about the album than that of the UK, embracing The Beatles as spokesmen for the counterculture, and dissecting the lyrics for messages and prophecies. As *Time* magazine said: 'The Beatles are where music is right now.' And, adding to the band's street cred, the BBC banned three of the tracks for containing alleged drug references.

It was the Beeb who, in 1966, conceived the idea of a live, global TV broadcast, transmitted to 24 countries using the latest satellite technology and featuring top acts from fourteen nations. Inevitably, the UK representatives were The Beatles, who were asked to pen a suitably uplifting and positive song for the event. Both John Lennon and Paul McCartney wrote one each, finally opting for Lennon's 'All You Need Is Love' over Paul's 'Your Mother Should Know'. Thanks to that wise decision, the *Our World* programme – broadcast on 25 June 1967 – is chiefly remembered for The Beatles' sequence, in which they performed to a pre-recorded backing track, assisted by members of The Rolling Stones, The Who and The Small Faces.

Once again, it was a case of the right song at the right time. The Vietnam War was raging, the Summer of Love was at its height, and The Beatles themselves were the most popular band in the world after the release of *Sgt. Pepper*. 'All You Need Is Love' may not be the best song The Beatles ever wrote – *Rolling Stone* magazine slots it in at 21 in their list of the fab four's 100 greatest – but it said what needed to be said. It was all about love – not sappy boy-meets-girl stuff, but the universal love espoused by psychedelic rockers everywhere.

For a song that was supposed to have a direct, unambiguous message, it's surprisingly cryptic, with its asymmetrical verse time signatures and rather dense lyrics. McCartney said: 'The chorus is simple, but the verse ['Nothing you can do / But you can learn how to be you in time / It's easy'] is quite complex. I never really understood it.' The genius was in the anthemic 'All you need is love – love is all you need' payoff, the French national anthem intro to emphasise the international nature of it all, and the extended coda that offered snatches of Glenn Miller's 'In the Mood', 'Greensleeves', Bach's 'Invention No. 8 in F major', and The Beatles' own 'She Loves You'.

The band and their guests turned the TV broadcast into a psychedelic event, dressing up in multi-coloured clothes, with balloons, flowers, streamers and 'Love' graffiti festooned around Abbey Road's EMI studio. George Harrison even painted his guitar for the occasion. This was, unfortunately, somewhat lost on the estimated audience of 400,000,000, as it was filmed in black and white (but later artificially coloured). Oh, and the Eastern Bloc countries didn't get the love message, as they pulled out days before in protest at the Six-Day War between Israel and Jordan, Egypt and Syria.

The single, predictably, went to number 1 in music charts all over the world, and, along with *Sgt. Pepper,* became symbolic of the Summer of Love: its message encapsulating the optimism and hope of the time. As The Beatles' manager Brian Epstein said in a Melody Maker interview, 'It was an inspired song, and they really wanted to give the world a message. The nice thing about it is that it cannot be misinterpreted. It is a clear message saying that love is everything.'

It was one of his last interviews. On 27 August, Epstein was found dead in his London flat from an accidental drug overdose. He was just 32. The Beatles responded by throwing themselves into even more work, recording the tracks that would eventually appear in their poorly-received Boxing Day special, *Magical Mystery Tour*. Once again, the demand to put out another single resulted in the November release of two tracks: the chirpy 'Hello Goodbye' and the barmy but brilliant 'I Am the Walrus'.

The A-side need not detain us long. Catchy and commercial, yes, in a simple-minded way with its theme of duality and contradiction, along with the by-now-obligatory coda. Instead, it's the flipside that we will focus on as a psychedelic rock classic and the culmination of John Lennon's nonsense-lyrics period. 'I Am the Walrus' was inspired by LSD trips, Lewis Carroll's poem 'The Walrus and the Carpenter', and was an attempt to bamboozle fans who were trying to find hidden meanings in Beatles songs.

Other, more specific musical and lyrical inspirations came from such mundane things as an overheard police siren to which Lennon sang the lines 'Mister city policeman', a childhood poem that included the phrase 'yellow matter custard', and Sergeant Norman Pilcher of the London Drug Squad, who became 'semolina pilchard'. The suggestion that the lyrics were a deliberate attempt to fox fans came from writer Hunter Davies in his 1968 book *The Beatles*. He was present when the song was being written, and claims Lennon said, 'Let the f***ers work that one out'.

The song uses major and major seventh chords from every letter of the musical alphabet: A to G. It has a childlike, almost plodding rhythm and ends on something called a Shepard tone – where the music appears to go up and up and up endlessly, with low notes coming in to replace the high ones as they disappear. Lennon's voice sounds a bit like a manic robot, switching between just two notes for much of the verse, while George Martin has once again thrown an orchestra at it, along with the Mike Sammes Singers going 'ho ho ho, hee hee hee, ha, ha, ha' and 'oompah, oompah, stick it up your jumper' (there are two of the Moody Blues there as well). Adding to the fun are short recordings from a radio broadcast of Shakespeare's *King Lear*.

'Hello Goodbye' never made it into *Magical Mystery Tour*. The Beatles were filmed performing it in Sgt. Pepper military uniforms. But 'I Am the Walrus' is the best part of the film, shot at West Malling Air Station in Kent, with the band in psychedelic jackets, in walrus costumes, swaying on a concrete anti-blast wall, and as eggmen. Oh, and there were four hand-holding policemen.

The film was first shown in black and white on BBC One on Boxing Day 1967, then repeated in colour on BBC Two in the new year, and was panned by viewers and critics. It was The Beatles first major critical disaster. But its psychedelic credentials were immaculate – the idea was to recreate the cross-country US bus tour made by writer Ken Kesey and his Merry Pranksters in 1964, coupled with the idea of popular coach tours from Liverpool to see the Blackpool lights.

The whole thing was improvised from start to finish, with the cast and crew – including The Bonzo Dog Doo-Dah Band, actor Victor Spinetti and Scottish singer Ivor Cutler – told to get on the coach on the morning of Monday 11 September, and see what happens. According to Ringo Starr, 'Paul had a great piece of paper – just a blank piece of white paper with a circle on it. The plan was, 'We start here, and we've got to do something here...'. We filled it in as we went along.'

The plot was something to do with Ringo and his 'Aunt Jessie' taking a coach tour that is sabotaged by five magicians. But this was really just an excuse to string a series of bizarre scenes and sketches together that included an impromptu race in which everyone uses a different form of transport, John shovelling mountains of spaghetti onto Aunt Jessie's dining table, and a tug of war involving twelve children and assorted blindfolded vicars.

It was a magical mystery trip that basically introduced drug-induced hallucinations into the living rooms of the turkey-stuffed British public. No wonder it was panned.

The songs, however, were a different matter. Recorded through the latter half of the year, they were released in the UK as a double EP and in the US as a full-length album coupled with the year's singles. One had already been aired – the spectacular 'I Am the Walrus' – but it was in good company with the upbeat title song, Paul's whimsical 'The Fool on the Hill', the trippy instrumental 'Flying', and George's drone-like, contemplative 'Blue Jay Way'.

Once again, the band filled their songs with psychedelic sounds, adding echo effects on pianos, electronic tape loops, swirling Hammond organs, trumpets, flutes, recorders and cellos. Like the film, the 'Magical Mystery Tour' song itself was virtually made up as they went along, with the band thinking up lines in the studio, while 'Blue Jay Way' is performed entirely in the key of C, using flanging, phasing and other audio effects to create a sense of dislocation and unease. The EP came with a 24-page booklet with stills from the film and the story, told with a mixture of text and cartoon images drawn by British caricaturist Bob Gibson. In the US, it was LP-sized: another good reason to have the album rather than the double EP.

It is fitting that the EP ends with Harrison's disturbing 'Blue Jay Way' – the psychedelic year was coming to a close, and an unease about the casualties of increasing drug use was beginning to set in. As Harrison sings, 'There's a fog upon L.A. and my friends have lost their way'. The Beatles, too, appeared to have lost their way as their relationships fragmented. But in 1967, they were still fab.

# The Doors

Key personnel:
Jim Morrison: lead vocals, harmonica, percussion, Moog synthesizer
Ray Manzarek: keyboards, keyboard bass, vocals, marimba
Robby Krieger: electric guitar, vocals
John Densmore: drums, percussion, backing vocals

## History

Formed in 1965 in Venice Beach, Los Angeles, by Jim Morrison and Ray Manzarek, both students at the UCLA School of Film, Theater and Television. Manzarek was in a band called Rick & the Ravens – Morrison joined, followed by drummer John Densmore, and they renamed themselves The Doors after Aldous Huxley's book *The Doors of Perception*. They were signed to Elektra Records in 1966 after being spotted supporting Them at L.A. club the Whisky A Go Go.

## Key releases in 1967

### **The Doors** (album)

All songs by The Doors except as noted.
Label: Elektra
Release date: 4 January 1967
Charts: US: 2; Canada: 15 (It failed to chart in the UK until 1991)
Side 1: 1. 'Break on Through (to the Other Side)' 2. 'Soul Kitchen' 3. 'The Crystal Ship' 4. 'Twentieth Century Fox' 5. 'Alabama Song (Whisky Bar)' (Bertolt Brecht, Kurt Weill) 6. 'Light My Fire'. Side 2: 1. 'Back Door Man' (Willie Dixon, Howlin' Wolf) 2. 'I Looked At You' 3. 'End of the Night' 4. 'Take It As It Comes' 5. 'The End'.

### **'Light My Fire'/'The Crystal Ship'** (Single)

Label: Elektra
Release date: 24 April 1967
Charts: US: 1, Canada: 2, UK: 29

### **Strange Days** (album)

All songs by The Doors.
Label: Elektra
Release date: 25 September 1967
Charts: US: 3
Side 1: 1. 'Strange Days' 2. 'You're Lost Little Girl' 3. 'Love Me Two Times' 4. 'Unhappy Girl' 5. 'Horse Latitudes' 6. 'Moonlight Drive' Side 2: 1. 'People Are Strange' 2. 'My Eyes Have Seen You' 3. 'I Can't See Your Face in My Mind' 4. 'When the Music's Over'

Some bands became psychedelic; others had psychedelia thrust upon them. The Doors were created to be psychedelic. Born out of university arts courses, steeped in literature, poetry, classical, blues and jazz, they were never going to be Engelbert Humperdinck. But The Doors were psychedelic rock's dark side – moody, unpredictable and dangerous. No walrus suits or Victorian brass band uniforms for them – they represented the rage of the counterculture, the part of the hippie movement that wanted to tear down the old society, not just sit and look at it through fragrant cannabis fumes. The Beatles were day-trippers on magical mystery tours to Penny Lane – The Doors sang about the night, and funeral pyres, and riding the snake, and killing your parents. And they said 'f*ck' a lot.

The band took its cue from its leader and lyricist Jim Morrison, an unpredictable and erratic young man who epitomised the sexy, scandalous rock star. A military brat, his father was in command of US forces during the so-called Gulf of Tonkin incident in 1964, in which American and Vietnamese ships clashed, providing a pretext for the US to send the first combat troops into the Vietnam War. So young Jim didn't have to go far to find something to rebel against.

An avid reader, he was influenced by philosophers such as Friedrich Nietzsche and, while at university, the surrealist theatre of French director Antonin Artaud. He was also heavily into alcohol abuse – his first arrest came at the age of nineteen for drunkenly disturbing the peace at a sports game. So by the time he joined the band that was to become The Doors, he had the poetic sensibility to write dense, twisted lyrics, the theatrical knowledge to be an imposing frontman on stage, and a dark, damaged, almost schizophrenic personality that attracted trouble like a moth to a flame. He also looked like a rock god.

Morrison was lucky enough to fall in with three contemporaries who, with powerful, aggressive jazz-rock, had the musical chops to bring his visions to life. There was Ray Manzarek, whose Vox Continental organ dominated the band's sound (and he also played bass with his left hand on a separate Fender Rhodes keyboard); guitarist Robby Krieger could bounce around all sorts of genres, and play some mean slide with a broken bottle, while drummer John Densmore was inspired by jazz and world music.

Manzarek said the following in a 2013 interview with *THC Expose* magazine:

> It was going to be poetry together with rock 'n' roll ... and our version of rock 'n' roll was whatever you could bring to the table. Robby, bring your flamenco guitar. Robby, bring that bottleneck guitar, bring that sitar tuning. John, bring your marching drums and your snares and your four-on-the-floor. Ray, bring your classical training and your blues training and your jazz training. Jim, bring your southern-gothic poetry, your Arthur Rimbaud poetry. It all works in rock 'n' roll.

As stated before, the two albums The Doors released in 1967 pretty much bookend the year. In fact, 1967 was just four days old when their debut LP was unveiled, along with the opening track 'Break On Through (to the Other Side)' as a single. Neither made much impact at the time, but that changed when 'Light My Fire' was released in April as their second single. It climbed steadily to number 1 in the US charts, where it stayed for three weeks, pulling the album along with it.

'Light My Fire' became one of the most played singles of the year – part of the soundtrack to the Summer of Love – but it's an ambiguous song that veers from minor-key mystery to major-key exultation. Written originally by Krieger – who had the first verse and chorus – Morrison completed the lyric, while Manzarek created the swirling circle-of-fifths opening that moves through seven different chords in a matter of seconds.

It ostensibly sounds like a guy trying to persuade a girl to get jiggy with it. But there's a suggestion of a death wish there, that their love could become a 'funeral pyre', like the Indian custom of a wife throwing herself on the funeral pyre of her dead husband. 'Try to set the night on fire', Morrison sings, but he could well be talking about arson rather than sex – you can almost imagine him standing there with the light of the inferno dancing in his eyes.

The track was shortened for single release simply by cutting out the extensive solos that make the album version a seven-minute monster. Released in January 1967, it was a slow burner, creeping steadily up the charts before hitting number 1 in July. Then it seemed to be everywhere that summer, selling more than a million copies by the end of the year. The Doors even played it on *The Ed Sullivan Show*, infuriating TV producers by refusing to change the word 'higher', which the producers thought was a drug reference.

The album that spawned 'Light My Fire' displays an interesting mix of influences, from blues and jazz to Brechtian theatricals and Greek mythology. Unlike British psychedelic groups, however, The Doors didn't trade on rose-tinted nostalgia or pretend their drug-taking was as safe and harmless as sipping a cup of tea – their psychedelia was sometimes a bad trip through an acid-drenched hell. Writer and magazine editor Rob Hill said, 'The Doors' music was for the nighttime – music meant to send you off into a carnival dreamland of deserts, endless midnights, whisky and acid wildernesses, and cinematic verse. It was different – and strange'.

To be fair, there are songs that you could dance to on the debut: the poppy 'Soul Kitchen' and 'Twentieth Century Fox', for example. But tracks like 'The Crystal Ship' and 'End of the Night' lurch like Frankenstein's monster, while 'Alabama Song (Whisky Bar)' – Bertolt Brecht's 1927 composition originally sung by Lotte Lenya – drips with menace.

The album's most different and strange track was the nearly twelve-minute closer, appropriately titled 'The End'. Initially about a breakup with a girlfriend, the lyrics take on a much darker hue with overtones of *Oedipus Rex* (Morrison had worked on a student production while at university), as the singer introduces 'the killer before dawn, he puts his boots on'. Then he goes to his parents' room and says 'Father? I want to kill you...' before suggesting an altogether different criminal act with his mother. The song ends with about twenty 'f**k's and the exhortation to 'kill, kill, kill, kill'. The first public performance of the song – at the Whisky A Go Go – got The Doors banned from the venue.

Manzarek has explained in Ben Torres-Fong's book, *The Doors*, that Morrison 'was giving voice in a rock 'n' roll setting to the Oedipus complex: at the time, a widely-discussed tendency in Freudian psychology. He wasn't saying he wanted to do that to his own mom and dad. He was re-enacting a bit of Greek drama. It was theatre.' Morrison himself explained when quoted in *Creem* magazine:

> Sometimes the pain is too much to examine, or even tolerate ... That doesn't make it evil though, or necessarily dangerous. But people fear death even more than pain. It's strange that they fear death. Life hurts a lot more than death. At the point of death, the pain is over. Yeah – I guess it is a friend.

Spookily, 'The End' was the last song Morrison sang with the band before his death in 1971.

The debut was generally well-received, with Paul Williams of *Crawdaddy* saying it was 'an album of magnitude. Thanks to the calm, sure-footedness of the group, the producer, the record company, there are no flaws'. But others dismissed the long, final track as a 'dirge' and Morrison's lyrics as self-indulgent. Posterity has been kinder, ranking it as one of the greatest albums ever made, and, for some reviewers, the best album from The Doors. In 1967 it leapt to number 2 in the US charts, held off the top spot (as so many albums were that year) by The Beatles' *Sgt. Pepper*. But the album had to wait until 1991 before it charted in the UK, boosted by the release of Oliver Stone's film on the band.

By the time of the second album *Strange Days* – as so often happened to groups signed to produce two LPs a year – the band was recording in between tour dates (from May to August). This time, the Doors had eight tracks to play with, and they took full advantage of the sonic possibilities this leap in recording technology provided. Ray Manzarek explained in his memoir *Light My Fire: My Life With the Doors*:

> And thus began our plunge into the laboratory. We were making a record, making music, but we were also mad scientists manipulating the aural spectrum for our diabolical creations ... (we had) songs from the terminus. Songs from the endpoint of the west. From the meeting point of the continent and our mother, the sea. Songs from the end of the western dream of expansion...

They didn't just have four more tracks to play with, they had one of the first Moog synthesizers, they had pianos played backwards, a harpsichord, marimba, and a pre-release copy of *Sgt. Pepper* to inspire them. The result is a follow-up that sounds even more assured than their first, that marries their doom-laden rock poetry with more overtly psychedelic influences, producing an album that took time to be recognised as a masterpiece.

*Strange Days* doesn't dilute the band's dark, aggressive musical approach but does add moments of surprising beauty – such as the twangy lead guitar break in 'You're Lost Little Girl' and the jaunty, Beatley bounce of 'Love Me Two Times'. 'Unhappy Girl' contains the backwards piano, which Manzarek had to perform forwards to the sound of the backing track playing backwards in his headphones.

'Horse Latitudes' is a poem about horses being thrown overboard from transatlantic sailing ships bearing cargo to the New World, set to windy, screeching sound effects, while Manzarek hammers the strings of a grand piano with mallets, and Morrison slams coconut shells on the parquet flooring. The single 'People Are Strange' is almost Morrison's self-diagnosis in a quirky, Brechtian setting, complete with honky-tonk piano and massed chorus vocals, while 'Moonlight Drive' masquerades as a blues with an off-kilter rhythm and Krieger's eerie slide guitar.

Like its predecessor, *Strange Days* ends on a long track: the eleven-minute 'When the Music's Over', but this has a more insistent, almost samba-like beat. Led by Manzarek's organ playing little more than the alternating chords of E minor and A major, Morrison utters the disturbing lines, 'Cancel my subscription to the Resurrection', and 'What have they done to our fair sister? / Ravaged and plundered and ripped her and bit her / Stuck her with knives in the side of the dawn.'

By the end, he is screaming at us – 'We want the world and we want it now!' – as Robby Krieger offers up an incendiary guitar break, and Morrison reminds us that 'music is your only friend until the end'. Manzarek said of the recording session, 'We were in the divine moment, and all pretence was abandoned. We were our real, naked selves and we were playing our instruments with our souls.'

With no 'Light My Fire' to set the charts alight, *Strange Days* was seen at the time as a disappointment but has since been reassessed as The Doors' forgotten masterpiece. Yes, it's strange – not least the album cover of circus freaks with the title tucked away as a peeling poster behind the weightlifting strongman – but it's chock full of catchy melodies and fascinating sonic experiments.

It didn't quite do as well as its predecessor in the US charts – stalling at number 3 – but *Rolling Stone* magazine said it 'has all the power and energy of the first LP, but is more subtle, more intricate and much more effective'. It has fared even better in hindsight – on the 40th anniversary of its release, Sal Cinquemani wrote in *Slant magazine* that 'While *The Doors* had more frequent, obvious peaks, the quirky *Strange Days* is a more ambitious, unified work. There are fewer filler tracks, and each song carries as much weight as the one before and after it.'

The Doors would reach the height of their fame in 1968 when that year's disintegration of the hippie dream probably fit their music a bit better than 1967's starry-eyed optimism. But they showed that psychedelic music could have a dark, menacing core. It didn't have to be all Victoriana and flowers – it could be multicoloured, so long as every colour was black.

# The Jimi Hendrix Experience

Key personnel:
Jimi Hendrix: guitar, vocals
Noel Redding: bass
Mitch Mitchell: drums

## History

Born Johnny Allen Hendrix in Seattle, Washington in 1942 (his father changed his first names to James Marshall in 1946), he picked up the guitar at fifteen and played in countless short-lived bands, invariably getting the sack for missing the tour bus, refusing to wear the matching outfits, or playing too damn loud and flashy. He joined the army to avoid a prison sentence for stealing cars, but he didn't like it, and the army certainly didn't like him. He played in backing bands for, among many others, the Isley Brothers and Little Richard, before being spotted by Chas Chandler of The Animals, who became his manager. Moving to England in late 1966, Chandler recruited guitarist Redding to play bass, and drummer Mitchell, who'd just been fired by Georgie Fame and the Blue Flames. The Jimi Hendrix Experience released their first single, 'Hey Joe' on 29 December 1966, and prepared to take 1967 by storm.

## Key releases in 1967

### 'Purple Haze' / '51st Anniversary' (Single)

Both songs by Jimi Hendrix.
Label: Track (UK), Reprise (US)
Release date: 17 March 1967
Charts: UK: 3; Austria: 7; Norway: 7; US: 65 (where B-side was 'The Wind Cries Mary')

### 'The Wind Cries Mary' / 'Highway Chile' (Single)

Both songs by Jimi Hendrix.
Label: Track (UK), Reprise (US)
Release date: 5 May 1967 (UK); 19 June 1967 (US – as B-side to 'Purple Haze')
Charts: UK: 6

### Are You Experienced (Album)

All songs by Jimi Hendrix.
Label: Track (UK), Reprise (US), Barclay (France and Benelux countries)
Release date: 12 May 1967 (UK); 23 August 1967 (US)
Charts: UK: 2; US: 5; Norway: 3
(UK release) Side 1: 1. 'Foxy Lady' 2. 'Manic Depression' 3. 'Red House' 4. 'Can You See Me' 5. 'Love or Confusion' 6. 'I Don't Live Today' Side 2: 1. 'This May Be Love' 2. 'Fire' 3. '3rd Stone From the Sun' 4. 'Remember' 5. 'Are You Experienced?'
US version includes 'Purple Haze', 'The Wind Cries Mary' and 'Hey Joe' (Billy Roberts): losing 'Red House', 'Can You See Me' and 'Remember'.

## **Axis: Bold as Love** (Album)

All songs by Jimi Hendrix except as noted.
Label: Track (UK), Reprise (US)
Release date: 1 December 1967
Charts: UK: 5; US: 3
Side 1: 1. 'EXP' 2. 'Up From the Skies' 3. 'Spanish Castle Magic' 4. 'Wait Until Tomorrow' 5. 'Ain't No Telling' 6. 'Little Wing' 7. 'If Six Was Nine' Side 2: 1. 'You've Got Me Floating' 2. 'Castles Made of Soul' 3. 'She's So Fine' (Noel Redding) 4. 'One Rainy Wish' 5. 'Little Miss Lover' 6. 'Bold as Love'

The Rock Gods assembled in London's Bag O' Nails nightclub could scarcely believe their eyes – and, especially, their ears. Here was this virtually unknown black man playing electric guitar with a ferocity, inventiveness and dexterity they could only dream of. John Lennon, Paul McCartney, Jeff Beck, Pete Townshend, Brian Jones – if you could've heard any noise in the club other than Hendrix's six-string roar, it would've been the sound of celebrity jaws hitting the floor. The kings were dead – long live The King.

Eric Clapton was there, but he had already been on the receiving end of Hendrix's sonic assault. The previous month he was playing at a London college with his new band Cream, and was asked if Jimi could sit in on a number. The song was Howlin' Wolf's 'Killing Floor', which Clapton had only just mastered. Hendrix played it at breakneck speed, behind his head and with his teeth. Halfway through, Clapton stopped playing and walked off stage with his hands shaking.

Word had spread, and at the Bag O' Nails, British rock's great and good piled in to see precisely what the fuss was about. Peter Jay and the Jaywalkers' singer Terry Reid was quoted in Philip Norman's Hendrix biography:

> Here comes Jimi, hair all over the place, pulls out this left-handed Stratocaster, beaten to death, looks like he's been chopping wood with it. And he gets up, all soft-spoken, and all of a sudden WHOORRAAWWR! He breaks into 'Wild Thing' and it was all over. There were guitar players weeping. They had to mop the floor up. He keeps piling it on, solo after solo. I could see everyone's fillings falling out. When he finished, it was silence. Nobody knew what to do. Everyone was dumbstruck, completely in shock.

Jimi Hendrix was a US-born musician who had to move to the UK to find fame – and then returned to conquer his homeland. The Experience was formed to show off his talents as a guitarist – and what a guitarist he was! He played as if he was torturing his instrument on behalf of the CIA, wrenching sounds out of it that had never been heard before. He used feedback, plenty of tone pedals (one band leader complained that when it came to Hendrix's solo, he spent most of it choosing the right pedals to press), and turned his amplifier volume up to eleven. He is now regarded as one of the most influential guitarists in the history of popular music.

Little of what Hendrix did was actually original. Playing guitar behind his head? That came from T-Bone Walker. The teeth thing? Alphonso Young (who was in a short-lived band with Jimi, The King Kasuals) did it first. But Jimi did it while being note-perfect – even though his fingering looked sloppy as hell – and turned the guitar almost into a living, roaring beast. Somehow, he had entered into some kind of pact with the spirit of his Stratocaster – you touch me any way you want to, and I'll play the sounds in your head.

His sidemen were well-chosen by manager Chas Chandler – Noel Redding was a guitarist who auditioned for The New Animals, and impressed Hendrix with his knowledge of blues progressions. His playing wasn't flashy or aggressive – in fact, he could barely play bass at all, and Hendrix had to teach him. But he knew his job was to anchor a song, while the frontman performed his guitar pyrotechnics over the top. Mitch Mitchell, on the other hand, had a hard, driving jazz style that more than held its own. It also helped that both men had big Afro haircuts, just like Jimi, who modelled his own on Bob Dylan's.

The first single 'Hey Joe' – released in the closing days of 1966 – was a cover of a rock standard written by Billy Roberts and inspired by a slow version from folk singer Tim Rose. It hit number 6 in the UK in February 1967 but went absolutely nowhere in the US. Neither did the follow-up 'Purple Haze' (In fact, all his singles performed pretty badly in the US; his fans were album buyers), but it showed Hendrix was more than just a loud blues guitarist – its mixture of sonically-treated guitar, vocals coming from what sounds like the bottom of a well, and those hippy-trippy lyrics (including the hilariously misquoted 'Excuse me while I kiss the sky'), all scream psychedelia. Some critics even compared the words to James Joyce's famously unreadable *Ulysses*.

Depending on which Hendrix story you believe – and he delighted in giving different answers in different interviews – the song was either inspired by *Night of Light,* a 1966 science-fiction novel by Philip Jose Farmer, that depicts a planet drenched in mania-inducing purple haze from sunspots, or it was a dream he had about walking under the sea. It certainly seems the riff came first, and Chas Chandler claims the credit for spotting it as the next single, telling Hendrix to go off and write some lyrics.

Recorded on four-track equipment at De Lane Lea Studios in London – eight-track didn't become widely used in the UK until 1968 – Chandler added echo effects and guitar parts recorded at half-speed. It also featured the first use on record of the Octavia: a foot pedal designed by acoustical engineer Roger Mayer, that not only added fuzz and distortion but could lower or raise guitar notes by an entire octave. Jimi loved it.

Forget 'Hey Joe' – 'Purple Haze' is really the first proper musical expression from The Jimi Hendrix Experience, opening with a powerful, fuzz-laden eight-note riff that was destined to be practised by every would-be guitarist for the next 50 years, with Jimi's added orgasmic grunts and sighs. Unlike 'Hey Joe'

– which contained a sensible, restrained guitar solo in the middle – 'Purple Haze' fades out on Hendrix's Strat screaming in agony or ecstasy. It's a raw, dirty and slightly chaotic track that hit number 3 in the UK, has been dubbed the number-one guitar song by *Q* magazine and was inducted into the Grammy Hall of Fame.

'Purple Haze' was still in the charts when third single, 'The Wind Cries Mary', was released, revealing another side to the guitar-wrangler – the ability to create soulful ballads, inspired by one of his heroes, Curtis Mayfield. Its inspiration has been claimed by Jimi's then-girlfriend Kathy Etchingham – they had a bust-up over her cooking, resulting in him locking her in the bathroom of their London flat, before she escaped and fled to a friend's. As an apology, Hendrix wrote the song dedicated to 'Mary' – Kathy's middle name – and included references to the crockery that got broken during the row.

Chas Chandler said it was recorded in just twenty minutes after cutting the album track 'Fire', adding that Mitchell and Redding hadn't even heard it. He said: 'They played it once through (and Hendrix then suggested overdubs). In all, he put on four or five more overdubs, but the whole thing was done in twenty minutes. That was our third single.' Taken at a similar pace to 'Hey Joe', 'The Wind Cries Mary' dials down on the effects, concentrating on Hendrix's soulful delivery and a lovely, funky guitar solo shorn of sonic effects. His US label Reprise – founded by Frank Sinatra – didn't think that much of it, hiding it on the B-side of the American release of 'Purple Haze'. But Hendrix liked it enough to perform it live through 1967 and the following year.

It was on the band's debut album *Are You Experienced*, that Hendrix showed his ability to combine blues, jazz, soul and raga rock in a psychedelic stew. The singles weren't on the album's UK version – a convention started by The Beatles, who didn't want their fans to pay twice for the same song. So British record buyers got eleven brand new tracks recorded over a five-month period between October 1966 and April the following year. Jimi's full-on, effects-drenched playing presented the engineers with a challenge as they attempted to capture his sound on four-track recorders. Apparently, the volume in the studio was so huge, the microphone was placed twelve feet away from his speakers – on tracks like 'Red House', you can really hear the instruments bouncing around the studio.

The album takes the 'Purple Haze' template but lays on the fuzz, distortion and echo even thicker. 'Foxy Lady' (spelt 'Foxey' on the US version) opens with gradually-increasing feedback before melting into a heavy rock riff, with Hendrix salaciously whispering 'Foxy!'. The overdubbed guitar solo is short but oh, so sweet, ascending up the neck until the song plunges back into the heavy riff again.

'Manic Depression' sees guitar and vocals in melodic unison, while Mitchell appears to be anticipating noted Muppets drummer Animal on a track that has a distinctive Jack Bruce feel. In the ballad 'May This Be Love', slide guitar phrases are heavily laden with echo, while there are all sorts of delicious effects on the spacey '3rd Stone From the Sun'. 'I Don't live Today' referenced Hendrix's native-American heritage; 'Can You See Me' sounds like a frantic pop single (he called it a song for teenyboppers), and 'Fire' is driven along by Mitchell on overdrive.

The trippiest track is the title cut, 'Are You Experienced?' (with a question mark this time, pedantry fans), which is based mostly on one chord, with a repeated piano octave over a drone-like backing. It opens with backwards-taped drums, with a backward lead guitar break that includes fret-squeak as Hendrix runs his fingers up and down the neck.

Hendrix's lyrics were a mixture of standard blues cliches and disturbing images seen through the distorting prism of the many drugs he ingested during his short, tragic career. He was known to use marijuana, LSD and cocaine, although he denied taking heroin, despite being busted for possession in 1970.

Those who worked with him said he was never stoned in the studio; otherwise, he wouldn't have been able to play with such invention and precision. But lines such as 'Purple haze all around / Don't know if I'm coming up or down' and 'Must there be all these colours without names, without sounds' strongly suggest that – closeted in a room with a guitar and pen – Jimi was channelling the effects of various chemical substances.

Recorded in just ten days and costing £1,500, *Are You Experienced* hit number 2 in the UK, kept off the top spot by the sales roadblock that was *Sgt. Pepper*, while the US version, which included the three singles, reached number 5, thanks to plenty of promotion by record company Reprise and a barnstorming performance at the Monterey International Pop Festival.

Hendrix wasn't the first choice for the festival – the brainchild of John Phillips of The Mamas & the Papas – and was only included because Beatle Paul, one of the organisers, insisted. He was still a virtual unknown in the US, although some of the other musicians on the roster knew what he was capable of and that his act was likely to be a showstopper. Nobody wanted to follow him, particularly Pete Townshend of The Who, who won a coin-toss to perform first. In a 2007 *Mojo* interview, Townshend recalls, 'We went on first; he then announced that if we preceded him and set the crowd alight with our destruction act, he too would set them alight. So the crowd got two mind-fucking sets'.

It wasn't the first time Hendrix had set fire to his guitar. He'd done it to end a show in London after a suggestion from a journalist on how to top The Who's notorious instrument destruction. That time it had taken buckets of lighter fluid and three matches, and the guitarist burned his hand.

At Monterey, the burning was an altogether more successful climax to his performance. He had just produced the most astonishing sounds from his guitar, rubbing it against the amplifiers, bashing it on the stage floor, sitting astride it in an act of mock copulation, before setting it alight with the help of several squirts of accelerant.

There is spectacular footage of Hendrix from that performance, on his knees, arms raised in worship, face contorted in ecstasy, as his Fender Stratocaster burns on the stage before him, and the audience looks on, bewildered and shocked. As the *Los Angeles Times* reported, during that single performance, Jimi Hendrix went 'from rumour to legend'. And he did it all in a fabulous psychedelic outfit of ruffled silk shirt, velvet pants, ostrich boa, Mongolian vest, Spanish hat, and western boots, all draped in handmade jewellery.

*Are You Experienced* was an immediate critical and commercial success. *Melody Maker* praised the way the songs 'stop, start, fade, fizzle, simmer and burn in a cauldron of beautiful fire'. *NME* called it 'A brave effort to produce a musical form that is original and exciting'. Posterity has been even more gushing, variously dubbing it one of the most distinctive albums in psychedelic rock, a landmark in a summer of landmark albums, and, from *Guitar World* magazine, 'The measure by which everything in rock and roll has been measured since'. *Rolling Stone* put it as number 30 in the 500 Greatest Albums of All Time, and third in the Best Debut Albums. It's the greatest guitar album of all time, according to *Mojo* magazine, and is one of the 50 recordings chosen by the US Library of Congress for being 'culturally, historically or aesthetically significant'. Sales matched the superlatives, with the album shifting a million copies in just seven months.

It's no surprise, therefore, that the follow-up *Axis: Bold as Love* doesn't quite measure up. It was recorded in between gigs in Europe and the US, so the band was tight and firing on all cylinders, but it left Hendrix with little time to fully develop his musical ideas as he had done with the debut.

It was preceded by the single 'Burning of the Midnight Lamp', which failed to match the chart success of its predecessors, but, from a psychedelic point of view, is notable for its use of harpsichord on the intro, wah-wah guitar chords and angelic choir backing. Indeed, its little known B-side 'The Stars That Play With Laughing Sam's Dice', not only has a drug-influenced psychedelic title ('Stars That Play' and 'Laughing Sam's Dice' abbreviate as hallucinogens STP and LSD), but turns into a raucous, mock-live finale full of whistles, shouts and laughter provided by Frank Zappa, among others.

The second album showed Hendrix branching out instrumentally, incorporating harpsichord, recorder and glockenspiel, and opening the album with a bizarre mock-interview followed by weird and wonderful sounds supposed to depict a flying saucer taking off. This merges into 'Up From the Skies', in which Jimi once again plays a visiting alien wanting to know about 'the new Mother Earth' and 'the rooms behind your minds'.

'Spanish Castle Magic' references one of Hendrix's teenage haunts – the Spanish Castle ballroom in Washington state – and is a return to his heavy blues riffs. 'Wait Until Tomorrow' is a rather limp story about an attempted elopement. 'Little Wing' – the album's 'The Wind Cries Mary' – and 'Castles Made of Sand' draw from his own life, with references to the father who dominated him, the mother who died of cancer, and his brother, who ended up in jail. Oh, and Noel Redding supplies a Who-ish pop song, 'She's So Fine', with Mitch channelling Keith Moon.

Apart from the opening track, 'If Six Were Nine' is probably the album's most psychedelic moment, with Hendrix using fuzz, echo and reverb to create a maelstrom of noise, while Redding is uncharacteristically busy all over it, and various people – including Graham Nash of The Hollies – supply stomping footsteps.

It's a less aggressive album than *Are You Experienced*, and the songs don't sound as developed as they should. Some of them come and go without making much impact, with one clocking in at a meagre 1:50. But there is a spaced-out lightness to it all, Hendrix's guitar work is superlative, as usual, and there are plenty of his psychedelic lyrics to puzzle over:

> Anger, he smiles
> Towering in shiny metallic purple armour
> Queen Jealousy, envy waits behind him
> Her fiery green gown sneers at the grassy ground

Then there's the cover showing the band as various incarnations of the Hindu god Vishnu – which angered Hendrix because it wasn't part of his heritage, angered Hindus for cultural appropriation, and angered the Malaysian government, who banned it in 2014 to 'protect religious sensitivities'.

The album was well-received, described by Nick Jones of *Melody Maker* as 'the culmination of all Jimi's blues, all his soul, all his urging, all his crying, all his shouting, all his grooving, all his everything'. *Rolling Stone* called it 'the finest voodoo album that any rock group has produced to date', dubbing it the number-one stoner album.

But there are some dissenters, particularly among more contemporary reviewers looking back at Hendrix's body of work, who praise the guitar work and drumming but criticise the songs' brevity. Nevertheless, it still ranks high in various lists of best albums, and certainly worked its magic in 1967.

By the end of the year, *Melody Maker* voted Hendrix the 'World's Best Pop Musician'. The talented but insecure dreamer from Seattle had finally made it.

# Jefferson Airplane

Key personnel:
Marty Balin: vocals, guitar
Jack Casady: bass, rhythm guitar
Spencer Dryden: drums, percussion
Paul Kantner: rhythm guitar, vocals
Jorma Kaukonen: lead guitar, vocals
Grace Slick: vocals, keyboards, recorder

## History

Formed in San Francisco by Marty Balin and Paul Kantner to play folk-rock – inspired by The Beatles, The Byrds and Simon & Garfunkel – at Balin's club The Matrix. They recruited vocalist Signe Toly Anderson, blues guitarist Jorma Kaukonen, drummer Jerry Peloquin and acoustic bassist Bob Harvey for their live debut on 13 August 1965. Peloquin and Harvey were soon replaced by Skip Spence and Jack Casady. A friend of Kaukonen jokingly dubbed him 'Blind Thomas Jefferson Airplane': a play on US blues legend Blind Lemon Jefferson. Stuck for a name, the band took Kaukonen's suggestion of Jefferson Airplane. Live performances enhanced their reputation and they signed a contract with RCA Victor, releasing their first single 'It's No Secret', in 1966, followed by their debut album *Jefferson Airplane Takes Off*. Signe left the band after giving birth to her daughter, and was replaced by Grace Slick (who was lead singer of local folk-rock group The Great Society), while the drummer's chair was taken over by Spencer Dryden.

## Key releases in 1967

### **Surrealistic Pillow** (album)

Label: RCA Victor
Release date: 1 February 1967
Charts: US: 3
Side 1: 1. 'She Has Funny Cars' (Jorma Kaukonen, Marty Balin) 2. 'Somebody To Love' (Darby Slick) 3. 'My Best Friend' (Skip Spence) 4. 'Today' (Balin, Paul Kantner) 5. 'Comin' Back to Me' (Balin) Side 2: 1. '3/5 of a Mile in 10 Seconds' (Balin) 2. 'D.C.B.A.–25' (Kantner) 3. 'How Do You Feel' (Tom Mastin) 4. 'Embryonic Journey' (Kaukonen) 5. 'White Rabbit' (Grace Slick) 6. 'Plastic Fantastic Lover' (Balin)
The UK release replaced 'She Has Funny Cars', 'White Rabbit' and 'Plastic Fantastic Lover' with 'Don't Slip Away' (Balin, Spence), 'Chauffeur Blues' (Lester Melrose) and 'Come Up the Years' (Balin, Kantner).

### **'Somebody To Love'** (D. Slick) / **'She Has Funny Cars'** (Kaukonen, Balin) (Single)

Label: RCA Victor

Release date: 1 April 1967
Charts: US: 5; Canada: 1

**'White Rabbit'** (G. Slick) / **'Plastic Fantastic Lover'** (Balin) (Single)
Label: RCA Victor
Release date: 24 June 1967
Charts: US: 8; Canada: 1

**After Bathing at Baxter's** (Album)
Label: RCA Victor
Release date: 27 November 1967
Charts: US: 17
Side 1: Streetmasse 1. 'The Ballad of You & Me & Pooneil' (Paul Kantner) 2. 'A Small Package of Value Will Come to You, Shortly' (Spencer Dryden, Gary Blackman, Bill Thompson) 3. 'Young Girl Sunday Blues' (Marty Balin, Kantner) The War Is Over 4. 'Martha' (Kantner) 5. 'Wild Tyme (H)' (Kantner) Hymn to an Older Generation 6. 'The Last Wall of the Castle' (Jorma Kaukonen) 7. 'rejoyce' (Grace Slick) Side 2: How Suite It Is 1. 'Watch Her Ride' (Kantner) 2. 'Spare Chaynge' (Jack Casady, Dryden, Kantner) Shizoforest Love Suite 3. 'Two Heads' (Slick) 4. 'Won't You Try / Saturday Afternoon' (Kantner)

**It's hard to imagine Grace Slick being scared of anything. But she was terrified when she first sang live with Jefferson Airplane. Not because she didn't know the songs – her band The Great Society had supported the Airplane so many times, she was word-perfect. She had also listened to the debut album and attended as many gigs as possible as part of the gradual changeover from departing lead singer Signe Anderson.**

**As Slick revealed in her autobiography *Grace Slick: Somebody to Love?: A Rock-and-Roll Memoir* (which is mostly about all the men she shagged), she was thrust onstage at the Fillmore one night in 1966 when Signe failed to turn up:**

> My problem is that I detested performing without lots of rehearsals, without meticulous preparation ... but there I was, ready to start singing, with very little preparation, and, hence, no self-assurance. Even so, I stepped out on stage with plenty of attitude, calculated, looking casual, careful to keep my hands relaxed and by my sides, no fingers twitching. I gave the audience a smile and a silent look that said, 'I know I'm new, I know you're used to Signe, but I'm here now'. Of course, inside I was a nervous wreck.

**She needn't have worried. Slick quickly established herself as a powerful, ballsy, uninhibited lead singer who injected a new energy and purpose into the band.**

If The Beatles were the flag-wavers for British psychedelia, Jefferson Airplane were their West Coast equivalent. They didn't just make psychedelic music; they were heavily involved in promoting it and staging it. In 1965, Marty Balin opened a club – The Matrix, in San Francisco, in a former pizza parlour – and this became a testing ground for many early psychedelic bands. He was also instrumental in persuading Russian immigrant Bill Graham to open the Fillmore ballroom: the premier psychedelic showcase for San Francisco.

Jefferson Airplane came to the genre from a different direction than The Beatles – from folk rather than pop – but like them, the Airplane injected whimsy, surrealism and literary references into their music, lifting them above many of their contemporaries. They weren't as experimental when it came to song structures and instrumentation, but they were much better musicians and improvisers – listen to Jorma Kaukonen's wild guitar solo at the end of 'Somebody To Love', his gorgeous twelve-string instrumental 'Embryonic Journey', and Spencer Dryden's muscular drumming on nearly everything – and they had the powerful, unmistakable voice of Grace Slick, who roughed up the soft edges and gave each song a sense of urgency and earthy sexiness.

Their 1966 debut album *Jefferson Airplane Takes Off* was a modest success but sold mainly around their home city. It was the two albums and some of the singles they released in 1967 that cemented their reputation as one of America's premier psychedelic acts and told the rest of the world that Frisco was the centre of the psychedelic musical universe. They became the go-to band for festivals, ushering in the new year at the Human Be-In in January, and unofficially headlining the Monterey International Pop Festival in June.

Surprisingly, they failed to make any impact on the UK charts until the release of *Bless Its Pointed Little Head* in 1969, and they had to evolve from an Airplane into a Starship before getting a number 1 single either side of the Atlantic (although Canada was surprisingly fond of them).

There were links between Jefferson Airplane and Jerry Garcia – it was the Grateful Dead guitarist who gave them the name for their second album with his comment, 'as surrealistic as a pillow is soft'. He is credited on the sleeve as the band's 'musical and spiritual advisor', and lent his guitar talents to some of the tracks. In fact, according to Kaukonen, he was really the album's co-producer and arranger.

But it was the replacement of vocalist Anderson with Slick that helped the Airplane really take off. She brought with her two compositions that became the band's hit singles of 1967: the powerhouse rocker 'Somebody To Love' – penned by her brother-in-law Darby – and the dark and mysterious 'White Rabbit', inspired by Lewis Carroll's *Alice in Wonderland*.

Recorded in just two weeks, all but two of the tracks on *Surrealistic Pillow* were already staples of Jefferson Airplane's live set. Paul Kantner explained, 'Everything we did was based on the live experience and then taking it to the edge.' The stomping opener, 'She Has Funny Cars', begins with Spencer Dryden's almost tribal drumming, followed by band and vocalists playing and singing the same riff before suddenly launching into a quirky, minor-key verse and playing out on guitar improvisation. '3/5 of a Mile in 10 Seconds' was another stage favourite that owed a lot to Dryden's driving drums and a bluesy guitar riff.

Initially, the record company chose the safest sounding track – the Byrds-like 'My Best Friend' – as the first single, but it made little impact. Then came 'Somebody To Love', which shot into the US top 10, and became one of the sounds of the Summer of Love. Opening with slashing guitars, Dryden's pummelling drums, and Slick's urgent vocals, it's a song about searching and disillusion, but the catchy chorus gives it an optimistic, almost triumphalist air. Love will prevail... if you can find it.

The follow-up single, 'White Rabbit' – track ten on the album – borrows an insistent Spanish beat from Ravel's 'Bolero', married with druggie images from *Alice in Wonderland*: 'One pill makes you larger, and one pill makes you small'. And some pills help you to write songs like 'White Rabbit'. Slick penned it after listening to Miles Davis' *Sketches of Spain* for 24 hours non-stop during an LSD trip and insisted the song was about the hypocrisy of parents reading their children books laced with blatant drug references, then branding them dropouts and freaks for ingesting the substances themselves in later life. She told writer Mark Paytress:

> In all those children's stories, you take some kind of chemical and have a great adventure. Alice in Wonderland is blatant. Eat me! She gets literally high, too big for the room. Drink me! The caterpillar is sitting on a psychedelic mushroom smoking opium!

Others have seen Vietnam War references – the caterpillar represents the tracks of tanks, they suggest. In truth, it's a song that's open to all sorts of interpretations.

Record company RCA weren't entirely comfortable with Jefferson Airplane. They were signed because they were being talked about all over San Francisco, but RCA found their drug-taking, politics and, most of all, their long hair, threatening. They gave them a producer who they thought would keep them on a tight rein to produce family-friendly music, but he didn't know what the hell they were doing.

So RCA took to checking the band's lyrics for drug references, taking out anything slightly suspicious. In response, the band put in things for the record company to find, while sneaking other obscure references past them. So the track 'D.C.B.A.–25' – a jangly pop song with gorgeous harmonies – made it onto the album, despite the fact that the '25' is a reference to LSD 25: so-called 'purple acid'.

Like The Beatles, Jefferson Airplane were blessed with three great singers, in Slick, Balin, and Kantner, and they harmonise to impressive effect on tracks such as 'How Do You Feel', and '3/5 of a Mile in 10 Seconds'. But it was

Grace's voice that made the band stand out, whether it was bluesy wailing over thrashing guitars or providing understated, moody vocals on tracks such as 'Today' (originally written by Balin for Tony Bennett).

From stomping rock to the delicacy of the gentle ballad 'Comin' Back to Me' and Kaukonen's twelve-string instrumental 'Embryonic Journey', *Surrealistic Pillow* was a glorious mixture of folk, pop, and rock, drenched in acid-fuelled psychedelia.

But Jefferson Airplane had even deeper and further to go, releasing a second album in 1967 that inspired *Rolling Stone* to call them 'The best rock 'n' roll band in America'. Out at the end of November, *After Bathing at Baxter's* concentrated on the dark, dangerous elements of *Surrealistic Pillow* that worried RCA executives so much. There were no safe songs here. Instead, there were sprawling suites, with feedback, sound collages and talking voices drenched in echo – 'No man is an island-land-land-land…'!

It's interesting that none of the singles from this album did very well, because there really aren't any singles on it, certainly not with the immediacy of 'Somebody To Love' or 'White Rabbit'. Instead, songs dissolve into or out of jams, move through unexpected chord changes, or plough along using one chord for most of the time. Guitar solos are based on Indian ragas, fed through dense fuzz, and sometimes end by slowing down to a crawl.

First, the title. 'Baxter' was the band's code word for LSD – so the title really meant 'After Tripping on Acid', although the album frequently sounds like the performers are still in mid-trip. The tracks are split into suites, with the first three grouped together: 'Streetmasse', 'Martha', and 'Wild Tyme (H)' are labelled as 'The War Is Over', and the last two on side one called 'Hymn to an Older Generation'. On side two, the four tracks are split evenly between 'How Suite It Is' and 'Shizoforest Love Suite'.

*Surrealistic Pillow* was recorded in two weeks. *After Bathing at Baxter's* took seven months, albeit the time peppered with gigs, including the Monterey International Pop Festival. Paul Kantner, quoted in *Uncut* magazine, said recording the album was 'a little crazy and chaotic. We just went in and jammed. We were taking a lot of acid, both onstage and in the studio, and everywhere else.'

In the same interview, Kaukonen added, 'We were running two eight-track machines side by side. And because we'd had a hit with *Surrealistic Pillow*, we had an unlimited budget. So all of a sudden, we had all this money, all this technology, endless time to mess around and create things. The songs are long; they're convoluted, there's overdubbing up the wazoo.'

The band rented a Victorian mansion in Fulton Street – that's it depicted on the cover, with marijuana bushes growing out of the windows, only it has wings so it can be truly high. It had a pistol range and swimming pool, and according to Kaukonen, 'It was a non-stop carnival. Neil Young was there, Stephen Stills was there, Crosby was an old friend of Kantner's. And people you didn't even know.'

The drugs, money and technology allowed the Airplane to disappear up their own wazoo on 'A Small Package of Value Will Come to You, Shortly' – one and a half minutes of hallucinogenic sound effects – and to horrify RCA with the nine-minute free-form, some may prefer the description 'aimless', instrumental 'Spare Chaynge'.

But there were still plenty of great moments in the madness – the sloppy but exciting sprawl of 'The Ballad of You and Me and Pooneil'; the bluesy chug of 'Young Girl Sunday Blues'; the magnificent guitar work on 'The Last Wall of the Castle', and Grace Slick's mysterious James Joyce references in 'rejoyce' (a song that also offended the straights with the line 'I'd rather have my country die for me').

*After Bathing at Baxter's* has not received the same plaudits as its predecessor, but it's the sound of a band stretching out, experimenting and embracing psychedelia, and is as close as any band got that year to recreating the effects of taking acid on vinyl.

Jefferson Airplane were to combine their melodic and psychedelic influences more successfully on 1968's *Crown of Creation* – while Slick and Kantner began to squeeze founder member Marty Balin out of the songwriting stakes.

Sometimes, their 1960s work seems to be overshadowed by later pop success as Starship. But the two albums they released in 1967 captured the year perfectly, in all its multicoloured, stoned, ramshackle glory.

## Love

Key personnel:
Arthur Lee: guitar, vocal
Bryan MacLean: guitar, vocal
Johnny Echols: guitar
Ken Forssi: bass
Michael Stuart-Ware: drums, percussion

### History

Formed in Los Angeles in 1965 by singer/multi-instrumentalist Arthur Lee – originally Arthur Porter Taylor from Memphis, Tennessee – as The Grass Roots, changing their name to Love upon the appearance of another band with the same name. Other members to join were singer/guitarist Bryan MacLean, lead guitarist Johnny Echols, and drummer Don Conka, soon replaced by Alban 'Snoopy' Pfisterer. Signed to Elektra Records, they had a minor hit with a cover of Burt Bacharach's 'My Little Red Book', and released their self-titled debut album in March 1966. A second single, '7 and 7 Is', became their biggest US hit. Pfisterer moved to harpsichord, and was replaced on drums by Michael Stuart-Ware, while Tjay Cantrelli (born John Barbieri) joined on woodwinds. Their second album *De Capo* was released in November 1966.

### Key releases in 1967

### Forever Changes (Album)

All songs by Arthur Lee except as noted.
Label: Elektra
Release date: 1 November 1967
Charts: US: 157; UK: 24
Side 1: 1. 'Alone Again, Or' (Bryan MacLean) 2. 'A House Is Not a Motel' 3. 'Andmoreagain' 4. 'The Daily Planet' 5. 'Old Man' (MacLean) 6. 'The Red Telephone' Side 2: 1. 'Maybe The People Would Be the Times or Between Clark and Hilldale' 2. 'Live and Let Live' 3. 'The Good Humor Man He Sees Everything Like This' 4. 'Bummer in the Summer' 5. 'You Set the Scene'.

There wasn't a lot of love in Love. Some people thought the band should actually be called Hate, because they were so damn hostile and intimidating – 'a bunch of hoods', said fanzine *Mojo Navigator*. The chief hood was Arthur Lee, the pugnacious, egotistical, antisocial control freak who was guitarist, singer, chief songwriter and his own worst enemy.

Love were a multi-racial band – a rare thing in 1960s rock and pop – but not because Lee was making any great statement about racial harmony. It was because he loved the music of The Beatles and The Byrds and wanted to play their brand of folk-rock which, in those days, was more of a white man's thing.

Bryan MacLean joined because he wanted to be part of Lee's black folk-rock band, and Lee wanted Bryan because he used to be a roadie for The Byrds. An intense rivalry developed between them that MacLean put down to Lee's jealousy at the former's songwriting chops. But Love was Lee's band, and Lee usually got his way, even if it meant ruining a perfectly good album like 1966's *Da Capo* with an aimless side-long jam called 'Revelation'.

Their sole 1967 album release *Forever Changes* has been reassessed in the last half-century. At the time, the album didn't make much of an impact in the States, partly due to Lee's refusal to tour and the band being overshadowed by labelmates The Doors. It did better in the UK, but acknowledgement of its place in the pantheon of psychedelic albums has had to wait. Today, it's frequently ranked as the year's best release, and in 1996 was number 11 in *Mojo* magazine's list of the 100 greatest albums ever made.

And that's surprising because *Forever Changes*, while undoubtedly a psychedelic folk album, is not the hippy-trippy flower-power celebration you might expect. It's actually quite moody and sinister – even in harder-edged L.A., Love were seen as dangerous outsiders, dropping acid and experimenting with heroin in Bela Lugosi's mansion. Lee was cynical about the Summer of Love and its potential to cure the world's ills with sunshine; he was obsessed with his own mortality and his band was falling apart.

Look at some of the lyrics he penned for the album: 'More confusions, blood transfusions ... the water's turned to blood' in 'A House Is Not a Motel'; 'When you've given all you had and everything still turns out bad' in 'Andmoreagain'; 'I don't know if I'm living or if I'm supposed to be / Sometimes my life is so eerie' in 'The Red Telephone'. And try this from 'Live and Let Live':

Oh, the snot has caked against my pants
It has turned into crystal
There's a bluebird sitting on a branch
I guess I'll take my pistol
I've got it in my hand
Because he's on my land

Lee was influenced by *Sgt. Pepper*, as every psychedelic band was after June that year. But he was also writing about the Vietnam War, inspired by a veteran who returned from the conflict with horrific tales of young kids calling out their mothers' names as they died in killing fields far from home. And he was writing about himself and his own demons, his disillusion with the hippie movement and the tensions within the band itself.

Even the title was cynical – it came from a story Lee had heard about the breakup of a love affair. The woman complained, 'You said you'd love me forever'. The man replied, "Forever changes". Lee always insisted the album's full title was *Love Forever Changes*.

Love had already shown their psychedelic credentials on their second LP *De Capo*. That was mostly a harder electric album. But for *Forever Changes*, the record label persuaded lee to adopt a softer, folk-based approach. For a man who wasn't usually open to other people's suggestions, he surprisingly followed the advice.

However, early sessions were fraught. By 1967, internal dissension and large amounts of heroin were practically destroying the band. In Barney Hoskyns' book on Lee, MacLean said, 'You kind of didn't care. There was a little stigma attached to it (heroin) – it was a little deeper in. Arthur was the one who turned me on to it, though I was what you'd call a chipper or weekender. Johnny (Echols) and Kenny (Forsi) got real bad'.

With the band fragmented and virtually unable to play, producer Bruce Botnick called in session musicians from Phil Spector's legendary Wrecking Crew to get things started, recording two of the album's eleven tracks. In liner noters for a 2001 re-release of the album, Botnick said, 'The group were present, too. I remember (them) physically crying at this session. The band was so shocked, so put out, so hurt that it caused them to forget about their problems and become a band again'.

Despite his leadership of the band and songwriting dominance, Lee didn't pen the album's most well-known track. The Latin-influenced 'Alone Again, Or' came from guitarist Bryan MacLean, who had a songwriting rivalry with Lee akin to the later relationship between John Lennon and Paul McCartney, and MacLean's lyrics are more reflective of the band's name and the 1967 summer. It's a 'love's gone wrong' song, but one with a sense of anger and urgency that's tempered by the wash of strings and the pretty guitar phrases in D major. MacLean recycles that Dsus4 phrase in the gentlest song on the album – 'Old Man', a story of the redemptive powers of love.

But elsewhere, we are in Arthur Lee's dark, scary world. 'A House Is Not a Motel' is suitably aggressive and brutal, given its subject matter of the Vietnam War, and features a searing slice of lead guitar by Johnny Echols. 'The Red Telephone' contains strange, unsettling chord sequences and, as mentioned above, lyrics to make your blood run cold. 'Andmoreagain' is relatively gentle, with some beautiful melodic lines, while 'May the People...' could almost be Burt Bacharach, with some of his trademark horn riffs, were it not for the fact that it seems to be about Lee's feelings of dislocation and disassociation with the music going on around him in L.A. (The Whisky A Go Go club was on the corner of Clark and Hillsdale).

As for 'Bummer in the Summer', this was Lee's cynical view of the Summer of Love and its apparent futility. Writer Harvey Kubernick said, 'He described things that were very menacing. We're coming out of the Summer of Love, and he's singing "Bummer in the Summer". He's talking about racial tensions, tensions between men and women'.

Guitarist Johnny Echols added the following In a 2012 interview for Kubernick's book on 1967:

> There are others (songs) that speak to the insecurity of people, speak to the animosity that is happening to the kids growing up not trusting anyone other than people their own age ... One of the kind of prevailing things I've heard is 'This is the soundtrack of my life'. And I think that is the best definition of it. A soundtrack of the life. Because *Forever Changes* was a soundtrack of the times. The music reflected the times we were living in.

But the jagged edges were smoothed out by the strings and horns that wash across the album – Lee had all the orchestral backing in his head and sang the parts to arranger David Angel. Or Lee arranged them all himself – the arguments raged for years over who was or wasn't responsible for various elements of the album. Indeed, MacLean claims Lee deliberately sabotaged the album's best song – 'Alone Again, Or' – by mixing his harmony vocals louder and burying the writer's lead melody. So nobody has actually heard the melody of that song – instead, you hear the harmony.

Even the cover was ambivalent – there was the band name in an ornate, *Sgt. Pepper*-ish font with the multicoloured faces of the band members drawn by Bob Pepper (no relation), who was known as the illustrator for the Philip K. Dick novels. But the colours are frequently muted shades of blue, green and purple, with just the occasional flash of yellow.

*Forever Changes* was greeted with a fair amount of indifference when it came out. Gene Youngblood of the *L.A. Free Press* described it as 'soft, subtle. Forever changing in tonal color, rhythm patterns, vocal nuances, lyric substance. Exquisite nuances.' But the record-buying public, particularly in the States, were not interested in Lee's anger, fears and anxieties laid bare on record, even if they were sugarcoated with sweet strings.

And the album also broke the band. There was one more session in January 1968 that inspired rumours of a *lost* Love album. But with Lee's inability to hold things together, and two members irreparably hooked on heroin, MacLean was the first to quit – he said, 'Arthur was like, 'You can't quit, cause you're already fired!''. By mid-1968, only Arthur Lee was left with the Love name.

He had feared he would die after making *Forever Changes*, but he lived until 2006, by which time he had reformed Love two or three times and served a prison sentence for firearms offences. He survived long enough to see his 1967 album hailed as one of the best albums ever made, groundbreaking and a masterpiece, mixing folk with rock, pop and even Latin – admirers include Robert Plant, The Teardrop Explodes and Creation Records boss Arthur McGee.

An *Allmusic* review calls it 'an album of enduring beauty, but it's also one of the few major works of its era that saw the dark clouds looming on the cultural horizon, and the result was music that was as prescient as it was compelling'.

# Pink Floyd

Key personnel:
Syd Barrett: guitar, vocals, percussion
Nick Mason: drums, percussion
Roger Waters: bass, vocals, percussion, slide whistle, gong
Richard Wright: keyboards, cello, violin, percussion, vocals

## History

Architectural college students Nick Mason, Roger Waters and Richard Wright circulated around various short-lived bands before forming Sigma 6 (later The Tea Set) in London in 1963 with guitarist Bob Klose. Waters' childhood pal Roger 'Syd' Barrett joined, replacing Klose on guitar. He suggested the name The Pink Floyd Sound – after blues musicians Pink Anderson and Floyd Council – when they found themselves booked to play with another band called The Tea Set. Taken on by management team Andrew King and Peter Jenner, they became known for long, drawn-out instrumentals and rudimentary light shows. By 1966 they were part of the underground music scene, becoming the house band for the UFO Club in London.

## Key releases in 1967

### 'Arnold Layne' / 'Candy and a Currant Bun' (Single)

Both songs by Syd Barrett, credited to The Pink Floyd.
Label: EMI Columbia
Release date: 10 March 1967
Charts: UK: 20; Netherlands: 24

### 'See Emily Play' / 'The Scarecrow' (Single)

Both songs by Syd Barrett.
Label: EMI Columbia (UK), Tower (US)
Release date: 16 June 1967
Charts: UK: 6; Ireland: 10; US: 134

### The Piper at the Gates of Dawn (Album)

All songs by Syd Barrett except as noted.
Label: EMI Columbia
Release date: 5 August 1967
Charts: UK: 6; France: 10; US: 131
Side 1: 1. 'Astronomy Domine' 2. 'Lucifer Sam' 3. 'Matilda Mother' 4. 'Flaming' 5. 'Pow R. Toc H' (Syd Barrett, Roger Waters, Richard Wright, Nick Mason) 6. 'Take Up Thy Stethoscope and Walk' (Waters) Side 2: 1. 'Interstellar Overdrive' (Barrett, Waters, Wright, Mason) 2. 'The Gnome' 3. 'Chapter 24' 4. 'The Scarecrow' 5. 'Bike'

They were young, fresh-faced ex-college students with little musical ability and a limited repertoire of cover numbers. Yet, they became one of the biggest bands in the world.

Pink Floyd should really be a footnote in musical history if it wasn't for three things: a gentle arrogance that can only exist in the knowledge that you have well-off parents to fall back on; a charismatic frontman with a drug problem and penchant for writing childish, whimsical ditties; and a lot of luck. Oh, and they had a light show that was frequently better than the band.

They were in the right place at the right time and doing the right things, even though they didn't know it. Much of what made them successful came about by accident – for example, the lead guitarist couldn't play very well, so when it came to his instrumental break, he ran a metal cigarette lighter up and down his strings and fed the sound through an echo machine.

The result was something people had never heard before, and they reacted in one of two extreme ways. The hippies, druggies and freaks lay back and let it wash over them, believing it was opening up new sensory avenues. The straights hated it and denied it was really music – on one occasion, even a judge agreed with them.

Pink Floyd were also blessed with a management team that really liked them, looked after them and didn't attempt to just rip them off. Peter Jenner and Andrew King were good mates who had once shared a house together – Jenner had his own record label, DNA, while Andrew had a job with an educational training company. Jenner wanted the Floyd on his label, but what the band really needed was good management. Jenner and King thought it might be interesting, and nobody else was offering.

As 1967 arrived, Pink Floyd had a weekly residency at the UFO Club in London (short for Underground Freak-Out and pronounced Yoofoh) run by former Harvard graduate Joe Boyd and British photographer-cum-political-activist John 'Hoppy' Hopkins. According to *Town* magazine at the time, Pink Floyd were 'the underground's house orchestra. Their music sounds more like Thelonius Monk than The Rolling Stones. Projected slides bathed the musicians and audience in hypnotic and frenzied patterns of liquid-coloured light. Honeycombs, galaxies and throbbing cells whirl around the group with accelerating abandon as the music develops.'

The band had a tune written by Syd Barrett, 'Interstellar Overdrive', apparently inspired by Peter Jenner trying to hum Love's 'My Little Red Book' (or it may have been Barrett's attempt to play the theme from TV comedy series *Steptoe and Son*). It was little more than a descending series of major chords starting on B and finishing on E, sandwiching an instrumental freak-out section that lasted pretty much as long as the band could play it and the audience could bear it. Boyd recalled in his book *White Bicycles*:

> They would just jam for a long period of time, for ten minutes, fifteen minutes, and would get very abstract. I think that Syd's melodies – this playful, almost

folk, 19th-century type of almost like school kids rhyming songs, very melodic – made those improvisations work. If it'd just been a blues jam, a kind of sub-English extension of the Grateful Dead jamming on a blues, it wouldn't have been so interesting or so significant or given the whole scene its confidence. And that song, in particular, is a classic example of Syd's sort of collage-y approach to making music.

Boyd must be credited with kick-starting Pink Floyd's recording career. As a former A&R man for Elektra Records, he was keen to get them a deal and produced a recording session for a demo of tracks that were part of the band's repertoire at the time, including the aforementioned 'Interstellar Overdrive', a risque drug song called 'Candy and a Currant Bun' that had to have its lyrics watered down, and a quirky, disturbing little number entitled 'Arnold Layne'. Everyone involved was so confident of success, they even shot a promotional film to accompany the latter track.

A deal with Polydor was in the offing, one that would keep Boyd as an independent producer (encouraging him to start his own company, Witchseason Productions). But that changed when EMI showed an interest, offering money, studio time and the cachet of belonging to The Beatles' label. So it was goodbye Joe – who went on to produce The Incredible String Band and Fairport Convention – and hello Beatles engineer Norman Smith.

Ironically, even the hallowed surroundings of EMI's studios on Abbey Road in St John's Wood couldn't improve on Boyd's recordings, and the versions of 'Arnold Layne' and 'Candy and a Currant Bun' released in March, were his demos taped earlier at Sound Techniques (An EP was also released with versions made at EMI).

Even by psychedelic rock standards, 'Arnold Layne' is... strange. Chosen because it was one of the few tracks Pink Floyd had that could conceivably be whittled down from its live length of ten-to-fifteen minutes, it told the story of a cross-dressing thief stealing ladies' intimate apparel from their washing lines. The titular Arnold was, according to Roger Waters, based on a real thief who pilfered bras and knickers from female student lodgers at the Waters and Barrett homes.

Launching almost immediately into the first verse, Barrett seems to revel in the sleaze with his drawn-out syllables over a driving beat; Wright's cheap-sounding organ swoops in and out like the soundtrack to a UFO film; Mason's drums are front and centre of the mix and the whole thing is drenched in echo. Wright gets a short organ solo that was recorded separately and then edited in place.

'Arnold Layne' reached number 20 in the charts with a little help from Pink Floyd's management paying to boost its position, despite the fact that it was banned by the BBC, Radio Caroline and Radio London for sexual perversion. The song has since become a minor psychedelic classic, unlike its B-side, which wasn't nearly as entertaining nor as clever.

It was good enough for EMI to request a follow-up single, but the band had to troop back to Sound Techniques, this time with Norman Smith in the producer's chair. The chosen song was another Barrett composition, 'See Emily Play', which references Games for May – a Pink Floyd multimedia event organised by Jenner and King at the Queen Elizabeth Hall on London's South Bank: in fact, the band premiered the song there.

Games for May was the quintessential psychedelic experience – with a spectacular light show complementing the band's way-out music and the audience sitting to watch and listen rather than dance – and further helped cement Pink Floyd's position as the UK's premier *happening* group. They had also appeared on *Top of the Pops* – twice – before Barrett put his foot down.

'See Emily Play' had everything 'Arnold Layne' had and more, but without the sexual perversion. Waters' bouncing bass anchors everything, with powerful drumming from Mason, a great sing-along chorus and twinkly musical-box interruptions. Barrett produces a slide guitar sound with his electric lighter (or a plastic ruler – memories are hazy) and Wright once again gets a short but spirited keyboard solo.

The Emily in the title was said to be a girl that Barrett, during a psychedelic trip, had supposedly seen sleeping in the woods. She was later identified as The Honourable Emily Young – daughter of Wayland Young, 2nd Baron Kennett – who was a frequent visitor to the UFO club. The single, backed with a soon-to-be album track, soared to number 5 in the UK. Perhaps it would've gone further if the increasingly unpredictable Barrett hadn't put the kibosh on TV appearances. In fact, he tried to stop the single's release, believing it to be too commercial.

The recording was sandwiched between sessions for Pink Floyd's (they had dropped the 'The') debut album *The Piper at the Gates of Dawn* at EMI's studios. Life at the future Abbey Road Studios was not as free and easy for the Floyd as it was for The Beatles – recording was done in regimented three-hour blocks, with songs being finished in one or two days, overseen by men wearing white coats. On the positive side, the studios had an extensive library of recorded sound effects plus a collection of unusual musical and percussion instruments.

Nick Mason recalls the recording 'went pretty smoothly ... there was general enthusiasm from everybody, and Syd seemed to be more relaxed and the atmosphere more focused'. But in the December 2007 issue of *Guitar World* magazine, Norman Smith had a different take:

> The band would be in the studio recording a particular number. I would bring them back into the control room to listen to the playback. And I would suggest perhaps a little phrasing alteration in what Syd was singing. Syd was nodding. He didn't say anything, but he was nodding, like a 'yes' nod. He seemed to be paying attention, so I said, 'Okay, go back in the studio and we'll do another take'. So they go back in the studio and Syd did exactly the same thing he'd done on the previous take. I said to myself, 'I think I'm wasting my time here'.

However, the final result certainly wasn't a waste of time, not by a long shot. *The Piper at the Gates of Dawn* is an explosive debut, a barely-constrained mixture of

Pink Floyd's wild abandon and intricate chord structures, with songs that crash out of the speakers like a runaway juggernaut. 'Astronomy Domine' is the sound of some kind of UFO battle in space; 'Lucifer Sam' shows their ability to create memorable melodies out of apparent chaos, while the nine-minute 'Interstellar Overdrive' hints strongly at their challenging live performances.

Most of the songs were written by Barrett and display his childish whimsy, but they are given a sinister edge through the band's inventive musical flourishes and producer Smith's judicious use of sound effects. Nowhere is this more blatant than on tracks such as 'Flaming' – an unlikely US single – that combines lyrics about unicorns and buttercups with wordless vocal noises, cacophonous improvisations, and, apparently, windup toys; or the closer 'Bike', in which a nursery rhyme with a fairground backing morphs via ghostly footsteps into a minute and a half of rhythmic sound effects, random tuned percussion, and what sounds like a tape loop of disturbed quacking ducks.

If psychedelia was music inspired by LSD, then *The Piper...* was as psychedelic as you could possibly get. It was as way-out, wacky and weird as any stoned hippie could hope for. The album's reputation has grown in stature over the years – included in *Mojo* magazine's 50 Most Out There Albums of All Time, *Q* magazine's list of the 100 greatest British albums, and placed at 253 in *Rolling Stone*'s 2012 update of the 500 greatest albums ever.

In hindsight, the album's reputation as a psychedelic lodestone is buttressed by the sad decline of Syd Barrett because nothing says psychedelic like an acid casualty. As 1967 progressed, the band's lead singer and creative force began to unravel, missing gigs or, when he did make them, standing there with his guitar around his neck and his hands at his sides, staring vacantly into the audience. On one occasion, he failed to appear and was deputized by Davy O'List from The Nice.

Attempts to intervene by Syd's bandmates and friends proved of little value – it would've required a level of understanding and insight that just didn't exist in the popular music fraternity back then. And, as good middle-class English lads, the Floyd were adept at sticking their heads in the sand and hoping for the best.

But by December, it was clear something had to be done. It was suggested to bring in a second guitarist and singer to take the pressure off Barrett, much as The Beach Boys did with Brian Wilson. The Floyd contacted an old friend from Cambridge – an accomplished musician called David Gilmour who played with locally successful band Jokers Wild. So Pink Floyd ended the year as an unstable and uncomfortable five-piece, and it wasn't to last. As Nick Mason recounts in his autobiography, the band was on its way to a gig when someone said, 'Shall we pick up Syd?'. The response was, 'No, fuck it, let's not bother'. And that was the end of the 1967 lineup of Pink Floyd.

In later years, in times of greater maturity and understanding, Syd's decline and departure would haunt the band so much, they would compose a long track about him on one of their most successful albums. But they would spend the next seven years trying to match the sheer invention and psychedelic chutzpah of their celebrated 1967 album *The Piper at the Gates of Dawn*.

# Cream

Key personnel:
Ginger Baker: drums, percussion, vocals
Jack Bruce: bass, piano, vocals, harmonica
Eric Clapton: guitar, vocals

## History

**Regarded as the world's first supergroup, Cream were created by key players from two bands: John Mayall's Bluesbreakers, and The Graham Bond Organisation. Guitarist Eric Clapton came from the former and was chafing at the restrictions placed upon him. Ginger Baker was the drummer for the latter and was looking at forming a new band. However, he was surprised when Clapton insisted on recruiting Jack Bruce, who had played bass in both groups and, notoriously, didn't get on with Baker. Signed to Reaction Records, they had a minor UK hit single with 'Wrapping Paper', followed by 'I Feel Free', which reached number 11. Debut album *Fresh Cream* was issued in late 1966 in the UK, hitting number 6 in the charts.**

## Key releases in 1967

### Fresh Cream (Album - US version)

Label: Atco
Release date: January 1967
Charts: US: 39
Side 1: 1. 'I Feel Free' (Jack Bruce, Pete Brown) 2. 'N.S.U.' (Bruce) 3. 'Sleepy Time Time' (Bruce, Janet Godfrey) 4. 'Dreaming' (Bruce) 5. 'Sweet Wine' (Ginger Baker, Janet Godfrey) Side 2: 1. 'Cat's Squirrel' (Dr Ross, arr. Bruce, Baker, Eric Clapton) 2. 'Four Until Late' (Johnson, arr. Clapton) 3. 'Rollin' and Tumblin' (Hambone Willie Newbern) 4. 'I'm So Glad' (Skip James) 5. 'Toad' (Baker)

### Disraeli Gears (Album)

Label: Reaction
Release date: 2 November 1967
Charts: UK: 5; US: 4; Australia: 1; Finland: 1; Sweden: 1; France: 2; New Zealand: 4
Side 1: 1. 'Strange Brew' (Eric Clapton, Felix Pappalardi, Gail Collins) 2. 'Sunshine of Your Love' (Jack Bruce, Clapton, Pete Brown) 3. 'World of Pain' (Pappalardi, Collins) 4. 'Dance the Night Away' (Bruce, Brown) 5. 'Blue Condition' (Ginger Baker) Side 2: 1. 'Tales of Brave Ulysses (Clapton, Martin Sharp) 2. 'SWLABR' (Bruce, Brown) 3. 'We're Going Wrong' (Bruce) 4. 'Outside Woman Blues' (Arthur Reynolds, arr. Clapton) 5. 'Take It Back' (Bruce, Brown) 6. 'Mother's Lament' (trad arr. Bruce Clapton, Baker)

### 'Sunshine of Your Love' / 'SWLABR' (Single)

Song credits as above.
Label: Atco

Release date: December 1967
Charts: US: 5, Canada: 3

They started arguing at the very first rehearsal. Jack Bruce and Ginger Baker just seemed to rub each other up the wrong way, while Eric Clapton looked on in discomfort. But when they played together, it was magical. Everything seemed to work – those big, powerhouse drums slotted in perfectly with Bruce's virtuoso bass-playing. And as for Clapton, wasn't he already God?

His vision was to be a frontman like Buddy Guy, leading a blues trio. It soon became clear that Bruce and Baker were no one's backing group, and the sound they were after required the three of them to be contributing equally. Live, this meant heading off into extended jams and solos, with each group member apparently trying to outdo the others in virtuosity and decibels. This was the blues, played loud and heavy and seemingly endlessly.

But on record, where more discipline and brevity were required, Cream showed another string to their bow – the psychedelic side. Bruce was writing with poet Pete Brown, who would come up with quirky, surreal lyrics that Bruce would match with equally quirky music. So the first single, 'Wrapping Paper' was about as far from the blues as you could get, almost a music-hall number led by rolling, over-strung piano, close-harmony backing vocals and an instrumental section on cello. 'Spoonful' it ain't.

The follow-up 'I Feel Free' – another Bruce and Brown number – at least gave Clapton a little more to do, but is still a psychedelic pop song rather than anything resembling the blues, with humming, clapping, and a piano constantly hitting the same high note. At least the debut album – released in December 1966 in the UK, but a month later in the US – had Willie Dixon's 'Spoonful' on it (though it was left off the US release in favour of 'I Feel Free'), the traditional electric guitar workout 'Cat's Squirrel', plus some covers of old blues standards.

But there was also Bruce's 'N.S.U.', with its quirky chord changes and lyrics about... well, it was apparently something to do with a member of the band having a venereal disease. Another Bruce composition – 'Dreaming' – was a pretty pop song with rather random backing vocals and overlapping lead, while Ginger Baker's 'Sweet Wine' could've been a pop song by The Yardbirds.

So Cream were always more than a blues band, and their psychedelic credentials came to the fore on their second album *Disraeli Gears*, released in November 1967. By that time, the musical landscape had undergone an upheaval; everyone had turned on and tuned in to the Summer of Love, and *Sgt. Pepper* was encouraging musicians to march to a different beat. Clapton spoke of it in his autobiography:

> London in 1967 was buzzing. It was an extraordinary melting pot of fashion, music, art and intellect – a movement of young people all concerned in some

> way or another with the evolution of their art. There was an underground too, where you would get these seminal influences suddenly showing up out of nowhere like they had come out of the woodwork.

Clapton had his first acid trip at London club The Speakeasy, around the time *Sgt. Pepper* was released. Baker was already struggling with a heroin addiction from his days as a jazz drummer, while Bruce got into the drug as Cream were hitting their heights. So, with their minds expanded, they were ready to contribute even more self-penned material to the new album.

It was recorded in New York in May with a hot young producer called Felix Pappalardi, who had such an influence on some of the finished tracks, he actually received songwriting credits. In his autobiography, Clapton tells of one composition that the wunderkind changed beyond recognition:

> On the very first night, he took home with him the tape we had previously recorded of 'Lawdy Mama', which was a standard 12-bar blues, and came back the next day having transformed it into a kind of McCartney-esque pop song, complete with new lyrics and the title 'Strange Brew'. I didn't particularly like the song, but I respected the fact that he had created a pop song without completely destroying the original groove.

Clapton's main contribution was 'Tales of Brave Ulysses', written with the help of an artist called Martin Sharp, who scribbled down a verse for him on a napkin – surreal, evocative lines about riding 'upon a steamer to the violence of the sun / And the colours of the sea blind your eyes with trembling mermaids.' Clapton provided a descending tune that owed not a little to The Lovin' Spoonful's 'Summer in the City' (and would inspire The Electric Light Orchestra's '10538 Overture').

Clappers worked with Bruce and Pete Brown on what is arguably the most famous Cream song, 'Sunshine of Your Love', later covered live by Jimi Hendrix. In fact, the song was a tribute to the guitarist, Bruce having composed the riff after going to a Hendrix concert. The opening lyrics came about after an all-night session, as Pete Brown looked through the window at the world waking up and street lamps shutting down. 'It's getting near dawn', he recited, 'And lights close their tired eyes'.

'World of Pain' allowed Clapton to exercise his wah-wah pedal to great effect on another Pappalardi-reshaped pop song, while 'Dance the Night away' showcases Bruce's rubber band bass in a sort of twelve-string Byrds tribute, complete with totally out-of-his-skull lyrics by Pete Brown.

The cryptically-titled 'SWLABR' (it may stand for She Walks Like a Bearded Rainbow) is another slice of heavy pop psychedelia from Bruce and Brown and is apparently about a man who has been dumped by his girlfriend, so he goes around defacing pictures of her. 'We're Going Wrong' is a slow psychedelic blues that's lyrically quite sparse, but Bruce stretches the words out. Baker plays mallets throughout instead of sticks, and Clapton provides subdued guitar chords and occasional mournful lead.

The album is completed by a couple of bluesy numbers and then a little oddity: a two-minute rendition of a traditional Cockney ballad also known as 'Your Baby Has Gone Down the Plughole'. And the album title? It was a malapropism by one of the band's roadies – Clapton was talking about getting a racing bicycle, and the roadie said 'Disraeli gears!', meaning derailleur gears. Ginger Baker said, 'We all just fell over. We said that's got to be the album title'. Completing the album's psychedelic credentials is the cover designed by the aforementioned Martin Sharp: a multicoloured collage of trees, flowers and feathers almost obscuring the three band members' faces.

Cream played the Fillmore in San Francisco and toured the US later in the year, establishing themselves as a major musical force on both sides of the Atlantic, and helping to push their third single, 'Sunshine of Your Love' into the US top 10. They were to have even more success in 1968 with their double LP *Wheels of Fire*, but *Disraeli Gears* is the album that successfully merged their blues roots with their psychedelic leanings.

**Right:** The Beatles' hugely influential *Sgt Pepper's Lonely Hearts Club Band* - dubbed 'the Second Coming of the audio Christ'. *(Parlophone)*

**Left:** The Fab Four at their psychedelic peak - Paul, George, Ringo and John.

**Right:** Great album, shame about the film. The Beatles' Magical Mystery Tour. (*Parlophone*)

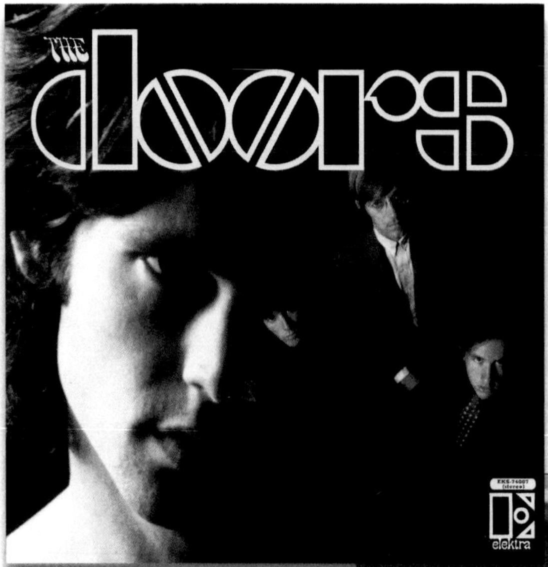


**Left:** This dark debut from The Doors opened 1967 and provided one of the anthems for the Summer of Love. (*Elektra Record*)

**Right:** The Doors in 1967 - Densmore, Krieger, Manzarek and Morrison.

**Left:** A strange cover for *Strange Days*, the second 1967 offering from The Doors. *(Elektra Records)*

**Right:** Jim Hendrix askes the question, *Are You Experienced.* (*Track*)

**Left:** Hendrix burns up the stage during his barnstorming performance at the Monterey International Pop Festival.

**Right:** *Axis: Bold As Love* annoyed Jimi with the inappropriate religious message on the cover. (*Track*)

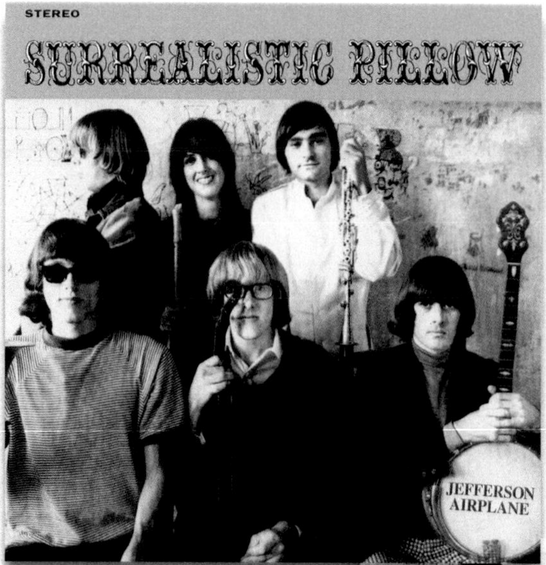


**Left:** Jefferson Airplane really took off with their second album, *Surrealistic Pillow*. (*RCA Victor*)

**Right:** The band with new girl Grace Slick, pictured in early 1967.

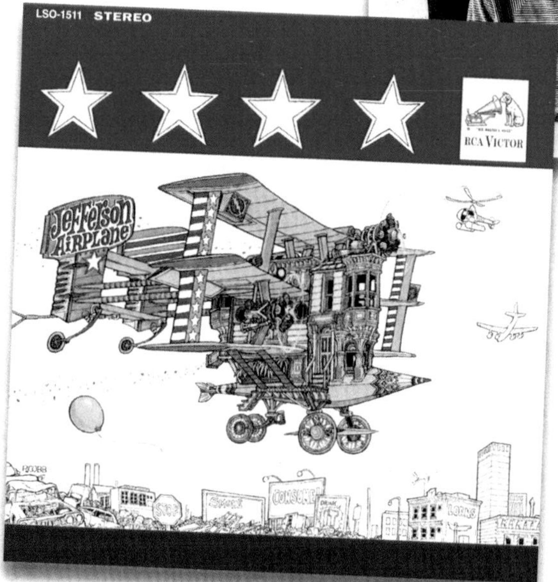


**Left:** The sprawling and undisciplined *After Bathing At Baxter's* was probably too psychedelic for its own good. (*RCA Victor*)

**Right:** Love's *Forever Changes* has become an iconic psychedelic album - but it is darker than you would expect. (*Elektra Records*)

**Left:** Arthur Lee with the Love line-up that recorded Forever Changes - but it wasn't to last.

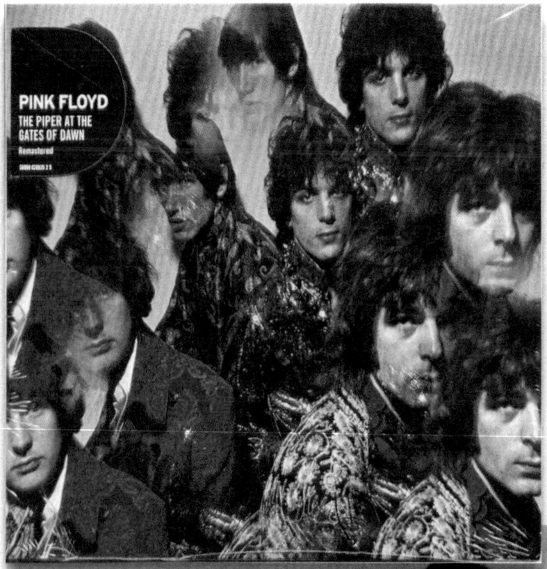


**Left:** The Pink Floyd debut *Piper At The Gates Of Dawn* showed Syd Barrett's collage-y approach to music. (*EMI Columbia*)

**Right:** Waters, Mason, Barrett and Wright - but only three of them would go on to make Pink Floyd one of the biggest bands in the world.

**Left:** The Floyd's delightful 1967 single 'See Emily Play'. (*EMI Columbia*)

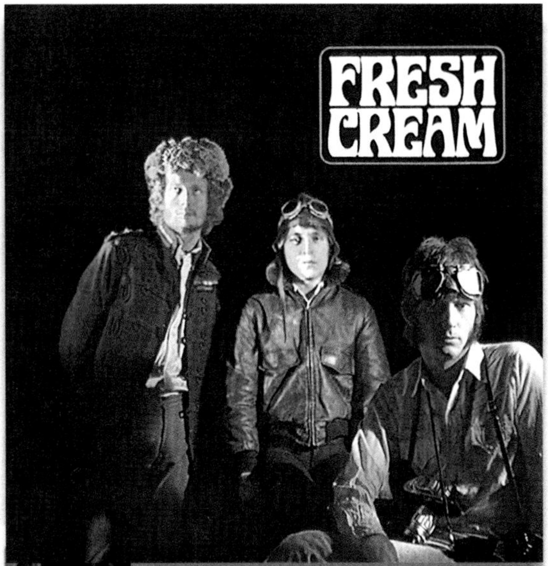


**Right:** Cream, the world's first supergroup, made their recording debut on *Fresh Cream*. (*Reaction Records*)

**Left:** Ginger Baker, Jack Bruce and Eric Clapton, looking about as flower-power as you can get.

**Right:** Cream's 1967 psychedelic tour de force, *Disraeli Gears*. (*Reaction Records*)

**Left:** The Byrds went through many musical changes, but in 1967 they were at the forefront of psychedelic rock with *Younger Than Yesterday*. (*Columbia*)

**Right:** So they wanted to be rock 'n' roll stars! The Byrds in 1967.

**Right:** *The Who Sell Out* was a loose concept album about pirate radio and advertising that extended to the hilarious cover. (*Track*)

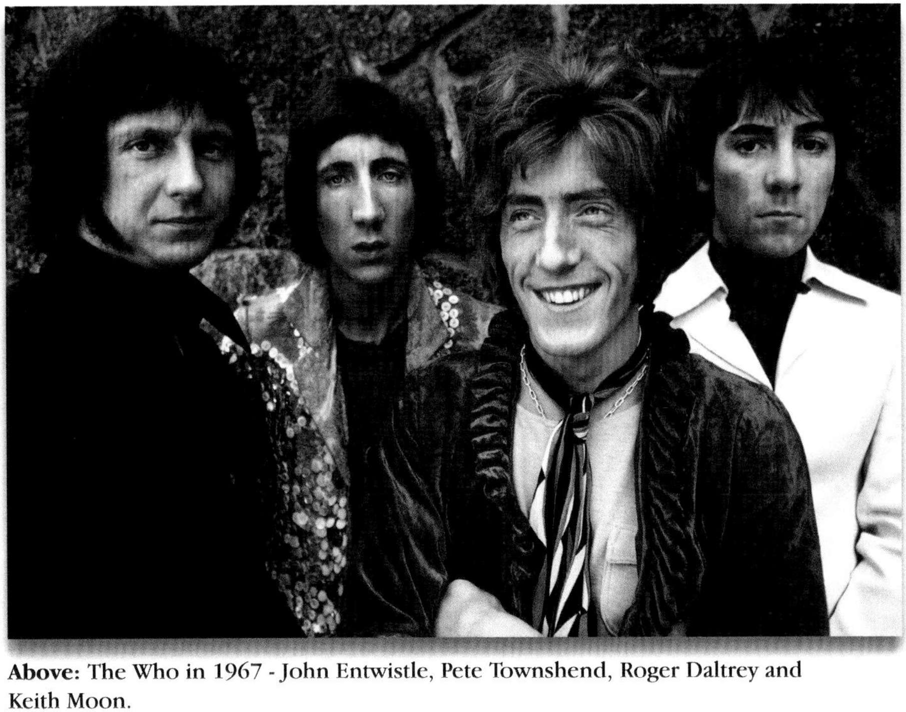

**Above:** The Who in 1967 - John Entwistle, Pete Townshend, Roger Daltrey and Keith Moon.

**Left:** The original artwork for the Beach Boys' 'lost' 1967 masterpiece *Smile*. (*Capitol*)

**Right:** The Beach Boys in 1967, with Brian Wilson in the middle.

**Left:** Smiley Smile, the Beach Boys album that finally surfaced in 1967, featuring 'Good Vibrations' and 'Heroes And Villains'. (*Capitol*)

**Right:** Regarded as one of the Rolling Stones' most successful albums, *Between The Buttons* successfully combined psychedelia with their brand of swaggering blues rock. (*Decca*)

**Left:** The Stones in 1967 - Keith, Brian, Charlie, Mick and Bill.

**Right:** The Stones go fully psychedelic and disappear down a musical rabbit hole on *Their Satanic Majesties Request.* (*Decca*)

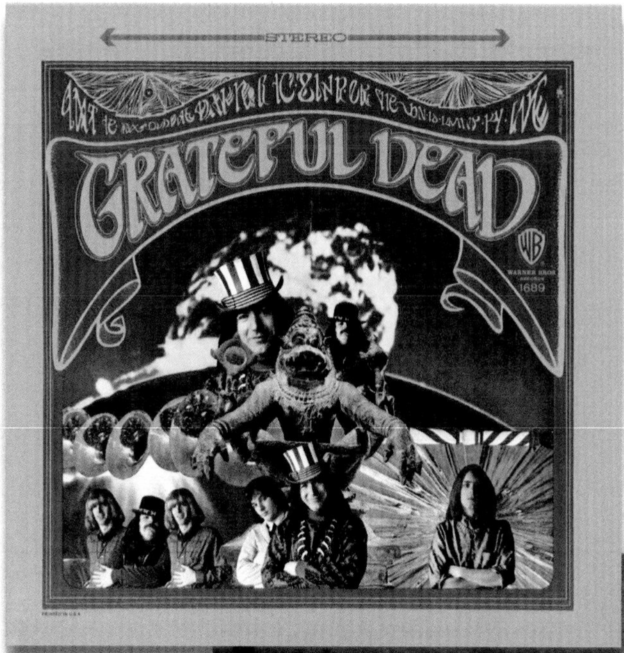


**Left:** The Grateful Dead's 1967 debut, showing just a hint of what a waaayyyy-out band they were to become. (*Warner Bros*)

**Right:** The Dead in 1967, ready to sweep all before them.

**Right:** Donovan's fourth album *Mellow Yellow* was only released in the US at the time because of a contractual dispute. (*Epic*)

**Left:** Troubadour Donovan Leitch with the year's must-have instrument.

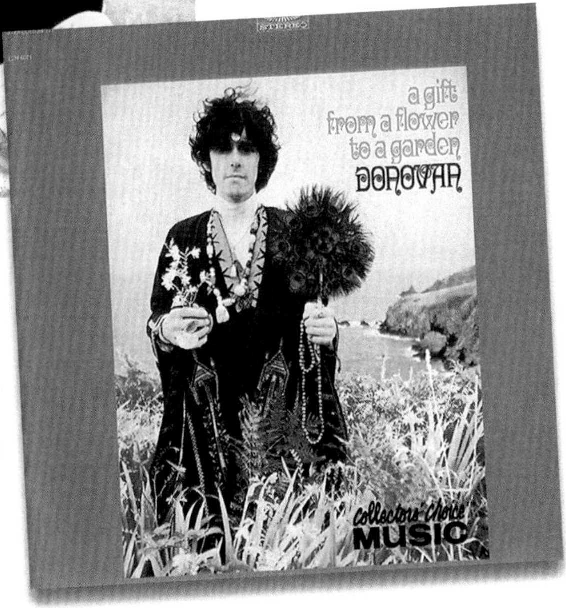


**Right:** *A Gift From A Flower To A Garden,* a double LP from Donovan that was originally released as two single albums. (*Epic*)

**Left:** The first – and best – album from Moby Grape. (*Columbia*)

**Right:** Moby Grape before it all went horribly wrong - full of talent, hope and ambition.

**Right:** A conceptual psychedelia masterpiece and arguably the first progressive rock album - *Days Of Future Passed* by The Moody Blues. *(Decca)*

**Below:** The Moodies in 1967, on the cusp of a long and successful career.

**Left:** Frank Zappa's *Lumpy Gravy* - a composer and musician who was ahead of his time and out on his own. (*Capitol, Verve*)

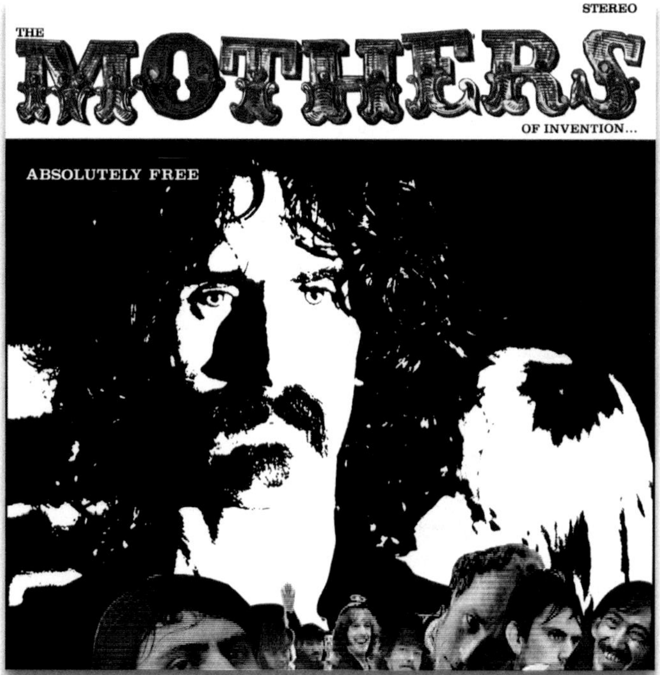


**Right:** Zappa's political, social and musical satire, the astonishing *Absolutely Free*. (*Verve*)

**Left:** The debut album by Procol Harum failed to capitalise on the band's single success. (*Regal Zonophone*)

**Right:** Procol Harum in 1967 - like the Moodies and Pink Floyd, they had a long and lucrative career.

**Left:** The single that became a hit around the world - the stately, elegant 'A Whiter Shade Of Pale'. (*Deram*)

**Right:** The title track of the album *I-Feel-Like-I'm-Fixin'-To-Die* became a Vietnam protest song for Country Joe & The Fish. (*Vanguard*)

**Left:** *Electric Music for the Mind and Body* was Country Joe's debut album. (*Vanguard*)

**Left:** Traffic's debut *Mr Fantasy* carried within it the seeds of the band's break-up. *(Island)*

**Right:** Traffic in 1967, fronted by Stevie Winwood.

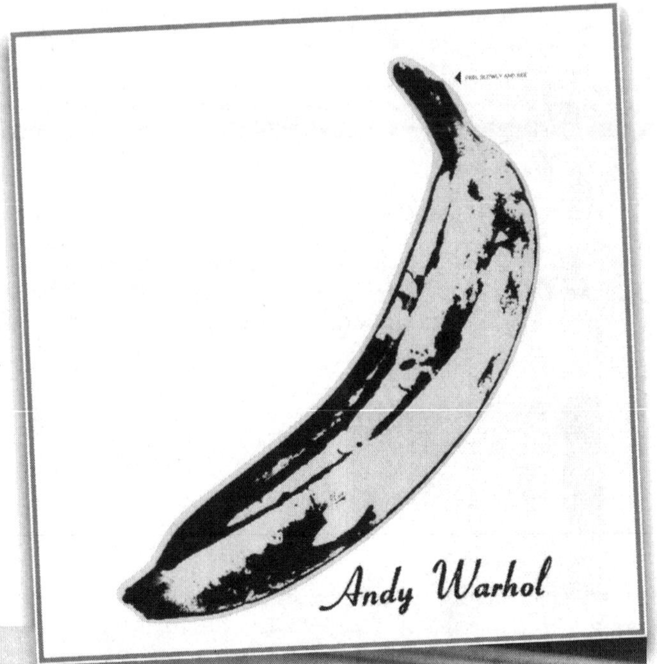


**Right:** *The Velvet Underground & Nico* didn't sell many copies but, allegedly, everyone who bought it started a band. (*Verve*)

**Above:** The Velvet Underground in 1967, before Nico was forced out and the band split from manager Andy Warhol.

## The Byrds

Key personnel:
Jim (later Roger) McGuinn: lead guitar, vocals
David Crosby: rhythm guitar, vocals
Chris Hillman: bass, vocals
Michael Clarke: drums

### History

Formed in Los Angeles in early 1964 when Jim McGuinn and Gene Clark started playing Beatles songs together in the bar of the Troubadour club, and David Crosby walked up and joined in on harmonies. They formed The Jetset and recruited drummer Michael Clarke and bassist Chris Hillman. Inspired by The Beatles, they renamed themselves The Byrds, and in 1965 released the Bob Dylan-penned 'Mr. Tambourine Man' as their second single, drawing on the Fab Four's jangly, twelve-string folk-rock sound on *A Hard Day's Night* and *Beatles for Sale* – they even bought the same instruments. The song hit number 1 in both the US and UK, while the Pete Seeger-penned 'Turn! Turn! Turn!' was a chart-topper in America. Record company Columbia was happy with the band churning out more Dylan covers, but album releases began to include more self-penned numbers, particularly from Clark. It was he who brought in the bare bones of 'Eight Miles High' – with contributions from McGuinn and Crosby, it became the band's seventh single, and was immediately banned from US radio because it had the word 'high' in it, and, as well all know, singing the word 'high' immediately turns listeners into hopeless junkies. The ban hit sales and kick-started a decline in popularity from which the band never really recovered – not helped by the departure of principal songwriter Clark in February 1966.

### Key releases in 1967

**'So You Want To Be a Rock 'N' Roll Star'** (Jim McGuinn, Chris Hillman) / **'Everybody's Been Burned'** (David Crosby) (Single)

Label: Columbia
Release Date: 9 January 1967
Charts: US: 29

**Younger Than Yesterday** (Album)

Label: Columbia
Release date: 6 February 1967
Charts: US: 24; UK: 34
Side 1: 1. 'So You Want To Be a Rock 'N' Roll Star' (Jim McGuinn, Chris Hillman) 2. 'Have You Seen Her Face' (Hillman) 3. 'C.T.A.-102' (McGuinn, Robert J. Hippard) 4. 'Renaissance Fair (David Crosby, McGuinn) 5. 'Time Between' (Hillman) 6. 'Everybody's Been Burned' (Crosby)

Side 2: 1. 'Thoughts and Words' (Hillman) 2. 'Mind Gardens' (Crosby) 3. 'My Back Pages' (Bob Dylan) 4. 'The Girl With No Name' (Hillman) 5. 'Why' (McGuinn, Crosby)

You have to hand it to The Byrds – they were instrumental (pun intended) in the development of no fewer than three popular music genres: folk-rock (the US kind), psychedelic rock, and country-rock. Yet, they had to sacrifice commercial success for artistic development.

In 1965 they were the most popular band in the US – hell, they were one of the most popular bands in the world, eclipsed only by The Beatles. The bright, jingle-jangle sound of Jim – later Roger – McGuinn's twelve-string Rickenbacker guitar, and the clear, close-harmony singing were like catnip to record buyers. Their second single, 'Mr Tambourine Man', was perfect for people who thought Bob Dylan songs were better performed by someone other than Bob Dylan. And the band influenced a Beatle – listen to George Harrison's 'If I Needed Someone' on *Rubber Soul* and hear the debt he owes to McGuinn.

Here's the thing, though – the fans wanted The Byrds to stay the same, to serve up their Dylan and Pete Seeger covers (and the occasional original that sounded like a Dylan or Pete Seeger cover) until the band members were drawing their pensions. But musicians are ornery folk who want to develop and progress as artists to show they can be successful on their own terms. Frequently, that's the point at which commercial and critical acclaim begin to diverge.

Take their groundbreaking 1966 single 'Eight Miles High'. We have already pointed out that it was a contender for the first psychedelic single, with its drug-influenced lyrics, raga-like drone backing and a lead guitar break deliberately played to sound like John Coltrane impersonating a sitar. But it stalled at number 14 in the US – a modest chart showing blamed on the song's nationwide broadcasting ban for allegedly encouraging drug use.

The album that followed – *Fifth Dimension* – fared even worse. Gene Clark quit the band (ironically, the chief composer of 'Eight Miles High' was mortally terrified of flying) and the rumour went around that The Byrds were breaking up. Someone remembers seeing McGuinn and Crosby fighting, rolling on the ground like little boys in a playground dustup.

In the midst of declining popularity and group fisticuffs came an album that is one of the best – if not *the* best – they ever produced. *Younger Than Yesterday* still had a Dylan cover that provided the title, but it was surrounded by some of the most trippy, exciting and thought-provoking compositions The Byrds had ever penned.

First out of the traps was 'So You Want To Be a Rock 'N' Roll Star', a gently caustic number with an instantly iconic opening riff that alternates between G and A, with trumpet flourishes from Hugh Masekela and screaming girls transported into the recording from a Byrds concert. The lyric pokes fun at the music industry and the bands that sell their souls for fame and fortune. Bud Scoppa commented in his 1971 book on The Byrds:

> McGuinn, especially, was turned off by excess of any kind – from the blatantly derivative Chicago blues style of many of the new bands, to the romanticized lyrics and messianic poses so common to San Francisco. If he looked down upon the exaggerated role of the rock hero, McGuinn rejected the bulk of the *new music* for essentially the same reason: he simply could not relate to overstatement.

So the song blasts the artificiality of appearances trumping content – 'And when your hair's combed right and your pants fit tight / It's gonna be alright' – the cynicism of the music business – 'Sell your soul to the company who are waiting there to sell plastic ware' – and finally, 'When you make the charts, the girls will tear you apart'.

It was a minor hit when released as a single in January 1967, backed with David Crosby's dark and foreboding 'Everybody's Been Burned'. Since then, 'So You Want To Be...' has become the go-to song for any artist wanting to bite the hand that feeds them, culminating in Patti Smith's gloriously agonised version on her 1979 album *Wave*.

It was the perfect opener for their fourth album, recorded at the end of 1966 and released in February 1967, and starts a seven-song run of almost perfect psychedelic pop. There's Chris Hillman's upbeat and McCartney-esque 'Have You Seen Her Face', with its glorious quick chord changes and sublime melodies: McGuinn's science fiction outing on 'C.T.A.-102', coupling fast-paced country rock with alien swoops and whooshes plus sped-up backward vocals; hippie drug anthem 'Renaissance Fair', with dreamlike lyrics and saxophone backing; Hillman's country rock of 'Time Between', a clear attempt to emulate The Beatles' version of 'Act Naturally' from the *Help!* Album; the aforementioned 'Everybody's Been Burned', sung with mournful passion by Crosby over shifting, fingerpicked electric guitar chords, and the exquisitely perfect 'Thoughts and Words', another catchy, irresistible Hillman composition with a backwards lead guitar break.

Things trip up a bit with Crosby's 'Mind Gardens' – probably the album's most self-consciously psychedelic track, and one that's easy to mock, as Crosby intones tuneless hippie platitudes over ham-fisted acoustic chords. Then there's the obligatory Dylan track 'My Back Pages', which became the band's second single of the year, and provided the album title from the line 'I was so much older then, I'm younger than that now'.

The album gets back on track with Hillman's Monkees-ish 'The Girl With No Name', and ends on a suitably high note with 'Why', which combines the chord structure of Martha and the Vandellas' 'Heat Wave' with a sitar-like raga rock lead break.

*Younger Than Yesterday* received mostly positive reviews when it was released, with *Billboard* optimistically predicting The Byrds would be 'riding high on the LP charts again'. But the record buyers didn't agree, taking the album no further than number 24 in the US, and an even worse 37 in the UK.

Since then, it's been ranked as one of the band's best efforts, with critic Richie Unterberger suggesting both *Younger Than Yesterday* and the following year's *The Notorious Byrd Brothers* as two of the most revered albums from the 1960s. It's number 127 in *Rolling Stone*'s 500 Greatest Albums of All Time.

Listening to the album again and knowing everything that followed it, there are three things that stand out. First, that Chris Hillman had grown into a fully-fledged pop songwriter, filling the void left by Gene Clark. His name was on no fewer than five of the album's eleven tracks, and his compositions sounded more like old Byrds than anything McGuinn and Crosby were doing. Second, that The Byrds were really frustrated country rock singers, and that would be their next musical direction. And third, by 1967, David Crosby's moody and self-absorbed compositions were a little bit out of step with the rest of the band, and it's no surprise he was the next to jump ship. He had long felt that his songs were sidelined for cover versions – unfortunately, 'Mind Gardens' wasn't a great example of what he could do – and when the band recorded his song 'Lady Friend' as their final 1967 single, it flopped miserably.

Back in the studio in June to work on the next album, Crosby balked at recording Carole King and Gerry Goffin's 'Goin' Back'. Crosby recalled in an interview with *Rolling Stone* writer Ben Fong-Torres:

> Roger and Chris drove up in a pair of Porsches and said that I was crazy, impossible to work with, an ego-maniac – all of which is partly true, I'm sure. (They said) sometimes, that I sang lousy, wrote terrible songs, made horrible sounds, and that they would do much better without me. Now, I'm sure that in the heat of the moment, they probably exaggerated what they thought. But that's what they said.

The Byrds did have one big hit in 1967: the *Greatest Hits* album that devoted side one to those jingle-jangle hits from the past. It showed that the problem wasn't just with the band but also with their fans. Unlike The Beatles, The Byrds were never able to take their fan base along with them on their musical journey. The record-buying public preferred it when they were 'Goin' Back', not moving forward.

# The Who

Key personnel:
Roger Daltrey: lead vocals
John Entwistle: bass, horns, backing and lead vocals
Keith Moon: drums
Pete Townshend: guitar, backing and lead vocals

## History

Grammar school dropout Roger Daltrey formed The Detours in Acton, West London in 1959. He played lead guitar and recruited John Entwistle after spotting him in the street carrying a bass. Entwistle suggested school pal Pete Townshend to complete a lineup that included Harry Wilson on drums and Colin Dawson on lead vocals. In 1962, Wilson was replaced by Doug Sandom, and Dawson quit, replaced by Daltrey on lead vocals, leaving Townshend as the sole guitarist. In 1964, they changed their name to The Who to avoid confusion with Johnny Devlin and The Detours, and Sandom was replaced by stand-in drummer Keith Moon. However, they briefly became The High Numbers for their flop debut single 'Zoot Suit' / 'I'm The Face' for Fontana Records. Back as The Who, filmmakers Kit Lambert and Chris Stamp took over their management and encouraged Townshend to write songs. Signed to Decca Records subsidiary Brunswick, singles 'I Can't Explain' and 'Anyway, Anyhow, Anywhere' reached the UK top 10 in early 1965, followed by the number 2 hit 'My Generation', which became the first album's title. Moving to Robert Stigwood's label Reaction, more singles followed – a UK number 5 with 'Substitute', number 2 with 'I'm a Boy' and number 3 with 'Happy Jack'. The second album, in 1966 (1967 in the US), included a nine-minute mini pop opera called 'A Quick One (While He's Away)'.

## Key releases in 1967

### **'Pictures of Lily'** / **'Doctor, Doctor'** (Single)

Both songs by Pete Townshend
Label: Track
Release date: 22 April 1967 (UK), 24 June 1967 (US)
Charts: UK: 4; US: 51; Netherlands: 5

### **'I Can See for Miles'** (Townshend) / **'Someone's Coming'** (John Entwistle) (UK), **'Mary Anne With the Shaky Hand'** (Townshend) (US) (Single)

Label: Track
Release date: 13 October 1967 (UK), 18 September 1967 (US)
Charts: UK: 10; US: 9; Canada: 4

### **The Who Sell Out** (Album)

All songs by Pete Townshend except as noted.

Label: Track
Release date: 15 December 1967
Charts: UK: 13; US: 48; Australia: 8
Side 1: 1. 'Armenia City in the Sky' (Speedy Keen) 2. 'Heinz Baked Beans' (John Entwistle) 3. 'Mary Ann With the Shaky Hand' 4. 'Odorono' 5. 'Tattoo' 6. 'Our Love Was, Is' 7. 'I Can See for Miles' Side 2: 1. 'Can't Reach You' 2. 'Medac (Entwistle) 3. 'Relax' 4. 'Silas Stingy' (Entwistle) 5. 'Sunrise' 6. 'Rael (1 and 2).

Pete Townshend feared he was losing his mind. He was sitting in his aeroplane seat listening to music on a headset, but he was also floating above himself in the tiny pressurised tube, watching as girlfriend Karen gently slapped his face, Keith Moon picked his teeth and John Entwistle read a magazine. Townshend recalled in his 2012 memoir *Who I Am*:

> I heard a female voice gently saying, 'You have to go back. You cannot stay here'. But I'm terrified. If I go back, I feel as if I'll die. 'You won't die. You cannot stay here.' As I drifted back towards my body, I began to feel the effects of the LSD kicking in. The worst seemed to be over; as I settled in, the experience, though extreme, felt more like my few trips of old: everything saturated by wonderful colour and sound.

It wasn't the first time Townshend had taken LSD (although it was the first inside a TWA first-class cabin), but it seems to have been the last – and the most profound. Not that it stopped him fretting over his role as a guitarist and songwriter, The Who's place in the pantheon of rock royalty and the meaning of the music they were producing – perhaps the drugs even exacerbated his fears and anxieties.

In 1967, The Who had a string of hit singles under their belts and two well-received albums in the UK, but they were still virtually unknown in the US: the holy grail of pop markets. They were seen as a mod band – followed by a British youth subculture obsessed with music, culture and fashion. Called 'Modernists' in the 1950s – because they listened to modern jazz – this subculture's musical horizons broadened to include soul, rhythm and blues, and ska. They would frequently clash with their bitter rivals, the Rockers, at otherwise sedate and old-fashioned seaside resorts such as Brighton.

Trouble is, The Who were never really mod – they rocked too hard – and Townshend resisted being straitjacketed by the term. He and the band were listening to more jazz, to Jimi Hendrix albums and, most of all, to The Beach Boys' *Pet Sounds* and The Beatles' *Sgt. Pepper* – Keith Moon even believed he was the 'Mr K' in 'Being for the Benefit of Mr Kite'. At a Pink Floyd gig, a group of mods exposed themselves to Pete's girlfriend Karen, then told him he'd let the side down. Townshend, wearing a long, psychedelic robe, replied that mod was finished. There was no argument: the gang simply zipped up and walked sadly away.

The mini-opera 'A Quick One, While He's Away' on the band's 1966 LP of almost the same name showed Townshend was more than a writer of two-and-a-half-minute wonders. Inspired by dark childhood memories of sexual abuse and parental neglect, the disturbing, fragmented nine-minute track strings together what are almost nursery rhymes, jarring uncomfortably against each other.

He knew he had more of this inside him, but how to get it out and do it without alienating the fans and, even the band, was something that eluded him until *Tommy* in 1968. But that is another story for another book. In 1967, he was mentally and physically thrashing around – The Who were becoming better-known for smashing up their instruments than for the music they were making. But even their position as rock's demolition experts was under threat – as Townshend watched Jimi Hendrix set his Stratocaster alight at the Monterey International Pop Festival, Mama Cass said to him, 'Hey, destroying guitars is *your* thing!'. Townshend replied, 'It used to be. It belongs to Jimi now.'

Two things seemed to keep him going during that year. One was a song he'd been working on since 1966 that he believed was going to be his crowning glory; a surefire number-1 hit. It was called 'I Can See for Miles' and was inspired by jealousy of his girlfriend Karen, who appeared to embrace the hippie concept of free love a little more comfortably than he did, coupled with the legalities of a case he was involved in: the first lyrics were written on the back of an affidavit. Musically, it was based on an E major raga rock drone – you move your chord shape up the neck of the guitar but keep that E bass string thrumming throughout – with a triumphant, acid-drenched chorus. He knew it would be the centrepiece of the band's third album, but he didn't want to expose it to the fierce critical light of the rest of the group. Not just yet.

The other was his growing interest in the philosophies of Meher Baba – an Indian spiritual teacher whose writings on how to become conscious of one's 'divinity' and the 'absolute oneness of God', seemed to chime with Townshend's own vague beliefs at the time. They were teachings that would find their full expression in *Tommy*.

Meanwhile, the commercial demands of the music market insisted that The Who release a single. 'I Can See for Miles' remained under wraps, so instead, he came up with another of his two-and-a-half-minute wonders: the catchy and slightly saucy 'Pictures of Lily'. It was inspired by a Victorian picture postcard on Karen's wall showing Prince Edward's scantily-clad mistress Lily Langtry. Townshend said in his memoir, 'My song was intended to be an ironic comment on the sexual shallows of show business, especially pop ... (it) ended up, famously, being about a boy saved from burgeoning adolescent sexual frustration when his father presented him with dirty postcards over which he could masturbate'.

As the single shot up the UK charts – but made barely a dent in the US – The Who flew to the States for one of those mismatched tours that seemed to happen quite frequently. Jimi Hendrix had toured with, of all people, The

Monkees; The Who found themselves on the same bill as pop's pretty boys Herman's Hermits (although Peter Noone was not nearly as innocent as he looked. But that's also for another book).

For ten weeks, they zigzagged across the continent, making fans in San Francisco and New York, but almost getting beaten up in conservative middle-America, where the locals thought their long hair signalled they were homosexuals. It ended in Florida, where Keith Moon famously plunged a Lincoln Continental into a Holiday Inn pool and covered the hotel room's floors, walls and ceiling with cake.

Roger Daltrey explained in a 2021 *Classic Albums* TV documentary on the making of *The Who Sell Out*:

> Breaking America wasn't just important for The Who; it was every rock band's dream. America was the land of steak – we were the land of suet and taxation. All we wanted was to earn a living doing this job that we loved so much, and America seemed to be the place that offered us the opportunity to readily do that.

Back in the UK, Townshend started writing more songs for the third album. 'Tattoo' was about the concept of manhood. What made a man? His hair? A tattoo? In the end, the tattooed narrator marries a tattooed woman, so go figure. 'Mary Anne With the Shaky Hand' is probably Townshend's second song about masturbation – 'What they've done to her man with those shaky hands' – performed with Everly-Brothers-style sweet harmonies and flamenco acoustic guitar flourishes.

'Our Love Was, Is' – later titled 'Our Love Was' – is clearly dedicated to Karen, but, despite repeating the word 'love' about 50 times, still manages to insert Townshend's insecurity in the lines 'Our love was famine, frustration / We only acted out an imitation of what real love should have been.' 'I Can't Reach You' is clearly about a communication breakdown and must have been personal to Townshend because he sings the lead vocal to a chirpy pop backing. 'Relax' is both musically and lyrically upbeat as the singer seems to be helping someone through an acid trip: 'Relax and settle down ... Open up your mind.'

There was one other song that helped dictate the album's direction: a hilarious advertising pastiche about a woman singer whose body odour lets her down because she didn't use a deodorant stick called Odorono. It was a real product, developed by Cincinnati physician Dr Abraham D. Murphey in 1909 to stop surgeons' hands from getting sweaty during operations. His daughter Edna discovered the red-coloured toilet water was also effective at sweetening female armpits – turning them, if you will, into charmpits – so she borrowed $150 from her father to launch the product, the name of which meant 'Odor! Oh no!'.

Perhaps Townshend came across the product while on The Who's US tour, and was inspired to write something emulating the catchy, witty advertising jingles on

TV. In fact, the band had already recorded a real advertising jingle for Coca-Cola – a fast guitar riff, pounding drums and the band singing 'Things go better with Coke' to images of swinging young things swigging the fizzy drink in London.

This kick-started the idea of making the next album all about advertising, with songs linked by the sort of jingles heard on pirate radio. In early 1967, there weren't many outlets for pop music – the BBC had the *Light Programme*, but you were more likely to hear big bands than rock bands. So, in defiance of British radio licensing laws, DJs started broadcasting from ships anchored at sea beyond the three-mile limit of Britain's legislative reach. The DJs on these illegal stations – such as Radio London and Radio Caroline – could play what they liked, and what they liked were the latest sounds from current bands such as The Who. Mixed in with the music were station idents – the jingles that reminded listeners who they were tuned into – and they became instantly recognisable aural icons. Later, the Labour government introduced laws to stop businesses advertising on pirate radio in an attempt to force them out of business. Townshend recalled in his memoir:

> One day I was in Soho and went to see (Who manager Kit) Lambert, and he said, 'I've got the album', and I said, 'You can't have because we haven't done it yet'. Then he presented me with the track list, which is very much like the track list on *The Who Sell Out*. But what was interesting was all that music was already recorded, and I said to him 'This is really not good enough'. We brainstormed for a couple of hours and came up with the idea of turning it into a radio show. John and Keith leapt on the idea and, inspired by 'Odorono', began making up advertising jingles for all kinds of things, like Medac spot cream, Premier drums and Heinz baked beans.

They were going to make the album sound like a pirate radio station broadcasting using the jingles from Radio London, and originally the idea was to sell the space between the tracks to various companies and write little commercials about their products. But the first company they approached, Coca-Cola, virtually put the phone down on them, so they decided to do it anyway without asking for money. That didn't stop Keith Moon getting sponsorship from Premier drums, and Entwistle did the same thing with Rotosound strings. Entwistle also offered up a very eccentric demo of 'Silas Stingy': one of his catchy nursery rhyme songs in the style of the second album's 'Boris the Spider'.

The opening number, 'Armenia City in the Sky', came from the pen of John David Percy 'Speedy' Keen, Pete Townshend's driver, and later, a member of Thunderclap Newman (Keen wrote their most well-known song 'Something in the Air'). It was inspired by a painting and was the first time The Who had used an original song from a non-group member. In an interview for the *Classic Albums* documentary, Daltrey said, 'It was always a bit of a mystery to me why we ever did this track that opens the album ... we had done a demo for him as a band. (Keen) had said 'Will you play it for me?', and we used Speedy's demo as the opening track on the album.' On the same programme, Townshend revealed, 'Years later, Speedy said, 'You got it all wrong, it wasn't 'Armenia City in the Sky' – it was I'm an ear sitting in the sky'. I think our version was better.' The Who's recording is dense and pounding, with backward tapes of Townshend's guitar creating space-age whooshes like a UFO soaring through the atmosphere.

With a rejig of 'Sunrise', a ballad Townshend had written years before for his mother, that left the final track, 'Rael', which carried some seeds for his next musical adventure. 'Rael', about Israel, was a fantasy in which the country is invaded by Red China (though quite why they would do that is not made clear). While not Jewish, Townshend had immense empathy for Israel – in his memoir, he recalls sharing a house with a big, joyous Jewish family, and his best friend, Mick Leiber, was of that faith. In a 2006 interview with *Rolling Stone*, Townshend said the following:

> Polish Jews were the kids I played with. They were my people. I remember saying to my mother, 'Aren't Polish people from Poland?', and she said, 'Yes, they were Britain's first ally in the war.' I'd say, 'But they're not like foreigners. They're just like we are,' and she said, 'Yes, they're just like we are.'

On the album, 'Rael' is subtitled '1 and 2' – on later releases, it would become part 1, and part 2 would be an outtake running to just one and a half minutes, opening with a hymn-like tribute to Israel before thundering into a mock advertising jingle for John Peel's BBC Radio 1 show *Top Gear*. Part 1, however, concludes with a lengthy instrumental section of chopping chords, pounding drums and wordless vocals that would make a reappearance a year later in two separate instrumentals on *Tommy*. But that, as I may have mentioned, is another story.

As this was an album about advertising, it was handed over to two advertising whiz kids, David King and Roger Law, who would later create the satirical British TV series *Spitting Image*. They came up with the title, *The Who Sell Out*, and the cover concept of the four band members promoting products. So Townshend stripped off to apply Odorono, Roger Daltrey sat in a freezing-cold bathtub of beans, Keith dabbed on spot cream, and John posed as a Charles Atlas bodybuilder with a scantily-clad girl.

*The Who Sell Out* was well-received by critics when it was released in December. They praised the songs, the musicianship, the concept and the sense of humour – even today it's seen as one of The Who's greatest achievements, a psychedelic pop-art masterpiece and one of the most successful concept albums, placed at 316 on *Rolling Stone*'s list of The 500 Greatest Albums of All Time.

But it sold poorly, as did the single 'I Can See for Miles' that Townshend thought would 'flatten the opposition'. He said, 'I couldn't work out what had gone wrong. I couldn't work out how we'd lost contact with our audience. I just thought, 'We're scuppered'.' It seemed the fans weren't keen to embrace The Who's gentle mockery and cynicism as readily as the critics, and the single's sheer energy and power weren't enough to lift it beyond the number 10 spot in the UK. On the bright side, they were the band's best-selling album and single in the US, boosted by an appearance on a big Sunday night show called *The Smothers Brothers Comedy Hour*.

Townshend said in his book, 'It was the last time we went into an album with smiles on our faces, having fun. After that, it all became a really deeply serious process, as we were hanging on to our audience and our hits and our gold albums by the skin of our teeth.' Towards the end of 1967, he wrote, prophetically, 'After wasting a lot of precious time, I think it's time for a real shake-up'. That shake-up was to come in 1968. But that's another story...

# The Beach Boys

Key personnel:
Al Jardine: guitar, vocals
Mike Love: vocals
Brian Wilson: vocals, keyboards, bass
Carl Wilson: lead guitar, vocals
Dennis Wilson: drums, vocals

## History

Formed in 1961 by brothers Brian, Dennis and Carl Wilson, who joined up with cousin Mike Love and Brian's high school classmate Al Jardine in Hawthorne, California, as The Pendletones, the name inspired by a type of popular shirt at the time. Dennis, the only surfer in the band, suggested the group write songs about the sport and lifestyle that went with it. Through ambitious father and occasional songwriter Murry, The Pendletones recorded a demo of Brian's song 'Surfin'', which got them a contract with Candix Records. The group discovered their name had been changed to The Beach Boys when 'Surfin'' was released as a single at the end of the year, reaching number 75. After Candix went bankrupt, the band moved to Capitol Records, and the second single, 'Surfin' Safari', was even more successful, hitting number 14. The third single, 'Surfin' USA' – a shameless steal from Chuck Berry's 'Sweet Little Sixteen' – peaked at number 3. Following singles showed increasing songwriting sophistication and Brian's growing production prowess, but a panic attack on a plane in 1964 forced him to stop touring (he was replaced on stage by Glen Campbell, then Bruce Johnston).

Inspired by The Beatles' *Rubber Soul* album, Brian spent most of 1966 in the studio creating *Pet Sounds* – now regarded as one of the most influential albums in rock – and the hit single 'Good Vibrations'.

## Key releases (and non-releases) in 1967

### Smile (Album)

Unreleased until 2011: The Smile Sessions (Capitol Records)
Suggested 1967 tracklist:
'Good Vibrations', 'Heroes and Villains', 'I'm in Great Shape', 'Wind Chimes', 'Wonderful', 'Cabin Essence', 'Child Is the Father of the Man', 'Surf's Up', 'Do You Like Worms?', 'Vega-Tables', 'The Old Master Painter', 'The Elements'

### 'Heroes and Villains' (Brian Wilson, Van Dyke Parks) / 'You're Welcome' (Wilson) (Single)

Label: Capitol/Brother
Release date: 24 July 1967
Charts: UK: 8; US: 12; Canada: 5; Sweden: 7

**Smiley Smile** (Album)
Label: Capitol/Brother
Release date: 18 September 1967
Charts: UK: 9; US: 41
Side 1: 1. 'Heroes and Villains' (Brian Wilson, Van Dyke Parks) 2. 'Vegetables' (Wilson, Parks) 3. 'Fall Breaks and Back To Winter' (W. Woodpecker Symphony) 4.'She's Going Bald' (Wilson, Mike Love, Parks) 5. 'Little Pad' (Wilson) Side 2: 1. 'Good Vibrations' (Wilson, Love) 2. 'With Me Tonight' (Wilson) 3. 'Wind Chimes' (Wilson) 4. 'Gettin' Hungry' (Wilson, Love) 5. 'Wonderful' (Wilson, Parks) 6. 'Whistle In' (Wilson)

**Wild Honey** (Album)
All songs by Mike Love and Brian Wilson unless otherwise stated.
Label: Capitol
Release date: 18 December 1967
Charts: UK: 7, US: 24
Side 1: 1. 'Wild Honey 2. 'Aren't You Glad' 3. 'I Was Made To Love Her' (Henry Cosby, Sylvia Moy, Lula Mae Hardaway. Stevland Morris) 4. 'Country Air' 5. 'A Thing or Two' Side 2: 1. 'Darlin'' 2. 'I'd Love Just Once To See You' 3. 'Here Comes the Night' 4. 'Let the Wind Blow' 5. 'How She Boogalooed It' (Mike Love, Bruce Johnston, Al Jardine, Carl Wilson) 6. 'Mama Says'.

The trouble with Brian Wilson is that he believed he was in competition with The Beatles – a contest he was very likely to lose. Now, had he been content to be in competition with himself, that would have been a different matter. As a songwriter, he had developed in leaps and bounds, from the Chuck Berry rip-off of 'Surfin' USA' in 1963, through exquisite mini-symphonies such as 'California Girls' and 'I Get Around', to his crowning achievement of 1966's *Pet Sounds* album and the songs 'God Only Knows' and 'Good Vibrations'.

The word 'genius' is bandied about too freely these days (as is the word 'legendary' – you need to have a doubtful existence to be a legend, like Robin Hood), but if it applies to anyone in the history of pop music, then Brian Wilson undoubtedly qualifies, along with Lennon, McCartney and Burt Bacharach. Wilson produced *Pet Sounds* almost single-handedly, as a riposte to The Beatles' *Rubber Soul*, and for a while, he actually topped them. Then they responded with *Revolver*, and Wilson knew he'd been knocked back into second place again. He had to come up with something better, a masterpiece of masterpieces, an album that would for once and forever elbow The Beatles off their perch. And that masterpiece would be *Smile*.

This is the only part of the book that deals with a non-existent album, but *Smile* has become legendary, certainly until Wilson re-recorded it as a solo album in 2004, followed by the release of *The Smile Sessions* in 2011. *Smile* is the album that destroyed Wilson's mental state and sent The Beach Boys on a long, slow decline. They never produced an album to match *Pet*

*Sounds* and only occasionally did their subsequent releases trouble chart compilers.

Were The Beach Boys psychedelic? Brian Wilson certainly thought so. In late 1966, he told a *Melody Maker* journalist, 'Psychedelic music will cover the face of the world and colour the whole popular music scene. Anybody who is happening is psychedelic.' When asked what he was, he replied, 'I'm psychedelicate!'. He had certainly taken all the right substances to qualify, starting with marijuana in 1964, moving on to LSD the following year: an experience that scared the shit out of him. The trouble was, Brian had an obsessive personality, whether it was over alcohol, drugs or tinkering endlessly in the studio to get the perfect sound. Once he started, he couldn't stop – it got to a point where he could hallucinate even without LSD.

His mental state became so fragile (he had undiagnosed schizoaffective disorder) that he stopped touring with the band, preferring to stay in the studio and mastermind the creation of the songs the rest of the guys would sing on the road. It may or may not have been the best thing for Brian, but it was a great move for popular music, enabling him to craft and shape *Pet Sounds*, playing many of the instruments and singing practically every vocal (the band members would come in to play or sing their parts, and sometimes Brian would wipe them and replace them with his own).

The album's success meant Capitol Records would pretty much bankroll anything he did, allowing him to give free rein to his musical ambition and fully unleash the delicate perfectionist within. Nobody was quite sure what to expect. Wilson recalled in his memoir *Wouldn't It Be Nice: My Own Story*:

> I didn't know what to expect either, though I knew the direction I wanted to head with the next album: up and farther out. Creatively, I was at the pinnacle of a streak that was heading into its third year. I'd climbed the ladder and stood at the top, all alone, imbibing on the thin air. But none of that satisfied my fundamental need to prove myself. I had to go farther. Now I wanted to jump off the ladder and... fly!

What he did know, is that it would be 'religious, white, spiritual music' – what he called 'a teenage symphony to God'. With lyricist Van Dyke Parks, Wilson spent endless hours writing and recording, unsure if what they had produced was a work of genius or complete rubbish, thanks to copious amounts of marijuana, speed and acid. Playing them to friends didn't help – they seemed confused by the fragmentary nature of what they heard.

Days blurred into nights, weeks into months, with The Beach Boys' mad scientist becoming ever more paranoid and fragile. On one occasion, arriving at the studio for a session with a very expensive orchestra, he refused to get out of the car for two hours. At a rescheduled session, he wore a red fireman's helmet.

Meanwhile, 'Good Vibrations' had been released and was a worldwide smash. Capitol Records no doubt breathed a sigh of relief that their open-ended investment was paying off, as the single became The Beach Boys' best seller ever, shifting 100,000 copies a day at the end of 1966. Encouraged, the record company scheduled *Smile* for a Christmas release and even printed up record sleeves.

But the festive season came and went with no sign of even a smirk, let alone a *Smile*. Wilson promised 15 January, but deep down, he knew that was impossible. He said in his memoir, 'Too much was working against me. For starters, the drugs. Speed let me see farther than I'd ever seen, but I couldn't get anyplace on it. I found it impossible to make the connections as naturally as I once did'.

Bringing in the rest of the band, as he did in February 1967, just made things worse. They ripped the music and lyrics to shreds, demanding explanations for some of Van Dyke Parks' poetic allusions, accusing him of trying to destroy The Beach Boys. Meeting Paul McCartney may have seemed like a great idea – one newspaper called it 'like Van Gogh meeting Constable meeting Turner meeting Rembrandt in a time machine fueled by adrenaline and Dexedrine'. But then the fab one played 'She's Leaving Home' and warned Brian that The Beatles had a new album coming out: *Sgt. Pepper's Lonely Hearts Club Band*. It was just what Brian didn't need – his chief songwriting rival casually tossing off a little masterpiece and fuelling Wilson's fear of failure.

The months rolled by, Parks left the project and Brian sank further into depression and creative stupor. Even moving home and installing a state-of-the-art recording studio didn't help. The music world was moving on and The Beach Boys were being forgotten, supplanted by newcomers such as Jimi Hendrix and Jefferson Airplane.

Pulling out of the Monterey International Pop Festival at the last minute didn't help, but Brian feared the band would sound twee and old-hat. *Sgt. Pepper* was released to universal acclaim, but Wilson denies suggestions that it was responsible for his ruin. He was already ruined by June when he announced to his dismayed bandmates that *Smile* was no more and everything he had created for it was now off-limits.

Everything, it seems, except the only track he really cared about and the first one he and Parks had written more than a year before. By now, there were several versions of 'Heroes and Villains', some of them lost in the mists of time, ranging from a 2:45 instrumental to an eleven-minute opus. But Brian decided to record it all over again – a truncated three-and-a-half-minute version destined to become the band's next single (because his astrologer told him so).

Backed with an acappella chant from the *Smile* sessions – 'You're Welcome' – 'Heroes and Villains' was released to such great anticipation that it was inevitably a disappointment. A rumination on the Old West and the origins of California, it failed to repeat the runaway success of 'Good Vibrations', with which it shares similar changes in pace, and a disjointed structure. Lyrically, it's miles away from the sunny but simple-minded romantic notions of 'Good Vibrations'. 'Heroes and Villains' deals with the epic subjects of tragedy and hope, and the upbeat melody – with shooby-doo-wah vocal backing and whooshes from what sounds like a swanee whistle – belies some of the grim content: 'Once at night Catillian squared the fight / And she was right in the rain of the bullets that eventually brought her down.'

Contemporary critical reaction was mixed. Some praised it as 'another masterpiece of production from Wilson and another move in his flowery progression' (Nick Jones, *Melody Maker*). But others decried it as 'disappointing ... one has, perhaps, just come to expect too much from The Beach Boys. And this isn't it' (Penny Valentine, *Disc and Music Echo*). The track was filled with the band's delicious harmonies, which were never less than perfect, but some unkind critics compared it to the sound of a barbershop quartet.

'Heroes And Villains' staggered to number 12 in the US and 8 in the UK, but the album that carried the track and 'Good Vibrations', managed to limp to a disappointing 41 in the States. By the time it came out – with the thoroughly inappropriate title of *Smiley Smile* – anyone who wanted the standout tracks had bought them as singles, and there was little left to encourage fans to open their wallets.

As a psychedelic album, *Smiley Smile* surely qualifies, with tracks about the importance of vegetables, complete with chopping sound effects recorded in a studio full of celery sticks, radishes and cherry tomatoes; women going bald, with bizarre sped-up vocals that sounded like The Beach Boys on helium, and the ridiculous 'Little Pad', a song drowned by what sounds like the band drunkenly giggling in the studio. The exquisite 'Wind Chimes' is the album's only other song that hints at the sonic possibilities Brian Wilson was groping for, but elsewhere, the album sounded nothing like the slam dunk that was supposed to top *Pet Sounds*. To quote Carl Wilson, it was a 'bunt'.

There was one more Beach Boys album in 1967 – *Wild Honey* – released a scant three months after *Smiley Smile*, as if in a bid to divert attention from the debacle of the latter. Mike Love was back as Wilson's main lyric writer, which meant a return to a more structured and disciplined way of working, but also a more pedestrian approach. Described as the band's R&B album – and a pioneer of so-called DIY pop – *Wild Honey* certainly isn't psychedelic and need not detain us here, except to point out that its sales were much healthier.

Later, when *The Smile Sessions* was released, listeners could decide for themselves whether it was a lost psychedelic masterpiece or a box of loose odds and ends that would never have made a coherent piece of work. My opinion tends towards the latter, and the only real regret is that Wilson never managed to complete the only other great song from those recordings – Surf's Up – until 1971.

The Beach Boys never did match, let alone surpass *Pet Sounds*, and their story is one of increasing musical irrelevance, with just a few bright spots to remind us of their past glories. For Brian Wilson, it was the start of a long battle with alcoholism, drug addiction and mental illness, at one point spending three years in his room. Psychedelic substances may have opened a few minds, but they destroyed many others, and Wilson is a prime example of someone for whom the drugs just didn't work.

# The Rolling Stones

Key personnel:
Mick Jagger: lead vocals, percussion
Brian Jones: guitar, keyboards, percussion, woodwind, brass, backing vocals
Keith Richards: guitar, backing vocals
Charlie Watts: drums, percussion
Bill Wyman: bass, percussion, vocals, keyboards

## History

In the mid-1950s, Mick Jagger had a group with friend Dick Taylor in Wilmington, Kent. Jagger met up with childhood pal Keith Richards at Dartford station in 1961 and, with Alan Etherington and Bob Beckwith, they called themselves The Blues Boys. At Ealing Jazz Club, they jammed with Alexis Korner's Blues Incorporated, which included pianist Ian Stewart, slide guitarist Brian Jones and drummer Charlie Watts. Jagger, Richards, Taylor, Jones and Stewart formed a group to play Chicago blues, with Tony Chapman on drums, later replaced by Watts. The new name was coined by Jones from a track on a Muddy Waters LP, 'Rollin' Stone'. With Andrew Loog Oldham as their manager (who, at nineteen, was younger than anyone in the band), The Stones were signed to Decca Records (who had foolishly turned down The Beatles). Stewart was dropped as a band member but remained as touring pianist. First single, Chuck Berry's 'Come On', reached number 21, followed by the Lennon/McCartney-penned number-12 hit 'I Wanna Be Your Man'. Then came the Buddy Holly cover 'Not Fade Away', which hit 3 in the UK and 48 in the US. Oldham encouraged Jagger and Richards to write, and they came up with their sixth single, 'The Last Time': the band's third UK number 1. A string of hit singles followed, including '(I Can't Get No) Satisfaction' and 'Paint It Black'. The first album solely written by the band, and considered their artistic breakthrough, is 1966's *Aftermath*.

## Key releases in 1967

### 'Let's Spend the Night Together' / 'Ruby Tuesday' (Single)

Both songs by Mick Jagger, Keith Richards.
Label: Decca (UK), London (US)
Release date: 13 January 1967
Charts: UK: 3; US: 1; Germany: 1; Netherlands: 2; France: 3

### Between the Buttons (Album - UK version)

All songs by Jagger, Richards.
Label: Decca
Release date: 20 January 1967
Charts: UK: 3; Germany: 2; Norway: 2
Side 1: 1. 'Yesterday's Papers' 2. 'My Obsession' 3. 'Back Street Girl' 4. 'Connection'

5. 'She Smiled Sweetly' 6. 'Cool, Calm & Collected' Side 2: 1. 'All Sold Out' 2. 'Please Go Home' 3. 'Who's Been Sleeping Here?' 4. 'Complicated' 5. 'Miss Amanda Jones' 6. 'Something Happened to Me Yesterday'

### **Between the Buttons** (US version)

All tracks by Jagger, Richards.
Label: London
Release date: 11 February 1967
Charts: US: 2
Side 1: 1. 'Let's Spend the Night Together' 2. 'Yesterday's Papers' 3. 'Ruby Tuesday' 4. 'Connection' 5. 'She Smiled Sweetly' 6. 'Cool, Calm & Collected' Side 2: 1. 'All Sold Out' 2. 'My Obsession' 3. 'Who's Been Sleeping Here?' 4. 'Complicated' 5. 'Miss Amanda Jones' 6. 'Something Happened to Me Yesterday'.

### **'We Love You' / 'Dandelion'** (Single)

Both songs by Jagger, Richards.
Label: Decca (UK), London (US)
Release date: 18 August 1967 (UK), 2 September 1967 (US)
Charts: UK: 8; US: 50; Netherlands: 1; Germany: 2; Australia: 4

### **Their Satanic Majesties Request** (Album)

All songs by Jagger, Richards, except as noted.
Label: Decca (UK), London (US)
Release date: 8 December 1967 (UK), 9 December 1967 (US)
Charts: UK: 3; US: 2; Australia: 1; France: 1; Norway: 2; Germany: 4
Side 1: 1. 'Sing This All Together' 2. 'Citadel' 3. 'In Another Land' (Bill Wyman) 4. '2000 Man' 5. 'Sing This All Together (See What Happens)' Side 2: 1. 'She's a Rainbow' 2. 'The Lantern' 3. 'Gomper' 4. '2000 Light Years From Home' 5. 'On With the Show'

Maybe it was the drugs that did it. Maybe it was the fault of The Beatles. Maybe it was a cunning attempt to get rid of their manager. Nearly 60 years on, the motivations are lost in the mists of time. But on one thing, Mick Jagger and Keith Richards are agreed: *Their Satanic Majesties Request* is a load of crap.

The record buyers didn't think so at the time – the album was a hit practically all over the world, with only Japan seemingly immune to its dubious charms. Contemporary critics were pretty damning, with one blasting it as 'ragged, monotone and off key'. But modern views have softened – as in this *AllMusic* review from Rich Unterberger:

> Without a doubt, no Rolling Stones album – and, indeed, very few rock albums from any era – split critical opinion as much as The Rolling Stones' psychedelic outing. Many dismiss the record as sub-*Sgt. Pepper* posturing; others confess, if only in private, to a fascination with the album's inventive arrangements, which

> incorporated some African rhythms, Mellotrons, and full orchestration. What's clear, is that never before or after did The Stones take so many chances in the studio.... In 1968, The Stones would go back to the basics, and never wander down these paths again, making this all the more of a fascinating anomaly in the group's discography.

The Stones were not a natural psychedelic band – their roots were in the blues. Sure, they were middle-class white guys playing black man's music, but they did it with a reverence and affection that many British bands had for the US's forgotten musical heroes. As the songwriting partnership of Jagger and Richards blossomed, they branched out into more mainstream music, releasing a string of great singles that successfully mixed rock aggression with melodic pop sensibilities. They were the band you loved if you found The Beatles a bit too squeaky-clean and sappy, and they were part of the British Invasion that stormed US charts and ears from 1964 onwards.

They weren't immune to the psychedelic elements that started creeping into British music in 1966 and even used that year's most fashionable instrument – the sitar – on the hit single 'Paint It Black' and a marimba on 'Under My Thumb'. Their songs' subject matter began to change, too, as they moved from singing about an inability to get satisfaction from their romantic partners, to discussions of mental breakdowns and drug abuse. But they used psychedelic elements as a garnish, not as a main ingredient, and were more likely to rough you up than put flowers in your hair.

The Rolling Stones entered 1967 with a bang, releasing the double A-side single 'Let's Spend the Night Together' / 'Ruby Tuesday'. The former was vintage Stones, a song unashamedly about enticing a young lady into sexual shenanigans. For the band's January appearance on *The Ed Sullivan Show*, a compromise was arrived at with Jagger forced to sing 'Let's spend some time together'. Even as late as 2006, puritanical Chinese authorities banned the group from performing the song because of its suggestive lyrics.

Because of this, 'Ruby Tuesday' got a lot more airplay. A song about Keith Richards' girlfriend, it featured the band's manager playing piano and recorder, and the composition credit really should've been shared with Brian Jones, because he contributed majorly to the melodic structure. Gentle and wistful, before bursting into a sing-along chorus, it stormed into the top 10 in most countries, topping the US chart.

The album that followed – *Between the Buttons* – is the perfect synthesis of psychedelia with The Stones' rough, biting rock. Following on from the pattern set by 1966's *Aftermath*, the traditional core of electric guitar, bass and drums is there, augmented by piano and an eclectic collection of other instruments, including organ, accordion, recorder, vibraphone, dulcimer, kazoo, tuba, trombone and trumpet: most of them played by the versatile Brian Jones. In fact, so busy is he tooting and plucking, that he only plays guitar on one track on the UK release: 'Miss Amanda Jones'.

The lyrics stay within the traditional blues trope of unreliable women failing to properly cater to the misogynistic rock star's needs. In 'Yesterday's Papers', Jagger compares his insatiable desire for a different woman every day with the discardable nature of old newspapers. You wouldn't read yesterday's papers, so why would you want yesterday's girl? It is blessed with catchy melodic riffs, with Jones providing tinkling vibraphone flourishes.

In 'My Obsession' Jagger lays claim to a young lady's, ahem, possessions 'til my mouth is soaking wet'. Too much information, Mick. The pretty and baroque 'Back Street Girl' features acoustic guitar, vibraphone, accordion and recorder, as the singer warns his 'common and coarse' mistress not to bother his wife. In 'All Sold Out', the woman is once again making life miserable for the sensitive lead singer, while 'Cool, Calm & Collected' is a Kinks-inspired portrait of an upper-class lady who 'always knows more than you do'.

To be fair, not all the songs on *Between the Buttons* put down women – 'Connection' details the stress of passing through airports on tour, 'She Smiled Sweetly' depicts religious faith as a comforting woman, and 'Something Happened to Me Yesterday' is about a shared LSD trip. But there's no raga-rock drones or chanting Tibetan monks, and most of the tracks bounce along with that honky-tonk rhythm that make Rolling Stones songs so appealing, and there's little in the way of audio trickery apart from a bit of echo, sped-up vocals and a spoken-word outro.

The album was a hit on both sides of the Atlantic and has variously been described as 'brimming with overlooked gems' (*Billboard*), and as one of The Stones' 'strongest, most eclectic LPs' (Richie Unterberger, *AllMusic*). It's in Rolling Stone magazine's 500 Greatest Albums of All Time and frequently appears in lists of the top psychedelic releases.

Perhaps it would've been best if *Between the Buttons* had remained The Stones' sole long-player for 1967. But in those days, bands were frequently signed to produce two albums a year, along with three or four singles – so the group spent several months going in and out of London's Olympic Studios, laying down tracks that would become *Their Satanic Majesties Request*.

There were reasons why the recording of The Stones' twelfth studio album was so piecemeal. For a start, there were the drugs…

It was Richards and Jones who first encountered LSD at a party thrown by Ken Kesey and the Merry Pranksters at the end of 1965. Mick Jagger waited until February 1967, when he sipped on a tea and acid cocktail at Keith Richards' house, along with George Harrison and his wife Patti. Later that day, nineteen police officers turned up and found illegal substances and a naked Marianne Faithfull wrapped in a fur rug.

Jagger and Richards were charged with drug offences, soon to be followed by Jones after a raid on his house discovered marijuana. At their trial, Jagger and Richards were convicted and both received prison sentences: Mick for three months and Keith for a year. They both spent a night in prison before being released pending appeal, and soon after, went into the studio to record a thank-you to their fans for their support – the anthemic 'We Love You', which opens with the sound of prison doors closing, and featured, uncredited, John Lennon and Paul McCartney on backing vocals.

Jagger and Richards also received surprising support from the usually straight-laced *Times* newspaper – in an editorial famously headed, 'Who breaks a butterfly upon a wheel?', editor William Rees-Mogg blasted the sentences as disproportionate, and on appeal, Richards' conviction was overturned and Jagger's reduced to a conditional discharge. The experience may not have changed Richards' behaviour – although he was always more together than he sometimes appeared – but the more cautious and conservative Jagger tried to make sure his drug use never became as public again.

There's no evidence that Bill Wyman or Charlie Watts ever touched serious drugs – Wyman has revealed only that he's partial to good white wine. But for Brian Jones, LSD was a disaster – during recording sessions for 'We Love You' and *Their Satanic Majesties Request*, he appeared so out of it, and was playing so badly, the rest of the band simply muted his amplifier so he couldn't be heard. The man who was once the guardian of The Stones' blues spirit and could've steered the music into a more believable direction, was now so groggy and confused, he made virtually no contribution whatsoever.

Then there were The Beatles. The media liked to portray the two bands as bitter rivals for pop supremacy, but in fact, they had become close friends – well, as close as you could be when your friends were your musical heroes. The drug busts also brought them closer together – they found common enemies in the Establishment and some of the media, who they saw as trying to knock them off their lofty public perches. Jagger, Richards and Marianne Faithfull were guests in the studio when the mad orchestral freak-out for 'A Day in the Life' was recorded, and also for the live broadcast of 'All You Need Is Love'; Lennon and McCartney reciprocated by singing on 'We Love You'.

In August, Jagger and Marianne joined the fab four on their famous trip to Bangor in Wales to be initiated into the mystical mysteries touted by the Maharishi Mahesh Yogi – it was the weekend that was cut short by news of the death of Brian Epstein. There were even clandestine talks about the two bands investing together in a studio with a hotel and a heliport.

All this fab hippiedom began affecting Jagger's view of The Stones' music, and the worldwide success of *Sgt. Pepper* made him want to do the same with his band's next album. After all, didn't it say 'Welcome the Rolling Stones' on the *Sgt. Pepper* cover, beckoning them to enter The Beatles' mystical, magical, flower-filled world? Author Philip Norman explained in his book *The Stones*:

> For Jagger, this entente with The Beatles was not without ulterior motive. His conversion to flower power made him hanker to turn The Rolling Stones into a psychedelic band such as The Beatles had effortlessly become. The Stones' long delay in finishing their album-in-progress, stemmed mainly from Jagger's insistence that it must touch all the same mystical chords as *Sgt. Pepper*.

For Keith Richards, the motivation was a bit more cynical. He says in his memoir *Life*, 'Much of the year, we haphazardly struggled to make *Their Satanic Majesties Request*. None of us wanted to make it, but it was time for another Stones album, and *Sgt. Pepper* was coming out, so we thought basically we were doing a put-on.'

The third influence was Andrew Loog Oldham: The Stones' flamboyant manager and producer. As Oldham grew wealthier and his business interests widened, the band began to feel he was neglecting them; while he was getting disillusioned with the group's public antics and the strange music they were producing in the studio. In 2011, Jagger told *Rolling Stone* magazine:

> The reason Andrew left was because he thought that we weren't concentrating and that we were being childish. It was not a great moment, really – and I would have thought it wasn't a great moment for Andrew either. There were a lot of distractions and you always need someone to focus you at that point, that was Andrew's job.

This resulted in *Their Satanic Majesties Request* being the first Stones album to be produced by the band itself rather than Oldham. Jagger and Co had complete musical freedom to do whatever they wanted. The lunatics had taken over the asylum.

Released in December, the album was originally slated to be titled *The Rolling Stones' Cosmic Christmas* – the eventual title was a twisting of the phrase 'Her Britannic Majesty requests...' written inside a British passport. In South Africa and The Philippines, it was called *The Stones Are Rolling*, because putting the word 'Satanic' on a record cover will turn all your children into Devil-worshipers. It sported the first 3D record cover – 'That was acid', remarks Keith – that showed The Stones wearing various forms of colourful fancy dress: Jagger in a tall black wizard's hat with a yellow moon on it; Keith in a yellow *Sgt, Pepper*-style uniform; Charlie looking like Leonardo da Vinci; Brian looking stoned, and Bill looking... well, stupid. Behind is a fantasy backdrop inspired by the band's trips to Morocco, with a minaret in the centre-background. Look closely, and you can see the faces of The Beatles scattered among the flowers, fruit, plants, stuffed camel and eastern musical instruments. To further cement the Beatles link, the picture was taken by *Sgt. Pepper* photographer Michael Cooper. He was also responsible for designing the cluttered photo collage inside that combines cut-ups of famous works of art with pictures of flowers, an observatory, the planet Saturn hovering over a cityscape, and a maze with the words 'It's Here' in the middle. You didn't need drugs – just looking at it would get you high (or give you a headache).

The music is as hard on the ears as the artwork is on the eyes, with opening track 'Sing This All Together' setting the standard – a shambolic, stoned sing-along led by ham-fisted honky-tonk piano and out-of-tune guitar, punctuated by out-of-place blasts of tinny brass, and an aimless instrumental section of random percussion, electric guitar and piano, all performed to a moronic thumping beat. It could be the worst three minutes and 47 seconds The Stones ever committed to tape – but worse is to come.

Second track 'Citadel' is a bit better – it has an electric guitar in it, Keith playing a four-chord sequence that sounds like The Stones of old and Jagger singing with real menace. The trouble is, it's overladen with extraneous tinkles, off-key saxophone farts and feeble attempts at backwards guitar. The sole non-Jagger-and-Richards track is 'In Another Land' – a dreary, forgettable little tune provided by Bill Wyman, in which his lead vocal has been sonically treated to sound like it's coming from deep inside a toilet bowl, on a composition clearly influenced by Pink Floyd's Syd Barrett. It ends with the sound of someone snoring – or that could've been me.

'2000 Man' has promising moments – the opening acoustic guitar figures are lovely and some of the sing-along sections have a bit of momentum. But the changing time signatures don't work, and Nicky Hopkins' organ is just too cheesy. Side one ends with undoubtedly the worst three minutes and 47 seconds – no, it's worse than that. It's *eight and a half minutes* of totally aimless banging, strumming, rattling, wordless huffs and screams, tuneless flute and Brian Jones' strained brass instruments repeating some of the musical phrases from the opening track. The reprise is subtitled 'See What Happens', but unfortunately, nothing much does.

It must've come as a relief to record buyers in 1967 to turn the album over and be greeted by the best track, and what should've been the album opener, 'She's a Rainbow'. You have to get past some pointless market-trader shouting before a gentle little music-box piano tune takes us into the opening verse, when suddenly the album bursts into life. Reminiscent of the chorus of 'Ruby Tuesday', the band sings of a girl who 'comes in colours everywhere / She combs her hair / She's like a rainbow.' It's not terribly deep and would've benefitted from a tighter arrangement with fewer stops and starts, but it's one of the album's few tracks that successfully blend The Stones' swagger with psychedelia.

'The Lantern' is fairly forgettable, as is the overlong and irritating (and poorly played – someone should've stomped on Jones's sarod, an Indian stringed instrument) 'Gomper'. We reach '2000 Light Years From Home', which has potential but is played as listlessly as Brian Jones after an acid binge. There's a promising little muted guitar riff in there that could've been built into something, but the ubiquitous Mellotron seems to drag it all down.

The album ends with its most blatant Beatles rip-off, in which Jagger's bizarre talking vocals are treated to sound like the captain on The Beatles' 'Yellow Submarine' – Jones frantically thrums a harp, there are chattering upper-class voices, a blast of horrible piano and then, mercifully, it ends.

*AllMusic*'s Richie aside, most critics hated this album – but none were more scathing than the band themselves. Jagger told *Rolling Stone* magazine:

> It's not very good. It had interesting things on it, but I don't think any of the songs are very good. There's two good songs on it. The rest of them were nonsense.

Richards was more succinct. He told *Esquire* magazine in 2015: 'The album was a load of crap.'

Too many drugs, too much time and no producer to rein them in: it was a recipe for disaster. And to that list must be added this: To make a truly convincing record, you have to believe in the music you are making, whether it's the blues or psychedelic rock. And The Stones didn't really believe in it. No wonder it gave so little satisfaction. As Rich Unterberger said, the Rolling Stones never strayed down pyschedelia's flower-strewn path again, returning to their commercial blues-rock formula with 1968's *Beggars Banquet* and staying with it for the next five decades.

# Grateful Dead

Key personnel:
Jerry 'Captain Trips' Garcia: lead guitar, vocals
Bill 'The Drummer' Kreutzmann: drums, percussion
Phil Lesh: bass, vocals
Ron 'Pigpen' McKernan: organ, harmonica, vocals
Bob Weir: rhythm guitar, vocals

## History

An array of misfits who congregated at a musical instrument shop – including Garcia, Weir and McKernan – formed folk group Mother McCree's Uptown Jug Champions, in Palo Alto, California, in 1964, so-called because the band's basic instruments included a jug which, when blown into, recreated a tuba-like bass sound. They recorded a live album not released until 1999. With the help of the shop's instruments, the group went electric and evolved into The Warlocks with the addition of Lesh and Kreutzmann. However, another group (the fledgling Velvet Underground) were also called The Warlocks, so Garcia found a new name in a dictionary: Grateful Dead, meaning a dead person showing gratitude to someone for arranging their burial. Nobody else liked it, but it stuck. The band was booked to appear at shows organised by *One Flew Over the Cuckoo's Nest* author Ken Kelsey, who had tried LSD, liked it, and wanted to spread it to other people through concerts known as Acid Tests. With financial backing from noted LSD manufacturer and supplier Oswald Stanley, Grateful Dead were signed to Warner Bros…

## Key releases in 1967

### The Grateful Dead (Album)

Label: Warner Bros.
Release date: 17 March 1967
Charts: US: 73
Side 1: 1. 'The Golden Road (To Unlimited Devotion)' (Grateful Dead) 2. 'Beat It On Down the Line' (Jesse Fuller) 3. 'Good Morning, Little School Girl' (Sonny Boy Williamson) 4. 'Cold Rain and Snow' (Obray Ramsey) 5. 'Sitting on Top of the World' (Lonnie Chatman, Walter Vinson) 6. 'Cream Puff War' (Jerry Garcia) Side 2: 1. 'Morning Dew' (Bonnie Dobson, Tim Rose) 2. 'New, New Minglewood Blues' (Noah Lewis) 3. 'Viola Lee Blues' (Lewis)

Here's your homework for tonight: Were The Grateful Dead really psychedelic? Answers on my desk first thing in the morning.

If you knew nothing about their history – and you were mysteriously robbed of the powers of hindsight – then your answer could well be 'no'. Listen to their debut album, and – apart from the closing ten-minute 'Viola Lee Blues' – there is nothing here that can be called psychedelic. Instead, we are talking about fairly unremarkable country rock with a smattering of blues, lifted by interesting lead guitar work from Jerry Garcia, intricate bass-playing from Phil Lesh, and some nice vocal harmonies.

They didn't even write all their own songs – only two of the nine tracks are originals, the rest taken or, ahem, adapted from various sources such as country blues singer Jesse Fuller, blues-harp player John Lee Curtis 'Sonny Boy' Williamson, 1930s guitar and fiddle group The Mississippi Sheiks and jug band musician Noah Lewis. There's no suggestion here that the band are fueled by anything more psychedelic than home-brewed whisky and perhaps a little weed.

Yet they became synonymous with psychedelic drugs and San Francisco's flourishing counterculture – they were right at the centre, where it was all happening, playing at psychedelic rock happenings throughout 1966, helping to bring hippies together into one acid-drenched movement.

Their financial backer – Owsley Stanley – was the acid king, an audio engineer and secret LSD manufacturer on an almost industrial scale, supplying, well, practically everyone. He also built the Dead the biggest and most powerful sound system then in existence and served as their sound engineer under the professional pseudonym Bear. The band immortalised him in the song 'Alice D. Millionaire': inspired by a newspaper headline that dubbed him the 'LSD millionaire'.

The Grateful Dead seemed to be everywhere in 1967 – playing at the Fillmore, at the Human Be-In at Golden Gate Park, at a Krishna Temple benefit at the Avalon Ballroom, headlining the Mantra-Rock Dance, doing a February benefit gig for the Council for Civic Unity, the First Annual Love Circus, the Monterey International Pop Festival and the Party for Chocolate George. From San Fran, they went to Los Angeles, Denver, New York, Boston, then on into Canada. Basically, if your show didn't have the Dead on the bill, then it couldn't really call itself psychedelic.

In true hippie style, the Dead also created their own commune, at 710 Ashbury, in the Haight-Ashbury district of San Francisco that would soon become the geographical centre of the Summer of Love. The Dead started moving into what was originally a college renting house, and all the other tenants wanted out, intimated by the LSD, loud music, and the sight of the hygienically challenged Pigpen.

In between, they went into RCA Studio A in Hollywood and started laying down tracks for their first album, completing it in just four days. They had cut a single the year before for local San Francisco label Scorpio, that was released in August but made little impact. However, in the same month, Warner Bros. Records' head honcho Joe Smith and his wife Donnie were persuaded by a local DJ to see the band at the Avalon Ballroom. In David Browne's book *So Many Roads: The Life and Times of the Grateful Dead*, Smith recalls, 'No-one my age had ever seen anything like that. People painting bodies and lying on the floor and smoking and, of course, the light shows.'

He had his reservations, particularly as the band were doing 'one of their 40-minute drone sets'. But he saw the way the wind was blowing in popular music and signed them up, believing they would add some street cred to the Reprise label: home to easy-listening squares Frank Sinatra and Dean Martin. When the band arrived in Los Angeles to begin recording, they discovered their deal didn't include creative control of their music – they wanted to recreate their trippy live show, but producer David Hassinger was intent on making a pop album that would sell.

In the same book, Garcia's girlfriend and eventual second wife Carolyn Adams (aka Mountain Girl) says, 'It wasn't exactly a fun trip. The expectations were so wildly different. The band wanted to be in-your-face outrageous, and the producer wanted pop that would sell – and who could blame him? There was more discussion than recording. It was pretty uncomfortable.'

Garcia later told *Rolling Stone*, 'At the time, it was unreasonable to do what we do, which would have been one LP, two songs or one song. Nobody would have gone for it. So we made the first record of songs we did.'

There's certainly plenty of energy in the recordings, fuelled perhaps by the drugs they were taking or the *musical differences* they were experiencing with the producer, and it works as high-octane country rock and blues. But few of the songs on the album captured even a shred of the band's live psychedelic magic – all except the aforementioned ten-minute version of 'Viola Lee's Blues'. One of two songs originally penned by Noah Lewis, this tale of someone being jailed for an unspecified offence was probably performed by the band when they were Mother McCree's Uptown Jug Champions, and the version recreated on vinyl was certainly part of their set in 1966.

Kicking off with a single mind-bending fractured chord – like a perverted version of the opening to The Beatles 'A Hard Day's Night' – it settles into a fairly swift, chugging rhythm, with verses punctuated by fluent lead guitar breaks from Garcia. After a couple of verses, the singing is abandoned, and we head into about seven minutes of Garcia's lead guitar. The backing starts speeding up and gets busier and more frantic, the guitar licks faster; the bass moves all over the place as if it's trying to get out of jail, and organist Pigpen seems to race up and down the keyboard like the swell of the ocean. At the eight-minute mark, there's another step up in speed with everyone playing the hell out of their instruments and Garcia providing lightning-fast, repetitive guitar phrases before everything falls back into the original rhythm and we get one more verse before the big finish.

The band played 'Viola Lee Blues' every night in the studio, and chose the one that seemed to hang together best. But even this palls when compared to a 23-minute live version bundled with a later release of the album: which would've been even longer if the first few minutes had been captured on tape. It starts at the end of the first verse, then moves fairly swiftly into a very long instrumental section that ebbs and flows in volume and intensity. Some sections seem to almost break down, as all semblance of rhythm and structure dissolve; then there are moments in which Garcia is virtually silent, letting bass, drums and organ take over before he crashes back in with fast, repetitive guitar phrases. And it goes on, and on, and on, either driving its listeners away into the night or into a drug-assisted trance as the relentless waves of music wash over them.

For the debut album's launch in March, the band organised a giant tub filled with dry ice and half-naked women – it was a message to the record company that the Dead would not be playing to their tune much longer. Indeed, their second album – 1968's *Anthem of the Sun* – contained just five tracks, one of them more than eleven minutes long, spliced together from live and studio recordings, and featuring such unlikely country-rock instruments as harpsichord, trumpet and guiro (a Latin American percussion instrument – you stroke the notches with a stick).

The debut album's cover was designed by Stanley Mouse and Alton Kelley, who produced psychedelic posters for rock events in San Francisco and went on to form their own design studio. Featuring cutouts of the band members and an alien fish monster bursting out of an egg superimposed over a solar flare, it was topped by a passage from *The Egyptian Book of the Dead*: 'In the land of the dark, the ship of the sun is drawn by the grateful dead.' But Garcia and the band thought it was pretentious and linked them to beliefs and ideas they didn't particularly share, so the text was stylised to be virtually unreadable.

The Grateful Dead were not very impressed with their first album, criticising it for feeling rushed and failing to capture the band's live spirit. It struggled to number 73 in the US charts, selling well in San Francisco but failing to make much impact elsewhere. Today, it's seen as one of the most important releases in 1967. Critic Robert Christgau wrote the following in his review of the 40 most essential psychedelic albums of the year:

> One of the year's few supposedly psychedelic LPs that wasn't actually a pop LP, the already legendary San Francisco band-collective's debut stood out and stands tall because its boogieing folk-rock epitomizes the San Francisco ballroom ethos: blues-based tunes played by musicians who came to rhythm late, expanded, so they were equally suitable for dancing and for tripping out. It's also the only studio album that respects the impact of Ron 'Pigpen' McKernan, who died in 1973 of cirrhosis of the liver. McKernan's organ is almost as pervasive as Jerry Garcia's guitar. And although Garcia and Bob Weir both take vocal leads, their singing styles are still in Pigpen's white-blues thrall.

There is, of course, a large dollop of hindsight here – as we know, the Dead went on to become one of America's most celebrated and best-loved bands, inspiring a devoted, fanatical following, thanks to their lack of commercial ambition, celebration of drug-taking (despite numerous busts) and the fact that every gig was different. Most bands performed an unchanging setlist night after night, but the Dead made it up as they went along, playing whatever they saw in their heads, and encouraged their audience to record the results. That's why there are at least five times as many live albums of the Dead as there are studio releases.

If the Dead had broken up in 1967 – and the band's future looked uncertain after the Ashbury house was raided and most of the members arrested on drug charges – their debut album would be just a footnote in history. But it deserves its place in this book because it launched the long, strange trip of, arguably, America's most psychedelic band.

## Donovan

Key personnel:
Donovan Phillips Leitch: vocals, guitar, harmonica

### History

Born in Glasgow in 1946, Donovan contracted polio when young (allegedly from a super-strength vaccine) that left him with a slight limp. Moving to Hertfordshire, he developed a love for folk music and studied the fingerpicking styles of the Carter Family, Doc Watson, Ramblin' Jack Elliott, and the songs of Davy Graham, Jessie Fuller, Woody Guthrie, Leadbelly, Big Bill Broonzy and Cisco Houston. Later, Bert Jansch would be a huge influence. Donovan was also influenced by trad jazz, visiting London clubs to soak in the sounds. Spotted by two music industry figures in a club in Southend-on-Sea, he was put on British TV music show *Ready Steady Go!* and signed to Pye Records. His first single 'Catch the Wind' hit number 4 in the UK and 23 in the US. The first album *What's Bin Did and What's Bin Hid* reached number 3 in the UK. In 1966, 'Sunshine Superman' gave him his first US number 1 – a contractual dispute resulted in an album of the same name being released that year in the US only.

### Key releases in 1967

**'Mellow Yellow' / 'Preachin' Love'** (Single)
Both songs by Donovan
Label: Pye
Release date: 3 February 1967
Charts: UK: 8

**Mellow Yellow** (Album)
All songs by Donovan Leitch.
Label: Epic (US)
Release date: February 1967
Charts: US: 14
Side 1: 1. 'Mellow Yellow' 2. 'Writer in the Sun' 3. 'Sand and Foam' 4. 'The Observation' 5. 'Bleak City Woman' Side 2: 1. 'House of Jansch' 2. 'Young Girl Blues' 3. 'Museum' 4. 'Hampstead Incident' 5. Sunny South Kensington'

**Sunshine Superman** (Album)
All songs by Donovan Leitch.
Label: Pye (UK)
Release date: June 1967
Charts: UK: 25
Side 1: 1. 'Sunshine Superman' 2. 'Legend of a Girl Child Linda' 3. 'The Observation' 4. 'Guinevere' 5. 'Celeste' 6. 'Writer in the Sun' Side 2: 1. 'Season

of the Witch' 2. 'Hampstead Incident' 3. 'Sand and Foam' 4. 'Young Girl Blues' 5. 'Three Kingfishers' 6. 'Bert's Blues'

### 'There Is a Mountain' / 'Sand and Foam' (Single)

Both songs by Donovan Leitch.
Label: Epic (US), Pye (UK)
Release date: 26 July 1967 (US), 20 October 1967 (Pye)
Charts: US: 11; UK: 8

### A Gift From a Flower to a Garden (Album)

All songs by Donovan Leitch except as noted.
Label: Epic (US), Pye (UK)
Release date: December 1967 (US), 16 April 1968 (UK)
Charts: US: 19
Side 1: Wear Your Love Like Heaven (First Part) 1. 'Wear Your Love Like Heaven' 2. 'Mad John's Escape' 3. 'Skip-a-Long Sam' 4. 'Sun' 5. 'There Was a Time' Side 2: 1. 'Oh Gosh' 2. 'Little Boy in Corduroy' 3. 'Under the Greenwood Tree' (Words by William Shakespeare) 4. 'The Land of Doesn't Have To Be' 5. 'Someone Singing'
Side 3: For Little Ones (Second part)
1. 'Song of the Naturalist's Wife' 2. 'The Enchanted Gypsy' 3. 'Voyage Into the Golden Screen' 4. 'Isle of Islay' 5. 'The Mandolin Man and His Secret' 6. 'Lay of the Last Tinker' Side 4: 1. 'The Tinker and the Crab' 2. 'Widow With Shawl (A Portrait)' 3. 'The Lullaby of Spring' 4. 'The Magpie' 5. 'Starfish-on-the-Toast' 6. 'Epistle to Derroll'

'Donovan? Who is this Donovan?' asked Bob Dylan. 'Is he any good?'.

There were times when Donovan seemed to be everywhere. He was backstage with Dylan in D.A. Pennebaker's film *Don't Look Back*: shot in 1965 but released two years later; he came up with the line 'Sky of blue, sea of green' for The Beatles' 'Yellow Submarine', and later accompanied the fab four to Rishikesh, teaching John Lennon how to play fingerpicked guitar. He also contributed two songs to the 1967 Ken Loach film *Poor Cow*.

Donovan was friends with Brian Jones of The Rolling Stones and pursued his ex-girlfriend, eventually marrying her. Donovan was also the first high-profile British pop star to be busted for drugs, and was in the same *News of the World* article that mistakenly quoted Mick Jagger as a self-confessed user of narcotics (The paper had actually spoken to Brian Jones, but the reporter couldn't tell the difference).

Not bad for a Glasgow lad with a limp who was regarded by some as the poor man's Bob Dylan. But then, influential British radio DJ John Peel called Dylan the poor man's Donovan. So it all balances out, really. There were similarities but also differences. Donovan was a better singer than Dylan, and a much better guitarist – perfecting a fingerpicking style that made him the envy of some of his contemporaries. But he lacked the political bite and arrogant swagger of Dylan, sometimes coming across as altogether too whimsical and fey for some tastes.

Having said that, Donovan was expanding his musical horizons by 1967, bringing in more instrumentation and influences from eastern music, jazz and psychedelia; while Dylan was going backwards to his mostly acoustic folk roots on *John Wesley Harding*. Donovan was stretching out, Dylan contracting.

Like Dylan, Donovan wrote poetry set to music. Unlike Dylan, Donovan's songs were mostly inspired by love: both the universal and the personal kind. In fact, many of his songs were attempts to communicate with the love of his life – Brian Jones' former girlfriend Linda Lawrence, who also bore the Rolling Stone member's fourth child.

In 1966, rumours broke that Donovan would be moving to Epic Records as part of a publishing deal with notorious US businessman Allen Klein, resulting in a contract dispute with Pye Records that meant none of his singles or albums were released in the UK for about a year. However, his US success was considerable, with the singles 'Sunshine Superman' and 'Mellow Yellow' and albums of the same name, all scoring high in the charts.

His 1967 UK comeback started with a sellout concert at the Royal Albert Hall: a multimedia event that included a tattooed dancing girl called Vali whose appearance fee was 'one Nubian goat'. That was followed by the release of the 'Mellow Yellow' single in the UK, four months after it appeared in the US. Originally written as a throwaway sing-along to play at parties, it provoked claims that Donovan was promoting the idea of smoking dried bananas as an unorthodox method of getting high (a joke originally suggested by Country Joe and the Fish as part of a PR stunt involving a giant carnival banana). In his memoir, Donovan explained:

> What I really meant by the phrase 'mellow yellow' was that I was a laid back kind of dude, smoking the safe little green herb. The electrical banana in my song was a reference to the vibrators which had become available through mail-order ads in the back pages of certain types of periodicals. Then a Boston radio station banned the song, saying I was singing about abortion. How bizarre.

Arranged by future Led Zeppelin bassist John Paul Jones, the song is a cheerful stomp, with electric guitar and bass, vamping muted horns and the sound of partying people (including Paul McCartney). It's impossible not to listen to it and smile.

The album that followed – but only in the US – saw Donovan mixing basic acoustic numbers with jazz, Latin, rock and poetry. His whimsical and fey reputation was enhanced by tracks such as 'Writer in the Sun' with its plaintive flute, and the acoustic 'Sand and Foam'. But 'The Observation' is a jazz number, driven by double bass, with stabs of piano improvisation, horns and little nods to the hit single. 'Bleak City Woman' mixes trad jazz with blues, 'House of Jansch' is Donovan's soundalike tribute to idiosyncratic folk troubadour Bert Jansch, and 'Sunny South Kensington' includes a mysterious bass intro, harpsichord, random harmonica and organ. By the way, Paul McCartney is on the album somewhere, adding uncredited bass and vocals.

In the UK, Pye Records decided to create a compilation album titled *Sunshine Superman*, combining seven tracks from that 1966 release with five from *Mellow Yellow*. Donovan's original albums were not released in the UK until 1994.

But back to '67, when Donovan toured Europe, Australia and the Far East. He would've been a shoo-in for the Monterey International Pop Festival if the US hadn't banned him because of his drug bust. Instead, festival organisers made him one of the twelve *governors* along with the likes of Mick Jagger, Paul McCartney and Roger McGuinn.

In August, Donovan released another single in the US (it was out two months later in the UK). 'There Was a Mountain' was inspired by a Buddhist saying by Qingyuan Weixin: a ninth-century philosopher who said there were three stages to understanding Zen – first, seeing a mountain as a mountain and water as water; second, seeing the mountain as *not* a mountain and water as not water, and third, seeing the mountain as a mountain and water as water once again.

So Donovan's lyric – set once again to one of his nursery-rhyme-style melodies – announces, 'First, there is a mountain, then there is no mountain, then there is'. Accompanied by simple percussion and clapping, it is flower power personified, in its apparent simplicity, hiding deeper truths. (Incidentally, Donovan claims the phrase 'flower power' was first used to describe his sellout concerts at the Hollywood Bowl that year, which used 7,000 irises to create a giant flower mandala.) Charting at number 8 in the UK and 10 in the US, it brought a little bit of Zen wisdom to the pop charts.

Also, in August, Donovan's then-girlfriend Enid gave birth to his first child, a boy. Full of parental love, he decided his next release would be a double album, one for the parents and another for their children. Recorded in October after a mammoth US tour, the first disc of *A Gift From a Flower to a Garden* was subtitled *Wear Your Love Like Heaven*, after the opening track that gave him another hit US single, and featured electric instrumental backing.

The second disc – *For Little Ones* – saw Donovan mostly recording on his own, showcasing his gentle fingerpicking with little in additional instruments except for flute and the sound of his own child crying on 'Song of the Naturalist's Wife'. Just what little ones made of song titles such as 'Epistle to Derroll' is not recorded, even though it was all about 'starry starfish'.

Of course, a lot of Donovan's songs sounded like nursery rhymes anyway, and the double album showed him at his fey, whimsical peak, creating gentle tunes and images for the stoned flower-power generation. The *adult* disc included pretty ditties about 'Mad John's Escape' and 'Skip-a-Long Sam', along with a song originally composed for Sir Laurence Olivier's National Theatre production of William Shakespeare's *As You Like It*.

Having said that, Donovan made a point of denouncing drugs in the album's liner notes. Instead, he promoted transcendental meditation, the result of an audience with the Maharishi Mahesh Yogi during a pause in the singer's West Coast tour. He saw it as the possible antidote to a malaise that he believed was creeping into the counterculture movement – that flower power was being commercialised and harder drugs were displacing marijuana and LSD.

The record company baulked at releasing the double-album box-set package, fudging the issue by issuing it first as two separate albums – once again prioritising the US over the UK. Sales were disappointing, so Donovan felt vindicated when, as a double LP, it eventually reached the top 20, selling half a million copies by 1970.

In his memoir, he pointed out that he was singing peaceful, childlike songs while the Vietnam War was raging, the Apollo 1 disaster killed its three-man crew, and China detonated a hydrogen bomb:

> Critics of my gentle approach to music were still missing the point. In contrast to the wild exuberance of rock and roll, I was soothing with my song. Peaceful music was needed then ... Soldiers returning from Vietnam met with me later and spoke of the effect the music had on them. Many returned damaged and became lost in the great peacetime which wanted to forget.

Donovan would go on to even greater fame and success in 1968 with the hit singles 'Jennifer Juniper' and 'Hurdy Gurdy Man', before joining The Beatles in Rishikesh and helping John Lennon to compose some of his best songs on the *White Album*. But, for Donovan, 1967 was a year of transition from folk singer to hippie balladeer and flag-waver for love. His music would never become as complicated as, say, The Beatles, but neither would it be as charmingly naive as it was in 1967. And neither would the rest of the world.

# Moby Grape

Key personnel:
Peter Lewis: rhythm guitar, vocals
Jerry Miller: lead guitar, vocals
Bob Mosley: bass, vocals
Skip Spence: rhythm guitar, vocals
Don Stevenson: drums, vocals

## History

Skip Spence and Matthew Katz had both been turfed out of Jefferson Airplane – the former was the band's drummer, the latter the manager. Katz encouraged Spence to form an Airplane-type band. Spence switched to guitar and enlisted bassist Bob Mosley after seeing him play with the Joel Scott Hill Trio in San Francisco. Mosley met fingerpicking guitarist Peter Lewis at an airport, and the quartet then went in search of a drummer. Mosley remembered Don Stevenson from an earlier band, The Frantics (now renamed Luminous Marsh Gas, and why not?), and got Don's fellow Gas man, guitarist Jerry Miller, as a sort of twofer. The three-guitar approach was unique, and all five members could sing and write songs. The only way, surely, was up.

## Key releases from 1967

### **Moby Grape** (Album)

Label: Columbia
Release date: 6 June 1967
Charts: US: 24
Side 1: 1. 'Hey Grandma' (Jerry Miller, Don Stevenson) 2. 'Mr. Blues' (Bob Mosley) 3. 'Fall on You' (Peter Lewis) 4. '8:05' (Miller, Stevenson) 5. 'Come in the Morning (Mosley) 6. 'Omaha' (Skip Spence) 7. 'Naked, If I Want To' (Miller) Side 2: 1. 'Someday' (Miller, Stevenson, Spence) 2. 'Ain't No Use' (Miller, Stevenson) 3. 'Sitting by the Window' (Lewis) 4. 'Changes' (Miller, Stevenson) 5. 'Lazy Me' (Mosley) 6. 'Indifference' (Spence)

There was a knock at the door. Roadie Tim Dellara opened it and there was Skip Spence, sweating and acting strange, wearing leather trousers, no shirt, and carrying an axe. 'Where's Don and Jerry?' he asked. Dellara rather foolishly told him (I mean, he was carrying an *axe*) that Don Stevenson and Jerry Miller were in their room. So Spence went to their room and hacked a hole in the door. Perhaps he put his head through and said, 'Heeeeeere's Skippy!'. Luckily, Stevenson and Miller had gone out, otherwise there could have been a bloodbath.

It turned out someone had filled Spence with bad acid, leading him to believe he was the Antichrist and that the only way to save himself was to cut Don Stevenson into tiny little bits. He was taken to Tombs jail in New York before being committed to Bellevue Hospital, and that was the end of his time with the band he had founded just a few short years before. Not long after, that was the end of the band.

Moby Grape was named after the gag. You know, what's big and purple and lives in the ocean? But we can change it a little. What's big and purple, lives in the ocean, released a classic psychedelic rock album in 1967, then was destroyed by questionable business decisions, bad luck, blunders and schizophrenia? The answer, sadly, is still Moby Grape.

When 1967 opened, they were the most sought-after band in San Francisco, with record companies waving their cheque books to sign them up. After all, Moby Grape had five songwriters, five singers capable of producing rich harmonies, and a unique triple-guitar attack that gave them an urgent, powerful sound. In just a few months, they had honed their act with regular gigs at venues such as The Ark, The Avalon, The Heliport and Bill Graham's Fillmore.

Here's what rock magazine *Crawdaddy* said about them:

> The Grape have enormous impact on an audience. Three guitars, a very talented bass, and a drummer (all of whom sing well), they come on like a flash flood. Guitarist Skip Spence ... radiates joy in all directions, turning on the group, turning on the audience, turning the whole performance into an event, a celebration. The Grape's music is excellent and is likely to get even better – the group is only a few months old, and when they really get it together, they'll be frightening.

The band were invited to Los Angeles to audition for various record labels, and the winner was Columbia, home of The Byrds. In hindsight – and, boy, does hindsight have to work overtime for Moby Grape – it wasn't necessarily the right decision. Peter Lewis summed it up in an interview with Jud Cost for The Rebel Hangs Ten In Hollywood, by saying Columbia was 'the worst place for us. You can sink or swim, and it doesn't matter to them.'

Here's another decision that had hindsight frowning and wagging a warning finger – when they signed with manager Matthew Katz, he demanded the rights to their name. Various members owed him money at the time, so went along with it – I mean, what's the worst that could happen? Within a few years, there were *two* Moby Grapes – the original band locked in a lawsuit with Katz, and a fake version their by-now ex-manager had sent out on the road.

But all that chaos was yet to come. In those early days, there was nothing but excitement and optimism as the band recorded demos for Columbia in between gigs up and down the West Coast. One of those appearances was at a benefit event to raise funds for a Krishna Temple in San Francisco; another was a fundraiser for a civil rights organisation that saw the Grape share the stage with the Grateful Dead.

On 11 March, they were in Columbia's L.A. studios, bright-eyed and bushy-tailed, ready to start laying down the songs for their new album under the steady, supportive gaze of producer David Rubinson. And what songs they had! The album bursts into life with 'Hey Grandma': a song you will recognise even if you think you've never heard any Moby Grape. Opening with Jerry Miller's screaming lead guitar, it's a joyful gallop with a catchy, stuttering chorus – this grandma is not a staid, white-haired old biddy knitting in a rocking chair; she's hip and trendy, probably what we nowadays call a *cougar*, as her 'old man's just a boy'. Written mostly by Lewis, it was also about the girls in San Francisco who would buy *granny clothes* from secondhand shops. In the final verse, it extols the virtues of Robitussin: a cough syrup that offered a cheap but effective high because of the codeine content.

'Mr. Blues' is, as the title suggests, a slightly slower, bluesier number, sung by Bob Mosley, but still defiantly optimistic, as he vows to 'put down' old Mr. Blues with the help of some alcohol. 'Fall on You' displays the band's vocal harmonies to the full – Peter Lewis takes lead vocal while the rest of the band chant 'Yes, I know, it's fallin' in yet another fast but criminally-short number (less than two minutes long) that marries blues-trope lyrics about breakups, cheating women and disconnected phone services to a relentlessly upbeat melody.

Things slow down for '805' – an absolutely gorgeous ballad led by Latin-influenced acoustic guitars and sung with the sort of sweet close harmonies The Beach Boys could produce after, say, seven months of recording (but the Grape recorded the entire album in six weeks).

'Come in the Morning' was one of the first tracks to be recorded: a Motown-influenced number about free love in which people come (oo-err!) and go with no regrets. 'Omaha', written by Skip Spence, fades in with ominous chords, before launching into an aggressive, Jefferson-Airplane-style rocker that fails to mention the Nebraska city, even in passing. The lyrics talk about universal love but are fragmented and jumbled, as if written during an LSD trip. Side one ends with 57 seconds of what sounds like a gentle country song, but one that extols the joys of walking naked down the street and getting high while penniless.

Side two opens with the gentle, contemplative 'Someday', originally written for The Frantics: a song that, like 'Mr. Blues' deals with loss, but without the upbeat defiance. Instead, you can feel the loss coming through the song, partly through its relatively slow, rambling nature and partly the unpredictable mix of major and minor chords. It fades out on a slightly out-of-focus guitar solo and, like most of the album's tracks, leaves you wanting much, much more.

'Ain't No Use' starts off as a fairly standard country-pop song but is interspersed with a sudden lurch into waltz time. 'Sitting by the Window' is another sad ballad about loss based on fingerpicked electric guitar, but one that moves into a more upbeat chorus, ending on a brief fingerpicked solo.

'Changes' was written and sung by drummer Don Stevenson, a difficult feat because it's a fierce, upbeat number with a Motown-style shouting vocal and lots of driving percussion, overlaid with Bob Mosley's almost non-stop lead guitar attack. 'Lazy Me' is a song of searching questions – 'Who holds the blank thoughts of people when nothing is said?' sings Mosley – but set to an upbeat, driving tune that fades out on a bass solo.

Finally, the album ends on the longest track: the powerful 'Indifference' that the Grape demoed for Columbia to seal their record contract. Featuring everything that made the Grape so appealing – the interweaving guitars, harmony vocals and breathless pace of attack – it's once again a song about questions:

> What's this song you're bringing?
> Just a bell ringing in my mind
> Is it forever ever?
> That's the part that blows my mind

After four minutes and sixteen seconds – a mammoth length for the Grape – it all seems to collapse at the end: foretelling, perhaps, the future of the band itself.

During those short sessions, there were other songs recorded that could've been included on the album – which runs at just over 31 minutes – and probably would've been if the Grape had been from Britain, where bands liked to give their fans a bit more value for money. *Sgt. Pepper*, for example, is nearly 40 minutes long and, you could argue, lasts forever if you leave the needle to pick up the strange voices in the run-out groove. Later *Moby Grape* reissues add the instrumental 'Rounder', audition recording 'Looper', and 'Bitter Wind': one of the earliest songs they'd written together.

Despite its paucity of running time and the fact that some of the tracks are criminally short, Moby Grape's debut is seen as a psychedelic masterpiece, with *Rolling Stone* in 1983 calling it 'as fresh and exhilarating today as it was when it exploded out of San Francisco during 1967's Summer of Love'. So its poor chart showing at the time – just number 24 in the States – is a puzzler until you learn about Columbia's marketing strategy for the album.

We have already noted a contrast in the way albums and singles were released and marketed in the US and UK. British bands and record labels feared their fans would baulk at paying twice for the same song, so their singles were rarely included on their albums. More than half The Beatles' UK singles were non-album tracks, while Jimi Hendrix's UK debut didn't feature his first three 45s.

But US labels feared albums wouldn't sell if they didn't include the hits. That's why Capitol Records reformatted The Beatles albums up to and including *Revolver*, and did the same with many British acts' releases. When it came to *Moby Grape*, Columbia made a decision that may have appeared to be a stroke of genius at the time but was actually an act of commercial insanity – they released nearly all the album's tracks on five singles simultaneously, along with the album, at a $100,000 launch concert that included Janis Joplin, hundreds of bottles of Moby Grape wine and a tsunami of purple orchids. Don Stevenson explained to author Cam Cobb:

> It's well known that Columbia's marketing and publicity strategy for our first album was about the worst thing that could've been done. Nobody knew out of the five singles that were all released at the same time, which one to play and which one not to play. And sometimes they didn't play any of them. Then people thought we were like The Monkees: that it was just a hype job. And some thought there were probably other musicians playing on the record and the singles ... You know, there are marketing strategies that make a difference. Columbia's marketing strategy made a big difference – just not the one we were hoping for.

Anyone who bought the singles wouldn't want to pay full album price for what would be just three additional tracks. And if you bought the album, why would you need the singles? The two releases cannibalised each other's sales – number 24 wasn't a bad achievement for a debut album, but it was hardly the slam-dunk super-hit everyone was expecting. And only two of the singles entered the charts, with best-performer 'Omaha' limping to number 88. It seems that the final track, 'Indifference', was eerily prescient of the public's reaction.

But there was worse to come. In the early hours of the morning after the launch party, Jerry Miller, Peter Lewis and Skip Spence were arrested on a charge of 'contributing to the delinquency of' three 17-year-old *flower girls*. Miller was also busted for possession of marijuana. The trio denied the charges, describing them as 'bullshit', but the resulting publicity undoubtedly trashed their reputations and damaged them commercially.

Then came the Monterey International Pop Festival fiasco. We have already visited this event, and we know that in the States, it made stars of Jimi Hendrix and The Who, and also launched the career of Janis Joplin. Moby Grape were top of the list for the festival organisers and were initially given a coveted Sunday time slot. But then their manager Matthew Katz started making extreme financial demands – some say he wanted $1,000,000 for his band – and as a result, the Grape were punished with a Saturday afternoon opening, warming up the incoming crowd for the bigger acts. They also failed to appear in the film of the event because the organisers explained, 'Matthew holds the paper on these guys. So we can't do that.'

Things went downhill from then. They were kicked off a tour after a tiff with Columbia labelmates The Buckinghams, and gigs had dried up because of the bad press from the arrests. Their panicking label forced them back into the studio to record their second album, but didn't like what they produced and put the sessions on hold. By the time they resumed later in the year, the band had started to fragment – the debut album had been recorded with everyone there at the same time, but the follow-up *Wow/Grape Jam* saw individual members coming in just to do their bit and then leave. Meanwhile, their relationship with Katz had deteriorated, and they replaced him with Michael Gruber. Later, Katz would sue them, claiming he had ownership of the band's name.

Meanwhile, the group was distracted by the impending court hearings on the underage sex and drug charges, which weren't all dropped until January 1968. And that important second album? It was smothered in strings and horns by producer Rubinson, and the band added a second disc of improvised jams. The debut album had taken thirteen weeks to record – *Wow/Grape Jam* took a year to reach the shops. It did marginally better than the debut, reaching number 20 when it was eventually released in June 1968, but by that stage, the steam had well and truly run out for the Grape.

From then on, it was all downhill, through court cases, drug-induced schizophrenia and plummeting sales, with the band eventually breaking up in 1969. Our focus is on 1967, so what happened to the band after then is not really part of this book. But it's impossible not to feel a sad sense of loss at the demise of a band with so much talent, so much promise. For many in that year, their psychedelic dreams would come true. For Moby Grape, those dreams turned into a nightmare.

# The Moody Blues

Key personnel:
Justin Hayward: acoustic and electric guitars, piano, sitar, vocals
John Lodge: bass, vocals
Mike Pinder: Mellotron, piano, tamboura, gong, vocals (including spoken)
Ray Thomas: flutes, percussion, piano, vocals
Graeme Edge: drums, percussion, vocals

## History

In 1964, Birmingham pals Mike Pinder and Ray Thomas formed The Krew Cats, before recruiting guitarist and singer Denny Laine, drummer Graeme Edge and bassist Clint Warwick, and changing their name to The MBs in the hope of getting sponsorship from local Mitchells & Butlers Brewery. They became The Moody Blues because they were interested in how music changes people's moods and because they were playing rhythm and blues at the time. Signed to Decca Records, the first single 'Steal Your Heart Away' failed to chart, but the follow-up 'Go Now' hit number 1 in the UK and 10 in the US. The debut album *The Magnificent Moodies* combined originals with R&B covers but failed to chart. Subsequent singles made less and less of an impact in the UK, although the band remained fairly popular in the US and Europe. In 1966, Warwick was replaced by Rod Clark, but he followed Laine out of the group about six months later. Recruiting old pal John Lodge on bass and singer/guitarist Justin Hayward, the Moodies relocated to Belgium for a while, where 'Boulevard de la Madeleine' had reached the charts.

## Key releases in 1967

### **Days of Future Passed** (Album)

Label: Deram
Release date: 10 November 1967
Charts: UK: 27; US: 3; Canada: 3; Australia: 10
Side 1: 1. 'The Day Begins' (Peter Knight, Graeme Edge) 2. 'Dawn: Dawn Is a Feeling' (Mike Pinder) 3. 'The Morning: Another Morning' (Ray Thomas) 4. 'Lunch Break: Peak Hour' (John Lodge) Side 2: 1. 'The Afternoon: Forever Afternoon (Tuesday?) 2. '(Evening) Time To Get Away' (Justin Hayward, Lodge) 3. 'Evening: The Sun Set, Twilight Time' (Pinder, Thomas) 4. 'The Night: Nights in White Satin, Late Lament/Resolvement' (Hayward, Knight, Edge)

### **'Nights in White Satin' / 'Cities'** (Single)

Both songs by Justin Hayward.
Label: Deram
Release date: 10 November 1967
Charts: UK: 19, Netherlands: 1
1972 re-release charts: UK: 9; US: 2; Canada: 1

By 1967, the Moodies were pretty much washed up. They had reformed with some new members, and a new sound that relied less on R&B covers and more on self-penned material. But the record-buying public – particularly in the UK – remained unimpressed. Justin Hayward revealed the following in Jon Brewer's 2005 TV documentary on the band, made as part of The Classic Artists Series:

> Our price had really dropped to about £25 a night, and I'd gone back to living with my parents. In a last desperate stab, we did some work in cabaret in the north of England ... and you had to do a bit of comedy and something else to make it work. On the Saturday night, we were at the Fiesta in Stockton – we'd finished our second set and there was a knock on the door, and this guy came in and he said, 'I thought I had to tell yer... yer the worst band I've ever seen in me life. You're effing crap' ... We were on our way back home in absolute silence, and from the back of the Transit, I heard this little voice from our drummer Graeme. He said, 'That bloke's right, you know. We *are* crap.'

The self-realisation could've destroyed a lesser band, but the Moodies had a core of steely determination that refused to let them give up. They threw away their blue stage suits and immediately started writing new material. Invited to Belgium by a rabid fan, they created a new stage show of music that they performed in Europe, particularly in France, where they were still popular.

Then came the call from Decca Records: Could they make a demonstration album for the company's new subsidiary Deram, a rock version of Dvorak's *New World Symphony*, to show off the Deramic Sound System audio gimmick? The Moodies couldn't really say no – their contract was about to expire and they owed the record company about £5,000 in advances. This would constitute their agreed second album, and all their debts would be forgiven.

The original idea was for the orchestra to play its version of the 1893 symphony, with the band rocking up Dvorak in between. The Moodies immediately said yes because they had nothing else, and the alternative was probably to beaver away in obscurity until the money finally ran out. Britain's then foremost orchestral arranger Peter Knight – who was tasked with providing the serious music content – went to see the band in concert and heard Pinder's 'Dawn Is a Feeling' and Hayward's 'Nights in White Satin': two new songs composed for their stage show. In the dressing room afterwards, Knight said, 'You know. I really like *your* songs', and poor Dvorak got the boot (he didn't complain, as he'd been dead for 63 years).

So when they entered the studio in May 1967, it was with a different format in mind – the band would play original songs and Knight would provide orchestral links using those themes. They had two or three compositions that had been part of their stage show – the rest were penned as they went along, with producer Tony Clark occasionally locking the musicians in a microphone cupboard until they had written the next track. At the end of the band recording, Peter Knight had a three-hour session with an orchestra to tape the musical links between the tracks, lifting key melodies out of the songs, so the album flowed from one track to the next with no break.

The orchestral backing on the actual songs came not from Knight, but from 1967's must-have instrument, the mighty Mellotron. Mike Pinder had actually worked at the Mellotron factory in Birmingham for eighteen months as a *test driver* of every new instrument that came off the production line. When he left to form The Moody Blues, his old boss found him an unused 'Tron languishing at the Dunlop Tyre Factory, where nobody knew how to use it.

With a few modifications, Pinder was able to produce a rich, lush orchestral sound that blended perfectly with Knight's orchestra – so well, in fact, that it was sometimes difficult to tell when one ended and the other took over. (Pinder's other claim to fame is that he introduced the instrument to The Beatles, who used it on their 1967 single 'Strawberry Fields Forever'.)

The result is an absolutely gorgeous blending of genres, with both rock band and classical orchestra working seamlessly to create a warm, bittersweet atmosphere. Knight's introduction opens with slowly-building timpani before dramatic minor-chord strings and woodwind introduce themes from some of the songs that are to follow, including moments from 'Nights In White Satin'.

But then it lowers the temperature a bit to introduce the poem – penned by drummer Graeme Edge – that opens and closes the album, recited by Pinder. 'Cold-hearted orb that rules the night, removes the colours from our sight,' he intones with a nice bit of bass to his voice. Edge explained in a 2018 interview with George Harris for *Jazz Weekly*:

> Our producer Tony Clarke said 'Can somebody do something about mornings?', because everything we'd got, being musicians, was about later. We never got up in the mornings; we wouldn't get up until around midday! We had plenty about evenings and afternoons and night, but no mornings. So, I sat down and tried to write something about the morning ... hoping that somebody could put music to it and make it a morning song for the album. When I got into the studio, I read it to them and they said, 'It's lovely, but there are way too many words for a song. You can't sing it with music; it's a poem, not a song.' Tony Clarke said, 'Let's just do it like that, as a poem!'. I had just smoked too many cigarettes, so my throat was too throaty and gravelly, so Mike Pinder read it with more gravitas.

It was a happy accident that became a tradition – from then on, most Moodies albums would include poetry from Graeme. The other happy accident was 'Nights in White Satin', the song now indelibly linked with The Moody Blues and one that became the first single from the new album. Penned by Justin Hayward, it was intended as a companion piece to Pinder's 'Dawn Is a Feeling', which the keyboard player had written on an upright red piano while gazing at dawn breaking over Barnes in West London. Hayward explained in the TV documentary:

> I sat down on the side of the bed and it literally took five or six minutes to write. A lot of things that were going on in my life, young love, and all people in love have the desire to tell the world about it, which was certainly my case. I was at the end of a big love affair, which I thought was devastating, and the beginning of another one, which I thought was wonderful, and all of these thoughts went into the song.

When he presented the song to the rest of the band, they appeared underwhelmed. But then Pinder asked him to play it again, and after each verse line, the keyboard player added a little seven-note motif that, along with Ray Thomas's flute solo, suddenly raised the composition to a whole new level.

Hayward also provided the more upbeat 'Tuesday Afternoon', which became the album's second single in 1968. Thomas came up with the jaunty 'Another Morning' and the swirling, trippy 'Twilight Time'; Lodge the fast-paced 'Peak Hour' and more contemplative 'Time To Get Away', and Pinder, the eastern-influenced, trance-like 'The Sunset'.

Rather than listing individual songs, the tracks are divided up into parts of the day, and everything is linked by Knight's expressive and melodic orchestral segues. It is truly a fully-fledged, no-nonsense concept album from start to finish.

When the Moodies delivered the finished album, record company executives were distinctly unimpressed. 'This isn't Dvorak', they complained. 'Where's Dvorak?'. But the band were saved by Walt Maguire – boss of Decca's New York subsidiary London Records – who said, 'I don't know about you guys, but give that to me and I can sell it in America'. Without him, the Moodies may have remained a tiny footnote in musical history – and certainly wouldn't be in this book.

The band went on to have a hugely successful recording career – *Days of Future Passed* and the five albums that followed are regarded as classic examples of a psychedelic and progressive rock hybrid that helped the Moodies sell more than 70,000,000 albums worldwide and enter the Rock and Roll Hall of Fame.

The album that saved their career received mixed reviews when first released, with *Rolling Stone* dismissing it as 'an English rock group strangling itself in conceptual goo'. But hindsight is a wonderful thing, and now the same magazine lists it as one of the most important albums of 1967.

For this listener, *Days of Future Passed* is the year's most perfect psychedelic concept album – and, take it from me, the surround-sound version will blow your mind.

> Cold-hearted orb that rules the night
> Removes the colours from our sight
> Red is grey and yellow white
> But we decide which is right
> And which is an illusion...

# Frank Zappa and the Mothers of Invention

Key personnel:
Frank Zappa: guitar, vocals
Jimmy Carl Black: drums, vocals
Ray Collins: vocals, tambourine, harmonica
Roy Estrada: bass, vocals
Billy Mundi: drums, percussion
Don Preston: keyboards
Jim Fielder: guitar, piano
Bunk Gardner: woodwinds

## History

Born in Baltimore, Maryland, in 1940, Frank Zappa was a precociously intelligent young man who was inspired by R&B and doo-wop, the modernist classical music of Igor Stravinsky and the sound experiments of Edgard Varese. Beginning his musical career as a drummer, Zappa switched to guitar, moved to Los Angeles and tried to make a living as a composer and producer.

He was briefly imprisoned after recording a fake erotic audio tape with a female friend. In 1965 he took control of local band The Soul Giants, renaming them The Mothers. They were spotted by record producer Tom Wilson, who signed them to Verve/MGM Records as The Mothers of Invention. The debut album *Freak Out!* was only the second rock double album.

## Key releases in 1967

### Absolutely Free (Album)

All songs by Frank Zappa.
Label: Verve
Release date: 26 May 1967
Charts: US: 41
Side 1: 1. 'Plastic People' 2. 'The Duke of Prunes' 3. 'Amnesia Vivace' 4. 'The Duke Regains His Chops' 5. 'Call Any Vegetable' 6. 'Invocation & Ritual Dance of the Young Pumpkin' 7. 'Soft-Sell Conclusion' Side 2: 1. 'America Drinks' 2. 'Status Back Baby' 3. 'Uncle Bernie's Farm' 4. 'Son of Suzy Creamcheese' 5. 'Brown Shoes Don't Make It' 6. 'America Drinks & Goes Home'

### Lumpy Gravy (Album, under artist name Frank Zappa)

All songs by Frank Zappa.
Label: Capitol (Verve, 1968 Expanded)
Release date: 7 August 1967 (4-track cartridge); 13 May 1968
Charts: US: 159
1. 'Sink Trap' 2. 'Gum Joy' 3. 'Up and Down' 4. 'Local Butcher' 5. 'Gypsy Airs' 6. 'Hunchy Punchy' 7. 'Foamy Soaky' 8. 'Let's Eat Out' 9. 'Teenage Grand Finale'.

There were hippies, and then there were freaks. Hippies were into peace and love and wore flowers in their hair. Freaks were known for sex orgies, wild free-form dancing, fantasy role-playing costumes and long, dirty locks.

The name was first used by artist and marathon dancing champion Vito Paulekas – also known as Captain Fuck – and his wife Zsou. They ran a clothes store in Hollywood but were better known for their sexual excesses and weird, acid-drenched, brain-damaged behaviour. Arthur Lee was probably more of a freak than a hippie. So were Frank Zappa and Captain Beefheart. Zappa explained it thus to writer Frank Kofsky in 1968:

> I was never a hippie. Always a freak but never a hippie ... because the whole hippie scene is wishful thinking. They wish they could love, but they're full of shit, and they're kidding themselves into saying 'I love! I love! I love!'. And the more times they say it, the more times they think they love. But it doesn't work, and most of them don't have the guts to admit to themselves that it's a lie.

Like Arthur Lee, Zappa ripped into the hippie scene but did it with a biting, satirical humour and spot-on musical pastiches. He was anti-drugs, so fails on one of the key requirements for psychedelic rock. But he makes up for it by his ability to mix genres into a dense, rich musical brew, using unusual instrumentation, creating strange song forms and eschewing the usual subject of boy-meets-girl, to explore politics, culture, sexuality and religion. Let's put it this way: It ain't The Monkees.

As you can see from his 1967 chart placings, the record-buying public had barely heard of him. But everyone in the music business *had*, and regarded him with a mixture of awe and fear. He was the musician's musician – a composer and performer of such rare ability, breadth and sheer brazen chutzpah, that few could hope to come close to him.

The fact that his debut album was not only a double, but contained a bewildering variety of musical styles – including twelve minutes of musique concrete in 'Return of the Son of Monster Magnet', and a track that simply repeats its title 'Help, I'm a Rock' – won admiration from his contemporaries for the fact that he could get away with it.

*Freak Out!* contained political tracks such as 'Trouble Every Day', but second album *Absolutely Free* was almost entirely an absurdist satire on US culture and society with all the songs segued together into two side-long suites. The first album was made in quite a leisurely fashion because the record company wasn't entirely sure what the band would produce. Once Verve realised The Mothers had absolutely no commercial potential, they clamped down on costs, forcing the follow-up to be taped in just four six-hour sessions.

*Absolutely Free* begins with the president of the United States attempting unsuccessfully to perform 'Louie, Louie': a simple three-chord R&B song best known as the 1963 hit single by The Kingsmen. Early versions of *Absolutely*

*Free*'s opening track 'Plastic People' would be 'Louie, Louie' with different lyrics. On the album, the song – if indeed you can call it that with its frequent interruptions and spoken-word sections – blasts the 'plasticity' of the average *normal* American:

> Take a day and walk around
> Watch the Nazis run your town
> Then go home and check yourself
> You think we're singing 'bout someone else
> But you're plastic people

'The Duke of Prunes' started life as the love theme for a 1962 film Zappa scored called *Run Home Slow*. According to the Zappa Fandom website, singer Ray Collins replaced the lyrics with absurdist nonsense about prunes, cheese and magic go-karts because, by then, Zappa hated love songs. The song is split by a brief interlude called 'Amnesia Vivace': an apparent cacophony of sound that includes references to Stravinsky's 'The Rite of Spring' and Gene Chandler's 1962 number-1 hit 'Duke of Earl'.

Then comes one of Zappa's most popular compositions: 'Call Any Vegetable'. In Absolutely Free: The Complete Libretto, he explained:

> The best clue to this song might lie in the fact that people who are inactive in a society ... people who do not live up to their responsibilities, are vegetables. I feel that these people, even if they are inactive, apathetic or unconcerned at this point, can be motivated toward a more useful sort of existence. I believe that if you call any vegetable, it will respond to you.

It was revived at various times during his career, and vegetables are mentioned quite frequently in other, possibly related, songs.

A screaming climax leads us into the seven-minute 'Invocation & Ritual Dance of the Young Pumpkin'. A pun on Stravinsky's names for some of his pieces, it's basically an instrumental in E minor, with electric guitar and Gardner's clarinet improvising at the same time, and occasional blasts from Stravinsky's 'Firebird Suite'. Side one then ends with 'Soft-Sell Conclusion', which is really another version of 'Call Any Vegetable'.

Side two opens with what appears to be a drunken attempt to croon a sad love song, originally called 'No Regrets', before segueing into another of Zappa's most celebrated tracks, the ridiculously catchy 'Status Back Baby': a song about acne and teenage angst, that ends with a brief quote from that Stravinsky fellow again. 'Uncle Bernie's Farm' rips into ugly Christmas toys and the ugly people who make them, as well as the ugly people who buy them:

> We gotta send Santa Claus back to the Rescue Mission
> Christmas don't make it no more

> Don't you know that murder and destruction scream the toys in every store
> (Think this'll sell in New York?)

In 'Son of Suzy Creamcheese', we come across a Zappa-ism that pops up all over his albums and songs, including in a 'letter' printed on the *Freak Out!* cover. In a 1974 interview for *Coq* magazine, Zappa explained:

> There never really was a Suzy Creamcheese. It was just a figment of my imagination until people started identifying with it heavily. It got to weird proportions in Europe, so that in 1967, when we did our first tour of Europe, people were asking if Suzy Creamcheese was along with us. So I procured the services of another girl named Pamela Zarubica, who was hired to be the Suzy Creamcheese of the European tour. And then she maintained the reputation of being Suzy Creamcheese after 1967.

Side two's longest track – 'Brown Shoes Don't Make It' – was inspired by the criticism levelled at President Lyndon B. Johnson for wearing brown shoes with a grey suit: an apparent major fashion *faux pas*. Amused by the small-mindedness displayed, Zappa wrote a song that, in his own words, is:

> ...about the people who run the governments, the people who make the laws that keep you from living the kind of life you know you should lead. These unfortunate people manufacture inequitable laws and ordinance, perhaps unaware of the fact that the restrictions they place on the young people in a society are a result of their own hidden sexual frustrations. Dirty old men have no business running your country.

'Brown Shoes Don't Make It' is quite explicit about the illegal and obscene fantasies obsessing these dirty old men – ending with the depressing image of 'TV dinner by the pool / I'm so glad I finished school / Life is such a ball / I run the world from city hall!'

The album concludes with a faster reprise of 'America Drinks', complete with indistinct party voices, including Terry Gilliam of *Monty Python* fame, to create a sort of drunken lounge-music vibe. The crowd noise was carefully orchestrated, with some people in the main studio reading lines on cue, and others enacting scenes such as Bunk Gardner trying to pick up two girls and Jimmy Carl Black and Ray Collins pretending to have a fight. In a 1967 interview in *Jazz & Pop* magazine, Zappa said, '...it's all happening in there, but you can't listen to it all. You've got to have it on ten tracks so you can walk around the room and see where it's all coming from.'

*Absolutely Free* is a fabulously inventive record and a stepping stone to what is regarded as Zappa's best early Mothers album: the following year's *We're Only in It for the Money*. If it all sounds like some insane off-Broadway musical, then you aren't far wrong – the band staged a theatrical performance called

*Absolutely Freeee* at the Garrick Theatre in New York, that ran through the Summer of Love from May to September. Visual stunts included encouraging a group of Marines to tear a doll apart as members of the audience cried, and spraying people with whipped cream from a huge stuffed giraffe.

After that, there was a short US tour, followed by their first gigs in Europe, playing the Royal Albert Hall where new member Ian Underwood clambered up to the 'mighty pipe organ' and played 'Louie, Louie' on the hallowed instrument. A *Melody Maker* review at the time said the following:

> Without doubt, this debut of The Mothers in England was one of the greatest live performances to have shaken this earth on this side of the Atlantic for a long long time. The eight or so Mothers on stage had a ball ... You can feel that they're digging, and their sheer maturity, experience and confidence adds shattering depth to their stage presence. Secondly, the Mothers are fine musicians. This, perhaps, was one of the most outstanding facets of these musical curios from the American jungle.

It was a busy year for Zappa. He married Gail Sloatman, who was pregnant with their first child Moon Unit (when quizzed about the supposedly strange names he gave his children, he pointed out it would be the surname that would get them into trouble), posed for an iconic photograph sitting naked on a toilet (captioned 'Phi Krappa Zappa') and started recording the third Mothers album.

In between, there was the single 'Why Don't You Do Me Right?' / 'Big Leg Emma', that fails to qualify as psychedelic rock because it was an attempt to make 'dumb' music for 'dumb' teenagers.

And, also in August, there was the release of Zappa's first solo album *Lumpy Gravy*, that got him into a small degree of legal difficulty. Capitol Records commissioned him to write something for an orchestra, to be issued on the four-track Stereo Pak cartridge format, and Zappa believed this would not infringe on his Verve/MGM contract so long as he didn't play anything on the recording.

He assembled a group of 51 classical musicians that he dubbed the Abnuceals Emuukha Electric Symphony Orchestra, and provided them with a dense 22-minute score split into nine sections, many using themes that would turn up in the following year's *We're Only in It for the Money* – particularly the song 'Oh No', repeated time and time again through *Lumpy Gravy* – and 'The Duke of Prunes' from *Absolutely Free*. There are also moments of avant-garde Varese-style dissonance, exquisite string melodies, horn freak-outs and hints of the future Mothers classic 'King Kong'.

One of the orchestra members – percussionist Emil Richards – recalls the bassoonist and bass clarinetist refusing to play their parts, claiming they were impossible. In an interview with David Fricke for the 2009 liner notes of *The Lumpy Money/Project Object* he revealed:

> Frank, with a real genteel manner and smile, said, 'If I play your part, will you at least try it?'. Frank then played the bassoon part, transposing it right there, on guitar. He played the bass clarinet part too. He freaked the shit out of them. Those guys immediately picked up their instruments and started shedding the parts. So did the rest of us.

The original *Lumpy Gravy* was released in limited quantities in August 1967 and was immediately followed by a lawsuit from MGM, claiming breach of contract. Zappa would completely expand and re-edit the album for a fuller release on MGM/Verve in 1968, and the 1967 version remained in the vaults until it was included in the 2009 box set *The Lumpy Money Project/Object*.

Frank Zappa's work in 1967, both solo and with The Mothers, showed him with so many feet in so many camps, he was like a musical centipede. For the sheer invention and audacity of his recordings, he deserves to be included in our roll call of psychedelic rock heroes – yet Zappa was not so much part of it as above it all, looking down at it through a jaundiced eye, occasionally swooping down to pick it apart and put it back together again as something totally unique.

## Procol Harum

Key personnel:
Gary Brooker: piano, vocals
Robin Trower: guitar
Matthew Fisher: organ
Dave Knights: bass
B. J. Wilson: drums
Ray Royer: guitar

### History

**Gary Brooker and Robin Trower formed The Paramounts in Southend-on-Sea, Essex, in 1960, playing R&B in Trower's father's cafe and eventually supporting The Beatles and The Rolling Stones. B. J. Wilson joined on drums in 1962, and the band was signed by Parlophone the following year. Early singles failed to set the charts alight, and the band broke up in 1966. Brooker concentrated on writing songs with a lyricist he'd met: Londoner Keith Reid. They decided to form a band to record one of their songs, and contacted Matthew Fisher from Croydon, who they'd spotted backing Screaming Lord Sutch.**

### Key releases in 1967

**'A Whiter Shade of Pale'** (Gary Brooker, Matthew Fisher, Keith Reid) / **'Lime Street Blues'** (Brooker, Reid) (Single)
Label: Deram (UK), London (US)
Release date: 12 May 1967
Charts: UK: 1; US: 5; Australia: 1; Belgium: 1; Canada: 1; France: 1; Germany: 1; Ireland: 1; Italy: 1; Netherlands: 1; New Zealand: 1; South Africa: 1; Spain: 1; Poland: 2; Norway: 3; Austria: 4

**Procol Harum** (Album, US version)
All songs by Brooker, Reid unless otherwise stated.
Label: Deram
Release date: 1 September 1967
Charts: US: 47
Side 1: 1. 'A Whiter Shade of Pale' (Brooker, Fisher, Reid) 2. 'She Wandered Through the Garden Fence' 3. 'Something Following Me' 4. 'Mabel' 5. 'Cerdes (Outside the Gates Of)' Side 2: 1. 'A Christmas Camel' 2. 'Conquistador' 3. 'Kaleidoscope / Salad Days (Are Here Again)' 4. 'Repent Walpurgis' (Fisher)

**'Homburg' / 'Good Captain Clack'** (Single)
Both songs by Brooker, Reid.
Label: Regal Zonophone
Release date: 22 September 1967
Charts: UK: 6, US: 34; Australia: 1; South Africa: 1; Netherlands: 1; Canada: 15

**Procol Harum** (UK version)
All songs by Brooker, Reid unless otherwise stated.
Label: Regal Zonophone
Release date: December 1967
Charts: UK: 26
Side 1: 1. 'Conquistador' 2. 'She Wandered Through the Garden Fence' 3. 'Something Following Me' 4. 'Mabel' 5. 'Cerdes (Outside the Gates Of)' Side 2: 1. 'A Christmas Camel' 2. 'Kaleidoscope' 3. 'Salad Days (Are Here Again)' 4. 'Good Captain Clack' 5. 'Repent Walpurgis' (Fisher).

Southend was my old stomping ground when I was a cub reporter back in the early 1980s. It is most famous for its pier, which sticks out a mile and a bit over the squelching mudflats of the Thames estuary. It's still there despite being burned, and bisected by boats on several occasions.

The town also gave us a number of rock bands, including Dr Feelgood and The Kursaal Flyers. But the most famous group to come out of Southend (so-named because it was the south end of Prittlewell, which was much more well-known in the 18th century), and is of interest to us on our time-travelling journey to 1967, is Procol Harum.

Yes, they gave us 'A Whiter Shade of Pale' – that evergreen psychedelic classic, one of the anthems of the Summer of Love and one of the biggest-selling singles of all time. Like 'Nights in White Satin' for The Moody Blues, it kick-started a long and successful career but saddled Procol Harum with a hit they could never quite match ever again. Oh, and it sparked a 2009 court case that meant Matthew Fisher's name is now on the songwriting credits. As they say, where there's a hit, there's a writ.

In Brooker and Reid's telling of the story, the lyrical ideas came from a passing comment at a party about someone looking pale. Reid took the comment and turned it into the phrase 'a whiter shade of pale', penning lines that were inspired by the paintings of Toulouse-Lautrec – he wanted the song to sound the way an abstract painting looked.

Brooker explained in a 2014 documentary for Dutch TV:

> I do remember having this musical idea which I worked out on the piano – 'Air on a G-String', which was a Bach composition. But when I got after about the first two bars, I think I got it wrong and just carried on in my own way. Then I wrote this sequence, which had a bit of a Bach-like melody over the top, bit 'Air on a G-string'y, just in that style. And I think it was about then that an envelope arrived that morning, and I opened it and it was some new lyrics from Keith, and the first one that I opened was 'A Whiter Shade of Pale'.

Other stories of the fortuitous overhearing suggest it was the band's manager Guy Stevens who made the comment to his wife Diane, and that he actually said the words that became the title. Neither Brooker nor Reid mention the role played by Matthew Fisher, who won 40 per cent of the royalties in a court case described by Brooker as 'a darker shade of black'. Fisher said the following in a BBC Radio 2 interview in 2000:

> The song used to be a lot longer. I mean it used to have four verses, and what used to happen was that Gary and I would take turns in between verses. I'd play a bit and then he'd play a bit, and it was all improvised. When it got to the point where we decided we wanted to make a demo of this, and we had to cut it down because it was about ten, twelve minutes long, you know, decisions were made that perhaps it would be better just to have the organ doing the solos; and then I made the decision that, well, if it was just gonna be me, then I would actually construct a definitive organ solo that would be the same every time, you know, that could be sort of a hook; and I did this by remembering all of my favourite bits that I'd played, and stringing them together, during the course of which I did actually come up with this idea of actually changing the bass line, and so the whole thing got a little bit changed at that point.

Wherever it came from, the song wasn't even written for Procol Harum. Brooker and Reid were signed to Essex Music publishers to pen hits for other people, offering their wares to The Love Affair, Dusty Springfield and The Beach Boys, with Brooker singing and playing piano on demos – very much the way Reginald Dwight and Bernie Taupin started out.

When it became clear that nobody was interested in singing Brooker and Reid songs, they realised the only way any of their compositions were going to see the light of day, was if they recorded them themselves.

In 2017, Brooker told *Classic Rock* magazine, 'We sat down and thought about the type of band we needed. It was kind of like the stuff we had been listening to at Guy Stevens' place – American gospel R&B using two keyboards. We wanted a more sophisticated sound with Hammond organ and piano'.

An ad in music magazine *Melody Maker* found Hammond-organ-player Fisher, guitarist Ray Royer and bassist David Knights. Stevens named the band after a breed of a friend's Burmese cat – Procul Harun – changing the final letter to an 'm' because of frequent misspellings. They recorded the song in April 1967 with a session drummer, and it was announced a surefire hit by a DJ who played the early acetate on air – finally persuading Decca Records, who thought it was too long, slow and gloomy. This is the same Decca Records who turned down The Beatles – so interesting to see their musical judgment hadn't improved in the intervening years.

When 'A Whiter Shade of Pale' was released a month later, its combination of stately baroque, classical organ and obscure, trippy but vaguely intellectual lyrics referencing Chaucer's *Canterbury Tales* (though denied by Reid, who said he'd never read 'The Miller's Tale') coupled with Brooker's impassioned, bluesy vocals, was a smash hit, reaching number 1 in most countries and, to date, selling more than 10,000,000 copies. Even Lennon and McCartney loved it. Brooker said in the Dutch TV documentary:

> I thought from the moment I wrote it, it was a good idea. It was a combination of a lot of influences, apart from the Bach inspiration; it also had a bluesy-soul vocal ... people didn't expect it at all, they hadn't even heard anything like that ... it never sounds dated when I hear it on the radio, it's a haunting thing that gets inside you.

By producer Denny Cordell's admission, it was an attempt to fuse the music from the Hamlet cigar ad and Percy Sledge's 'When a Man Loves a Woman' – and it worked a treat. The fact that the lyrics appeared either meaningless or meant anything you wanted – made even more obscure by Cordell cutting out verse two to make it a single-friendly length – mattered not a jot. It was all part of the trip, albeit a classy one.

'A Whiter Shade of Pale' is one of those songs that sounds like it was always there, floating about in the ether waiting for someone to pick it up and put it on a record groove, and will still be listened to in a hundred years time, if the human race manages to survive that long.

It was declared Song of the Year at the Ivor Novello Awards, is number 57 on *Rolling Stone*'s list of the 500 Greatest Songs of All Time, was voted Best British Pop Single 1952-1977 at the Brit Awards (jointly with Queen's 'Bohemian Rhapsody'), and was inducted into the Rock and Roll Hall of Fame in 2018.

The massive worldwide overnight success of the single meant an album was inevitable, and Brooker and Reid already had a clutch of songs nobody else wanted. With The Paramounts' drummer B. J. Wilson and guitarist Robin Trower back in the fold, Procol Harum returned to Olympic Studios to start work on their debut LP.

It opens with 'Conquistador', the song Brooker thought might be perfect for The Beach Boys. Unusually for the Brooker and Reid partnership, he had initially come up with the tune, and in his head, could hear Brian Wilson's harmonies over the chopping piano chords and slightly Spanish feel. In Reid's lyrics, the conquistador – Spanish for the explorers and conquerors who roamed the world in the 16th, 17th and 18th centuries – is a faded statue with a rusty scabbard. 'You did not conquer, you only die,' sings Brooker. There's little organ, and Trower's guitar plays a major part, with strong riffs leading the chord changes.

The organ takes centre stage for 'She Wandered Through the Garden Fence', a whimsical tale that could be about LSD – the lady of the title brings the singer a 'potion guaranteed to bring relief from all your suffering', but which then torments and tortures him.

'Something Following Me' appears to be about confronting one's own mortality – the singer sees his tombstone everywhere: in the street, at the dentist's, and in the movie theatre. This rather gloomy subject is supported by a rolling, bluesy tune that's mostly played on piano in a major key, with a dirty little guitar solo from Trower. 'Mabel' is a silly little throwaway track similar to a pub sing-along, with added swanee whistle, and it's mercifully short at less than two minutes. But even that has some disturbing lyrics, particularly in the lines 'In the cellar lies my wife / In my wife there's a knife'.

'Cerdes (Outside the Gates Of)' was one of several tracks here first attempted with the earlier Procol Harum lineup. It's a slow blues led by a simple ten-note piano riff and Trower's lead guitar, with some of Keith Reid's most surreal and evocative lyrics: 'Outside the gates of Cerdes sits the two-pronged unicorn, who plays at relaxation time a rhinestoned flugelhorn.' What? You could be forgiven for thinking these apparent stream-of-consciousness lyrics are inspired by LSD, but Reid has always attempted to be deliberately surreal.

'A Christmas Camel' has a title that appears to pun on Charles Dickens' 'A Christmas Carol'. The song seems to be set in Arabia, where the singer's 'Amazon six-triggered bride' is searching for a place to hide. There is a mention of Santa Claus, but no camel makes an appearance. Musically, it's a somewhat plodding, dramatic minor-key blues, led by Brooker's piano riff and featuring some excellent lead guitar from Trower.

On the US pressing, 'Kaleidoscope' and the following 'Salad Days (Are Here Again)' were merged into one track – the former is a simple upbeat throwaway with trippy, multicoloured lyrics that fades away on discordant organ, while the latter is a piano chord sequence that seems to be searching for a melody that Brooker can't quite grasp.

As for 'Good Captain Clack', this belongs in the same territory as 'Mabel', a possibly ill-conceived music hall sing-along about an Australian friend of the band. It is mercifully short.

Thankfully, the album ends on what's probably the best track here, and the only one that sounds a little like Procol Harum's big hit. Matthew Fisher's 'Repent Walpurgis' is based on Bach's 'Prelude No. 1 in C Major', Tchaikovsky's 'Piano Concerto No. 1', and a chord sequence from a Four Seasons song called 'Beggin'. Into that eclectic combination is thrown some portentous piano from Brooker, bluesy guitar by Trower and, finally, Fisher's organ all over it like something from *The Phantom of the Opera*. The title was originally going to be 'Repent', but Brooker added 'Walpurgis' because it evoked images of demons on Walpurgis Night (itself named after an English nun).

Procol Harum's debut – boasting a distinctive monochrome cover by Keith Reid's future wife, an artist known only as Dickinson – is not the best album they ever made but certainly passed muster as a follow-up to the big hit. But it pretty much flopped in the US and UK: number 26 for a debut album is not bad, but it's not number 1 all over the world. Why did *Procol Harum* fail to repeat the single's huge global success?

In hindsight, perhaps the band was too busy, not just changing the guitarist and drummer, but also the band's manager, who had booked them £60-a-night gigs in tiny UK venues. On top of that, the UK album release was delayed by record label shenanigans – some of the Essex Music artists, including Procol Harum, moved to Regal Zonophone, a process that took a few months to sort out.

So by the time the debut album was released in the UK in September 1967, the momentum was lost – the big hit had been followed by a smaller hit – 'Homburg' – and the fickle record-buying public had moved on to other things. This was also one of those rare times when *not* having the hits on the album probably worked against them in Britain.

Procol Harum's debut was generally well-received by critics, with Paul Williams of *Crawdaddy* saying it 'just keeps getting better and better', and comparing it to *The Doors*. Of course, he was reviewing the US version that wisely included the singles and lost some of the lesser tracks. Most people would go along with AllMusic's opinion: 'Not everything here works, but it holds up better than most psychedelic or progressive rock.' *Classic Rock* magazine lists it as one of the '50 Albums That Built Prog Rock', and it's one of *Rolling Stone*'s 40 essential albums of 1967.

Procol Harum would go on to have a long and eventful existence, recording a further eleven albums with only Gary Brooker as the constant member. But the band is still remembered for that perfect slice of psychedelic pop-rock in 1967; one of the songs that soundtracked the Summer of Love but did so with a rare touch of class.

## Country Joe and the Fish

Key personnel:
Country Joe McDonald: vocals, guitar, harmonica
Barry 'The Fish' Melton: lead guitar, vocals, bass
David Cohen: guitar, organ
Bruce Barthol: bass, harmonica
Gary 'Chicken' Hirsh: drums

### History

**The band was formed in Berkeley, California, in 1965 by folk musicians Country Joe McDonald – who edited a counterculture magazine called *Rag Baby* – and university dropout Barry 'The Fish' Melton, initially to produce an anti-Vietnam EP that included an early version of the future hippie favourite 'I-Feel-Like-I'm-Fixin'-To-Die Rag'. Deciding to form a proper band, they were joined by local jug band musicians Bruce Barthol, David Cohen, guitarist Paul Armstrong and drummer John Francis-Gunning. A second EP in 1966 showcased the group's psychedelic leanings, and in December that year, Country Joe and the Fish were signed by Vanguard Records, a folk music label keen to expand into the psychedelic scene.**

### Key releases in 1967

### Electric Music for the Mind and Body (Album)

All songs by Joe McDonald except as noted.
Label: Vanguard
Release date: 11 May 1967
Charts: US: 39
Side 1: 1. 'Flying High' 2. 'Not So Sweet Martha Lorraine' 3. 'Death Sound Blues' 4. 'Porpoise Mouth' 5. 'Section 43' Side 2: 1. 'Superbird' 2. 'Sad and Lonely Times' 3. 'Love' (Joe McDonald, Barry Melton, David Cohen, Bruce Barthol, John Francis-Gunning, Gary Hirsh) 4. 'Bass Strings' 5. 'The Masked Marauder' 6. 'Grace'

### I-Feel-Like-I'm-Fixin'-To-Die (Album)

All songs by Joe McDonald except as noted.
Label: Vanguard
Release date: November 1967
Charts: US: 67
Side 1: 1. 'The 'Fish' Cheer / I-Feel-Like-I'm-Fixin'-To-Die Rag' 2. 'Who Am I' 3. 'Pat's Song' 4. 'Rock Coast Blues' 5. 'Magoo' Side 2: 1. 'Janis' 2. 'Thought Dream' 3. 'Thursday' (Cohen, Hirsh) 4. 'Eastern Jam' (Barthol, Cohen, Hirsh, Melton) 5. 'Colors for Susan'

**By 1967, the Vietnam War had basically split the US into two camps: those who didn't want it but believed the only way out of it was victory through**

overwhelming and superior military force, and those who simply didn't want it. The previous year had seen more than 6,000 US citizens killed, in an estimated death toll of about 90,000 across the entire theatre of war.

By the time a Republican president pulled the US out of the conflict, more than 3,000,000 people had been killed, at least 58,000 of them Americans. To put that into some sort of perspective, that's like the US having twenty 9/11s. Even now, many decades later, the shadow of Vietnam hangs over the West as an awful warning against having blind faith in military force: a warning that's still frequently ignored.

The war provided a focal point for the counterculture – everything the young railed against, the suffocating rules, taboos, social mores and political beliefs of their parents, all swirled around the plughole of the conflict. It provoked demonstrations across the US that, in 1967, became more widespread and impassioned, and were being met with increasing levels of state violence.

It also encouraged some of the counterculture's musical spokesmen and women to write and sing about the war – though not as many as you would've expected. They were restrained by conservative record companies and radio and TV shows, who were both attracted to and repelled by the counterculture, attracted by its commercial possibilities, and repelled by the backlash its beliefs and actions could provoke from middle-America.

So it helped that one of the most popular protest songs of the year – Country Joe and the Fish's 'I-Feel-Like-I'm-Fixin'-To-Die Rag' – was dressed up in dark humour and a thoroughly acceptable country-rock sing-along backing. With its ironically cheerful refrain of '1-2-3, what are we fightin' for?', it was the sort of laid-back protest that appealed to hippies too strung-out on acid to do anything more focussed.

Country Joe was Joe McDonald, whose parents Worden and Florence were members of the Communist Party, and had to move to California from Washington, D.C. just after the war due to political differences with their neighbours. They named their son after Joseph Stalin, who was referred to during World War II as Country Joe, instead of the more accurate Mass-Murdering Madman Joe.

McDonald was himself a Vietnam-era vet – he did three years in the Navy, stationed in Japan, and was by all accounts a regular if unremarkable sailor, save for his unusual ability to play trombone as well as guitar. He enlisted purely because he thought he would be able to sail the seven seas and get laid in every port.

When he formed a band to play on his *Talking Magazine* EP, friend and co-publisher Eugene Denson leafed through Chairman Mao's *Little Red Book* and came across the phrase, 'The revolutionary is a fish that swims in the sea of the people'. Eureka! Let's call the band... Country Mao and The Fish! With a tiny bit of tinkering, the name became Country Joe and the Fish, serving the dual purpose of honouring McDonald's namesake while gently fooling some people into believing they were a harmless little jug band. And Barry became The Fish.

By 1967, CJ and the F had a record deal with Vanguard – signing a terrible contract for twelve albums over three years – and a growing reputation as an exciting live act in San Francisco. They had played the Human Be-In in January along with the Grateful Dead and Jefferson Airplane. They had also lost a band member in Paul Armstrong and replaced drummer John Francis-Gunning with the more rock-steady Gary 'Chicken' Hirsh.

Their debut album, *Electric Music for the Mind and Body*, was recorded at Sierra Sound Laboratories in Berkeley in May, with writer, musician and poet Samuel Barclay Charters IV as producer. Some of the tracks were remakes of songs released on the band's two EPs from 1965 and 1966. The oldest – 'Superbird' – rips into then-President Lyndon B. Johnson, who had authorised massive increases in the US presence in Vietnam, and whose wife Claudia was nicknamed Bird (a name she used on their marriage license). Depicting LBJ as a mock superhero, the song exclaims: 'It's a bird, it's a plane, it's a man insane,' before telling him 'Gonna send you back to Texas / Make you work on your ranch.' Short and sweet, played at a brisk pace with a standard blues construction, it's swamped with Melton's tasty lead guitar licks, and ends with the promise 'Gonna make him eat flowers / Yeah, make him drop some acid.'

Three more songs originate from the second EP. '(Thing Called) Love' – reduced to just 'Love' on the album – is credited to practically every member of the band, past and present, and features a false beginning, a few stabs of guitar, and Farfisa organ suddenly interrupted by a voice saying 'Oh, come on!'. Again, following a blues pattern, it has a typically-1960s vibe that wouldn't be out of place in an Austin Powers movie, with more of Melton's fantastic lead guitar.

'Bass Strings' is an ode to drugs – a slow, spaced-out dirge with lyrics that ask 'Hey partner, won't you pass that reefer round / My world is spinnin' / Yeah, just got to slow it down,' ending on repeated mentions of LSD, which McDonald and Melton had first tried in 1965. The remaining EP track, 'Section 43', is a Floydian experiment that pre-dates Pink Floyd – a disjointed, hypnotic seven-and-a-half-minute instrumental, with shimmering eastern-influenced organ chords, gently-picked guitar notes, laid-back rolling tom-toms and wailing blues harmonica.

Of the LP's new tracks, opener 'Flying High' is a cheerful tale of hitchhiking on a freeway and sharing a trip with the drivers of a Cadillac; 'Not So Sweet Martha Lorraine', a thinly-veiled description of the love-hate relationship with hallucinogens and the band's first 1967 single, just scraping into the *Billboard* top 100 at 98, and 'Death Sound': a slow but aggressive blues with such cheerful lines as 'I feel the black nails a-poundin' now into the coffin of our love'.

The oddly-named 'Porpoise Mouth' has a dark, circus-style waltz-time backing to tripped-out lyrics and lead guitar breaks based on eastern scales. There are sexual overtones here too, in the line 'I hunger for your porpoise mouth and stand erect for love'.

'Sad and Lonely Times' is, as the title doesn't suggest, quite upbeat and cheerful, while 'The Masked Marauder' is a danceable minor-key instrumental led by Cohen's organ, punctuated by psychedelic country guitar licks and child-like 'la la's.

The seven-minute closer 'Grace' was inspired by Jefferson Airplane lead singer Grace Slick but written at the time she was with The Great Society, named after a series of social proposals put forward by President Johnson. Hypnotic and dirge-like, 'Grace' is replete with spaced-out (and ungrammatical) lyrics such as 'Your silver streak flash across the tiny door of my eye'.

The album was supposed to contain one other track: the Vietnam War protest song that was first released in 1965 and was now a permanent fixture in the band's live set. But McDonald's website recalls, 'It was left off at the urging of the Vanguard's president Maynard Solomon, who felt that it would become a 'thorn in their side and prevent the band from getting any single played on the radio'.'

Released in May, *Electric Music for the Mind and Body* made its way to number 39 in the US charts: a reasonably respectable showing but unlikely to stop the Vietnam War in its tank tracks. Hindsighters such as *AllMusic* call it 'one of the most important and enduring documents of the psychedelic era', and it certainly shows that Country Joe was ahead of his time in some respects. But organist Cohen pointed out in a 2012 interview with *It's Psychedelic Baby* magazine:

> I had no idea what I was doing. None of us did! We were just making up this music, creating a sound and then it became real. Later the reviews said I had 'a unique style'. But I was just copying my own guitar riffs!

While Melton, quoted in a 2017 article on the Observer arts and entertainment website, says:

> We'd been a jug band, but we didn't play in a conventional way. We were doing something new. We deliberately walked a different path. It wasn't like we discussed it. We bridged folk and jazz with bluegrass, country and blues. It was an improvisational folk music, like what the Grateful Dead exploited commercially. When you're creating something new, you can't be held to any standard of criticism.

It took the Monterey International Pop Festival to make Country Joe and the Fish a national sensation, as it did to so many underground rock acts that summer. They did 'I-Feel-Like-I'm-Fixin'-To-Die Rag' followed by 'Please Don't Drop That H Bomb on Me, You Can Drop it on Yourself', ending with five minutes of the head-swirling 'Section 43'. But for McDonald, it proved to be a turning point in his attitude towards the drugs that washed through the psychedelic rock fraternity. In Ron Cabral's book *Country Joe and Me*, he said:

> (It was) the peak of my psychedelic period. I took STP the day before we played, and I was really stoned out. Monterey Pop was the end of childhood

for a lot of Bay Area bands. After Monterey, the big-time record industry really hit San Francisco. The music scene made the cover of *Time* magazine, and the whole business became commercial.

Some of McDonald's subsequent disillusion seemed to find its way into the band's second album that year, recorded just a month after Monterey. This time, the protest song got pride of place as the album title as well as the opening track. Far from being a thorn in the band's side, it had now become the year's anti-Vietnam anthem. On his website, Joe talks about how he wrote the song:

> I wrote 'Fixin'-To-Die Rag' in summer of 1965 after I had been discharged from the US Navy for several years. It just popped into my head one day and I finished it in about 30 minutes. I did not have a conscious purpose in mind, although I had been working on another song about the Vietnam War called 'Who Am I?' for several days, so I had the war on my mind. The 'Who Am I?' song was part of a play I was writing songs for titled *Change Over*, written by Fred Hayden and directed by Nina Serrano ... The song attempts to put blame for the war upon the politicians and leaders of the US military, and upon the industry that makes its money from war, but not upon those who had to fight the war: the soldiers.

The song was preceded by a live recording of 'The Fish Cheer' – on stage, the group would say 'Give me an F! Give me an I! Give me an S!' and so on, with the audience doing as they're told and finally shouting 'FISH!'. At a festival in 1968, the band encouraged the crowd to yell an alternative word beginning with F, propelling the song even further into the national consciousness but also earning them a ban from *The Ed Sullivan Show*. On the album, it closes with the sound of machine-gun fire and screaming jets.

Like the war, the song divided opinion between those who loved its black G.I. Joe humour and those who considered it an outrageous attack on the great US of A. But it became a favourite, not just of the anti-war brigade, but the soldiers themselves, who frequently heard the song being played through loudspeakers aimed at discomforting the enemy. US prisoners of war claimed the song was regularly played by their captors at North Vietnam's H a Lò Prison – ironically known as the 'Hanoi Hilton' – in an attempt to destroy morale, but the song had the opposite effect as the prisoners hummed along.

Sadly, much of the rest of the album failed to match the title track's mischievous spirit. That earlier anti-Vietnam war song McDonald mentioned – 'Who Am I' – is also on the LP. Unlike 'Fixin'-To-Die', it's an utterly unironic, earnest ballad led by acoustic guitar, in which McDonald castigates himself for 'the nothing I've made of life'.

'Pat's Song' is dreary and downbeat, matching psychedelic lyrics about dolphins, lemons and candles to a ponderous waltz-time rhythm, lifted only by

Cohen's organ and Melton's lead guitar. 'Rock Coast Blues' also fails to take off, as it lumbers unsteadily through its 6/8 rhythm with hoary, cliched lyrics about having a 'woman on my mind'. 'Magoo' is another contemplative dirge in a sombre minor key – 'Sometimes when I look into your eyes / The hurt and pain I see makes me want to cry', sings McDonald with just a little too much self-pity, with added crashing-wave sound effects.

It was, perhaps, the sound of a man getting over a love affair with a tempestuous woman. In early 1967, McDonald met Janis Joplin – the ballsy lead singer of Big Brother and the Holding Company – at a gig in San Francisco, and they lived together for three months. In *Country Joe and Me*, he said, 'It was just a very normal love affair between two people who shared exciting times in the Haight ... Soon I started spending nights with her at a flat she shared in San Francisco. Later I moved in with her for a while when she got her own place – actually, I didn't have any place to live at the time.'

To a waltz-time backing, McDonald sings of Joplin coming into his life 'on waves of electrical sound and flashing light' – their relationship had ended by this point, but he still sings about missing 'you and I'. The song was the band's second single that year, but failed to chart.

'Thought Dream' is a bit like the first album's 'Section 43' with lyrics, coming across as disjointed and depressing, while 'Colors for Susan' is the sound of stoned guitarists aimlessly strumming random chords for six minutes.

The second album didn't do nearly as well as the first, and 1968's *Together* is a much more, well, 'together' album, that gave Country Joe and the Fish their biggest commercial success. Indeed, they reached the peak of their popularity over the next few years, culminating in an appearance at Woodstock, caught for posterity in Michael Wadleigh's documentary film.

But 1967 was when the seeds of that popularity were planted and nurtured. Of course, a song can't stop a war, and the Vietnam conflict rumbled on until 1975. But the song symbolised the futility and madness of war, and helped Country Joe and the Fish become the counterculture's psychedelic heroes.

# Traffic

Key personnel:
Jim Capaldi: drums, percussion, vocals
Dave Mason: guitar, Mellotron, sitar, tambura, harmonica, bass, vocals
Steve Winwood: Hammond organ, guitar, bass, piano, harpsichord, vocals
Chris Wood: flute, saxophone, Hammond organ, percussion, vocals

## History

Birmingham-born Steve Winwood was lead singer of the hugely successful Spencer Davis Group, having joined at the tender age of fourteen. Dave Mason and Jim Capaldi – both from Worcestershire – were in local bands The Helions and Deep Feeling. Another Brummie, Chris Wood, was in Locomotive. Meeting up through Wood's sister (and Mason was briefly a roadie for The Spencer Davis Group), the quartet jammed together at The Elbow Room in Aston, Birmingham, before forming a band – the name was coined by Capaldi as they waited to cross a busy street. They rented a cottage in the Berkshire countryside to write and rehearse new music.

## Key releases in 1967

**'Paper Sun'** (Capaldi, Winwood) / **'Giving to You'** (Capaldi, Mason, Winwood, Wood) (Single)
Label: Island
Release date: 19 May 1967 (UK), July 1967 (US)
Charts: UK: 5; US: 70; Canada: 4

**'Hole in My Shoe'** (Mason) / **'Smiling Phases'** (Capaldi, Winwood, Wood) (Single)
Label: Island (UK), United Artists (US)
Release date: 25 August 1967 (UK), October 1967 (US)
Charts: UK: 2; Canada: 4; Netherlands: 9

**'Here We Go Round the Mulberry Bush'** (Capaldi, Mason, Winwood, Wood) / **'Coloured Rain'** (Capaldi, Winwood, Wood) (Single)
Label: Island (UK), United Artists (US)
Release date: 24 November 1967 (UK); February 1968 (US)
Charts: UK: 8

**Mr. Fantasy** (Album)
Label: Island
Release date: 8 December 1967 (UK)
Charts: UK: 16

Side 1: 1. 'Heaven Is in Your Mind (Jim Capaldi, Steve Winwood, Chris Wood) 2. 'Berkshire Poppies' (Capaldi, Winwood, Mason) 3. 'House for Everyone' (Dave Mason) 4. 'No Face, No Name and No Number' (Capaldi, Winwood) 5. 'Dear Mr. Fantasy (Capaldi, Winwood, Wood) Side 2: 1. 'Dealer' (Capaldi, Winwood) 2. 'Utterly Simple' (Mason) 3. 'Coloured Rain' (Capaldi, Winwood, Wood) 4. 'Hope I Never Find Me There' (Mason) 5. 'Giving to You (Capaldi, Mason, Winwood, Wood)

**Heaven Is in Your Mind** (Album)
Label: United Artists (US)
Release date: March 1968 (US)
Charts: US: 88
Side 1: 1. 'Paper Sun' (Capaldi, Winwood) 2. 'Dealer' (Capaldi, Winwood) 3. 'Coloured Rain' (Capaldi, Winwood, Wood) 4. 'Hole in My Shoe (Mason) 5. 'No Face, No Name and No Number' (Capaldi, Winwood) 6. 'Heaven Is in Your Mind' (Capaldi, Winwood, Wood) Side 2: 1. 'House for Everyone' (Mason) 2. 'Berkshire Poppies' (Capaldi, Winwood, Wood) 3. 'Giving to You' (Capaldi, Mason, Winwood, Wood) 4. 'Smiling Phases' (Capaldi, Winwood, Wood) 5. 'Dear Mr. Fantasy' (Capaldi, Winwood, Wood) 6. 'We're a Fade, You Missed This' (Capaldi, Winwood)

There was conflict at the heart of Traffic. You could tell just by looking at the song credits on their debut album. Six songs were by various combinations of Steve Winwood, Jim Capaldi and Chris Wood, and three by Dave Mason on his own. Only one song bore all four names, and that was obviously an improvised instrumental.

The divide was even more marked once you listened to the LP. The UK version – the one that left out the hit singles because, well, that's what they did in those days – showed three-quarters of the band had strong R&B leanings, while the other quarter produced cute, catchy, psychedelic rock songs. A split was inevitable.

But, in the beginning, it was meant to be four young musicians all pulling in the same direction. They even had a symbol – designed by Winwood's girlfriend Penny Massot – showing a wheel with four arrows circling a square axle that they used everywhere they went.

Inevitably, some of the members were more equal than others. Winwood, in particular, was already a minor pop star at the tender age of nineteen, having had hit singles as keyboard player and vocalist with The Spencer Davis Group. He felt stifled in a band that was strongly influenced by American R&B and liked to cover blues numbers, and he also wanted to work with people nearer his own age: everyone in The SDG was older than he was, including his brother Muff.

Compared to Winwood, the others were strictly amateurville – they'd been in various local bands, but hadn't had even a sniff of the kind of success Winwood had experienced. Mason wasn't even in a band at the time: he was The SDG's roadie. But Winwood was determined to make the break, and decided this was the right lineup at the right time.

In many ways, he was right, because what came out of this was an enduring and productive songwriting partnership with Capaldi that lasted until the very final Traffic album in 1974. Author John Van der Kiste, in his Steve Winwood biography, *While You See a Chance*, described how the pair used to work:

> Jim would jot words, lines, phrases or ideas down on a piece of paper, not arranged in a verse/chorus kind of way, and then they would go and jam. Steve stood the piece of paper on top of the piano or organ, then during the jam, when he felt it was appropriate, he would sing what Jim had written, and it always came out of a jam.

First, the band needed to find somewhere to rehearse and decided to escape the distractions and temptations of the big city, to hunker down in a cottage in the middle of nowhere, starting a trend that would be enthusiastically copied by many other bands, such as Fairport Convention and Led Zeppelin.

Traffic found a farmhouse near Aston Tirrold village – then in Berkshire but now in Oxfordshire – that had no indoor toilet and was rumoured to be haunted. There they set up their gear and jammed at all hours of the day and night, the only distractions being blackberry-picking and the locals' homemade apple pie. Word got around the UK music-making fraternity of these four crazy guys finding inspiration by getting back to nature, and stars such as Eric Clapton, Pete Townshend and Eric Burdon rocked up to see what was happening.

With their music booming across the countryside – and the cottage lit up by a multicoloured light show from an overhead projector – the band recorded hours of improvised music they called 'Traffic jams', and out of this, they crafted the songs that would make up their early singles and debut album.

While he was a member of The Spencer Davis Group, Winwood had agreed to write some music for a movie: Clive Donner's raunchy (for 1967) comedy *Here We Go Round the Mulberry Bush*, based on the book of the same name by future Beatles biographer Hunter Davies. The film – which made the name of English actor Barry Evans – was part of a progression in British cinema from gritty kitchen sink dramas towards *swinging London* sex comedies that would reach their zenith (or nadir, depending on your viewpoint) in the *Confessions* series.

Traffic recorded two songs for the film, including the surprisingly complicated title track. Led by fairground-style organ, the song has four distinct sections: a nursery-rhyme opening including a catchy chorus sung in the single chord of E flat; a more contemplative middle part over fingerpicked acoustic guitar, in which Winwood sings about the character's disillusion in his search to lose his virginity; a brief third 'marching beat' section in which Winwood tells of 'people running 'round and 'round / Bringing one another down'; and finally, a return to the opening and the chorus, ending on Capaldi's martial drum rhythm. Also in there somewhere were Wood's flute and Mason playing a sitar given to him by George Harrison.

But it would be another few months before 'Mulberry Bush' saw the light of day, as it was held back to coincide with the film's release. Instead, the band concentrated on creating what would become the A and B sides of their first single out of the Traffic jams they had taped. 'Giving to You' didn't seem to take much adaptation, as it was a mostly wordless flute, organ and guitar improv chugging along in C minor, topped and tailed by a few seconds of random conversations. But they knew 'Paper Sun' was going to be a hit almost as soon as they had put it together.

The lyrics came first, inspired by a newspaper article Capaldi had spotted, about a girl looking for work in Guernsey and ending up 'chasing the paper sun': a slang term for LSD. In Traffic's song, she is 'having good times with the boy that you just met', but she's also depressed and penniless, and the 'icicles you're crying down your cheek have just begun'. 'Ah, don't worry, have some LSD', the band appears to be saying.

Musically, it's a prime slice of British psychedelia, opening with an insanely catchy riff of descending sitar notes and featuring a soaring chorus with trippy, phased harmonies. It certainly sounded nothing like The Spencer Davis Group and everything like a bunch of young British lads soaking up the psychedelic vibes of the Summer of Love.

The single shot straight to number 5 in the UK, heralding the arrival of the new kids on the block and prompting record label demands for more of the same, please. Traffic responded with 'Hole in My Shoe'. But it was a song that was to highlight a growing rift within the band. Steve Winwood recalled In *Uncut* magazine in 2018:

> Dave very quickly started writing these quite poppy songs. But of course, we didn't know how to deal with that, as we didn't want to be a part of the pop world – Traffic for me was all about mixing jazz, folk, ethnic music, rock, R&B. We wanted to forge our own music, by trying to combine those different elements. We all wanted to write together, to write out of jams that we had, but Dave wasn't interested in that, he wanted to write his own songs, little arrangements in his head – which is fine, but I don't think it was right for Traffic.

Mason admitted he tended to be a loner when it came to songwriting, and he never really got to know Winwood, seemingly rubbing him up the wrong way. But he added, 'Who cares who writes the hit single? I don't give a damn'. The trouble was, Mason's idea of a hit single was different to the other three, and they hated the new song he had come up with: the first he had ever tried to write. 'Hole in My Shoe' seemed trite and meaningless, with faux psychedelic lyrics about 'bubblegum trees' and being shot at by tin soldiers, and a spoken-word section in the middle by Island Records boss Chris Blackwell's god-daughter Francine Heimann: 'I climbed on the back of a giant albatross, which flew through a crack in the cloud, to a place where happiness reigned all year 'round, where music played ever so loudly'. Mason says the song was inspired by a dream he had, and he wrote down random thoughts in the style of a nursery rhyme – and he wasn't on acid at the time. But the lyrics are clearly inspired by listening to 'Lucy in the Sky With Diamonds' from the *Sgt Pepper* album, which the future Linda McCartney had brought over one day while doing a photo shoot. As was his wont, Mason delivered the song to the band fully-formed, with no other member's input: something else that peeved Winwood. The others only agreed to record it after being persuaded by Blackwell and producer Jimmy Miller.

Musically, it has a lot of the elements that made 'Paper Sun' so memorable, including the heavy sitar presence. But the song is slower, with a galumphing beat, backward cymbals, Beatle-y piano chords, mystical Mellotron sounds, and vocals that appear to be coming from the bottom of a well. Three members of the band didn't want to release it as the next single – they preferred 'Coloured Rain': a bluesier, less commercial number that would've barely made the top 30 in the UK. Winwood later admitted that Mason had a more commercial head on him, but, at the time, the rest of the band looked down on pop, and wanted to carve a more unique musical furrow.

Mason's commercial instincts proved to be spot-on. The single – backed with the more mundane 'Smiling Phases' – hit number 2 in the UK, kept off the top spot by the Bee Gees' 'Massachusetts'. 'Hole in My Shoe''s psychedelic rock credentials are so up-front, almost to a cliched extent, that it was later recorded by Nigel Planer – Neil, the quintessential hippie in the 1980s British TV series *The Young Ones* – in 1984, once again reaching number 2.

Meanwhile, Traffic were recording their debut album in stops and starts from April to November 1967, interspersed with their live debut in Scandinavia. It's said they never played 'Hole in My Shoe' live, but Winwood's biographer contradicts that, claiming the band had no choice but to perform it, with an extended sitar opening by Mason, and rather muted, somewhat embarrassed accompaniment from the rest.

Following a triumphant gig at London's Saville Theatre, Traffic were invited to be part of The Beatles' *Magical Mystery Tour* movie. Footage was recorded of the band singing what was to be their next single 'Here We Go Round the Mulberry Bush', and doing silly pranks like pushing a globe downhill in the fields near their Berkshire cottage. But they were eventually cut out of the finished film – probably to their relief, considering the hammering it received.

Traffic released their first album *Mr. Fantasy* on 8 December (this author's birthday!), and it showed the band's schizophrenic nature. Anyone expecting something similar to the singles would've enjoyed Dave Mason's 'House for Everyone' – more nursery-rhyme-style lyrics set to a quirky, childlike little tune, with what sounds like the winding of a clock in the intro. It may be inspired by the band's communal countryside living, but this particular house is made of cheese, and 'my bed is made of candy floss'. There are shades of *Alice in*

*Wonderland* too – and perhaps a reference to Mason's imminent departure – in the lines, 'On the door of one was truth / On the other door was lies / Which one should I enter through? / I really must decide.' If the band hated 'Hole in My Shoe', they must've really despised 'House for Everyone'.

Mason also offered 'Utterly Simple', the only track on the UK album to use what by then had become the band's trademark sitar sound, set to an utterly simple waltz-time rhythm, repetitive melody, and a lengthy *sitar break* somewhat reminiscent of the one in the middle of George Harrison's 'Within You Without You'. Lyrically, it once again channels *Alice in Wonderland*, with some cod philosophy from a hermit dispensing wisdom in a cave. It doesn't sound like there are many of the other band members on it, so perhaps they found reasons not to be around while it was being recorded.

Finally, Mason's 'Hope I Never Find Me There' dials down the psychedelic element a bit, but still has those jabbing piano chords, phased vocals, treated guitar sounds and whimsical flute, while the writer sings such lines as 'The birds have flown / The sky's turned gray /The bees have ruffled by the flowers / Plastic plants that never die.'

The rest of the album is, well, mostly different: a mixture of light rock, R&B and jazz, dominated by Winwood's plaintive, bluesy voice. 'Heaven Is in Your Mind' is bright and catchy, with a double-speed chorus section and some nods to psychedelia in its ghostly harmonies, cries and yelps, and a long lead guitar outro. 'Berkshire Poppies' is probably the closest thing to Mason's songs that Capaldi, Winwood and Wood wrote – it even references a tramp with a hole in his shoe, with overstrung pub piano, a disorganised sing-along section, random spoken words and a kazoo. In fact, it's so obviously done, that one could be forgiven for suspecting a little bit of piss-taking here – Small Faces were recording their psychedelic hit 'Itchycoo Park' in the same studio and joined in with the general mayhem.

The album title comes from 'Dear Mr. Fantasy', a slow, bluesy rocker inspired by a Capaldi sketch showing a guitarist with puppet hands, along with the line 'Dear Mr. Fantasy, plays us a tune'. Was it a snide reference to guitarist Mason, his strings controlled by commercialism? Whatever it was, it was a simple repetitive three-chord song born out of a jam session – A, G and D, for those who care – with some spirited guitar work from Winwood: *not* from Mason, who played bass and harmonica.

Unusually, the song was recorded practically live instead of the musicians being in their own soundproofed booths, as was the usual practice. It also features producer Jimmy Miller on percussion. Engineer Eddie Kramer told writer Steve Jennings in 2003:

> We had the band set up on a riser at one end of the studio, which is a big room – maybe 65, 70 feet long by about 45 wide, with about a 30-foot ceiling. They were set up as if they were on stage, and I recorded them live straight to four-track ... We were in the middle of a take and there's a part where the tempo

> changes – it jumps – and I look around, and Jimmy Miller's not in the control room. The next thing I see out of the corner of my eye, is Jimmy hauling ass across the room, running full tilt. He jumps up on the riser, picks up a pair of maracas, and gets them to double the tempo! That, to me, was the most remarkable piece of production assistance I'd ever seen. They were shocked to see him out there, exhorting them to double the tempo. Their eyes kind of lit up. It was amazing. That was Jimmy!

*Mr. Fantasy* is completed by the gentle, dreamy ballad 'No Face, No Name and No Number'; the Spanish-influenced 'Dealer' (said to be about Chris Blackwell, although he didn't appear to notice); the jazzy 'Coloured Rain', and finally, a slightly altered version of the improvised jam that appeared on the B-side of 'Paper Sun'. US fans who bought the album when it was released in early 1968 – retitled *Heaven Is in Your Mind* – found two of Mason's three songs removed and replaced with the first two singles.

The album was generally well-received, with *Rolling Stone* calling it 'one of the best from any contemporary group'. But record-buyers were not so sure, sending the release to a disappointing number 16 – good for a debut from a new band, but not necessarily for one that was coming off the back of a number-2 hit and included the former lead singer of The Spencer Davis Group. In 1999, it was added to the Grammy Hall of Fame, and in lists of the best psychedelic rock albums of 1967, it hovers 'round about number 10 or 12.

The album suffers from that schizophrenic vision and the fact that by the time it was released, Dave Mason was already on his way out. He returned the following year for the second album, but, once again, his pop sensibilities clashed with the others' rock jams, and he was soon gone again, never to return.

Traffic showed that you had to be united in your vision to succeed as a psychedelic rock band. For a short period in 1967, their multicoloured flower bloomed. But they were never to achieve that level of commercial success again – without Mason, Winwood turned Traffic into the band he'd always wanted: one that refused to have anything to do with bubblegum pop.

# The Velvet Underground

Key personnel:
Lou Reed: vocals, lead guitar, ostrich guitar, sound effects
John Cale: electric violin, piano, bass
Sterling Morrison: guitar, bass, vocals
Maureen Tucker: drums, percussion
Nico: vocals

## History

In late 1964, New Yorker Lou Reed met Welshman John Cale when the latter was in the US studying classical music. They recruited Reed's college classmate Sterling Morrison, and Angus MacLise on percussion, forming a quartet that was eventually named The Velvet Underground, after a book about aberrant sexual behaviour. In 1965, MacLise was replaced by Maureen Tucker, who, unusually, played the drums standing up. They were introduced to Andy Warhol – a leading exponent of the pop art movement – who became their manager, secured them a recording contract with Verve, and suggested they use German-born singer Nico (alias Christa Päffgen), who had appeared in one of Warhol's films. They recorded their debut album in New York and Los Angeles in April 1966.

## Key releases in 1967

### The Velvet Underground & Nico (Album)

All songs by Lou Reed except as noted.
Label: Verve
Release date: 12 March 1967
Charts: US: 129; UK: 43 (In 1994)
Side 1: 1. 'Sunday Morning' (Lou Reed, John Cale) 2/ 'I'm Waiting for the Man' 3. 'Femme Fatale' 4.'Venus in Furs' 5. 'Run Run Run' 6. 'All Tomorrow's Parties'
Side 2: 1. 'Heroin' 2. 'There She Goes Again' 3. 'I'll Be Your Mirror' 4. 'The Black Angel's Death Song' (Reed, Cale) 5. 'European Son' (Reed, Cale, Sterling Morrison, Maureen Tucker)

The Velvet Underground were a strange band. They had a lead singer whose voice was more of a drone and who had tuned every string on his guitar to the same note. He wrote dark, hypnotic little songs about drug abuse, prostitution and sexual deviancy.

They had a classically-trained Welshman with a desire to mix rock and avant-garde, whose chief instrument was a viola fitted with metal guitar strings to get more volume. They had a female drummer – probably the only one in a major rock group at the time – who played standing up because she'd never been taught how to do it properly and didn't use cymbals. There was also a female singer who couldn't sing, and they had a bass player who hated playing bass.

Together, they produced one of the most disturbing and divisive albums of 1967 and one that was a total commercial flop – initial sales were something between 10,000 and 30,000. In fact, we wouldn't be discussing them here if it were not for the fact that hindsight and posterity have joined forces to declare that The Velvet Underground were one of the era's most influential groups. According to Brian Eno, not many people bought their debut album – but everyone who did started a band.

Were they even psychedelic? Well, they certainly weren't strangers to mind-altering substances – Lou Reed was heavily into heroin and amphetamines and helped introduce John Cale to his addiction by shooting him up for his first experience of smack. And their songs pulled no punches. Nobody wrote about drugs as openly as Reed: not just the *high* of taking them, but the grim, seedy business of buying and injecting them. They tick a lot of our other psychedelic boxes, particularly the ones about experimenting with song structure and content, and utilising the drones of raga rock. Stylistically, they are closer to the US West Coast psychedelia of acid-drenched guitars and dark, disturbing lyrical poetry, rather than the whimsical, nostalgic British brand.

But their debut, *The Velvet Underground & Nico*, is a difficult listen, particularly if you like your singers to be able to sing and the guitars to be in tune. There's an almost willfully anti-commercial approach that defies you to like this band, despite the fact that it was managed by one of the most commercially astute guys in the art business.

That was pop art legend Andy Warhol, who did the soup cans and Marilyn Monroe prints, and, in 1964, was looking to branch out into other forms of creativity, such as music – not to write it or play it, but to see if he could exploit it artistically and market it with the same level of success. The Velvet Underground appeared to be doing to music what he had done to art – flatten it, remove the elitism, make it about everyday things such as the Coca-Cola logo, dollar bills, sex and drugs: available and understandable to everyone whether they were a millionaire or trailer trash.

For the band, Warhol was, initially, a godsend. Nobody else was queuing up to sign them, and Reed had discovered early on in his career that his songs were considered too disturbing to be recorded. The band was a ship looking for a safe harbour, and Warhol was offering a very well-funded dock. But the deal came with a caveat. Warhol wasn't impressed with Reed's singing and insisted they use German-born model Christa Paffgen, who went by the stage name Nico. She had been introduced to the artist by Rolling Stones guitarist Brian Jones, and was working with Warhol on his experimental films. She actually had more recording experience than the rest of the band – she had released a single in 1965, produced by none other than Jimmy Page – despite being unable to sing in tune because she was deaf in one ear. She had a deep, gloomy, almost androgynous voice that fitted in perfectly with the generally seedy atmosphere of the songs Reed was writing.

As far as Warhol was concerned, The Velvet Underground were another artistic outlet – part of his mixed-media *happenings* that included film images being projected on the band members as they played. Initially called Andy Warhol, Up-Tight, the happenings toured the US in the spring of 1966, before heading back to New York as the hugely successful Erupting Plastic Inevitable, drawing several hundred people each night.

Then, in April that year, Warhol paid for the band to make a demo at Scepter Records' studio in New York, acting as producer in a vague, hands-off way, leaving most of the work to Norman Dolph. Lou Reed explained in a 1993 interview for German TV:

> The advantage of having Andy Warhol as a producer was, because he was Andy Warhol, they left everything in its pure state. They would say, 'Is that OK Mr Warhol?', and he would say, 'Uhhh...yeah…'. And so they didn't change anything. So right from the very beginning, we had the experience of what it was like to be in the studio and record things our way and have, essentially, total freedom. The record company never listened to the records in the first place, so they came out exactly like they'd been made.

John Cale added more in a 2017 *Rolling Stone* interview:

> He didn't say much, but he was there. That's usual with Andy. He'd say a few things, but they'd be effective at getting things done. Even when he was making his films, he didn't say much, but without him, they wouldn't have happened. But we were glad to have Andy because we thought he was somebody we could talk to, and what I mean by that is that we didn't say very much ourselves. We were pretty terse in our discussions of music. 'Just try this. Just try that.' That's about it.

In the same interview, Cale reveals that Warhol gave Reed a list of fourteen song titles and said, 'Now go away and write these songs' – reminding him to put in some dirty words. Cale added, 'It's very unorthodox and it worked perfectly'.

However, some of the tracks recorded for the demo pre-date Warhol's involvement with the band. 'Heroin' was one of the first songs Reed played to Cale when they met, and appeared on a 1965 rehearsal tape. Another early composition, 'Venus in Furs', was definitely around when the band chose its new name – the song is inspired by an 1870 novella written by Leopold von Sacher-Masoch, whose name gave rise to the term 'masochism'. 'I'm Waiting for the Man' was another drug song, but this one was about buying the stuff rather than using it, and the Velvets were playing 'The Black Angel's Death Song' at New York's Cafe Bizarre when Warhol first saw them. The disturbing monologue, referencing 'cut mouth bleeding razors' and 'the stools of your eyes', spoken to squealing viola accompaniment, was one of the reasons the club fired them soon after.

Other songs were more recent, written for Nico to sing, including 'Femme Fatale' and 'I'll Be Your Mirror'. The nine-track demo was completed with 'Run Run Run', another drug song, and 'European Son': little more than a guitar thrash with accompanying noises of scraping chairs and broken glass.

One other track was recorded at Scepter Studios that April: the musically accomplished but lyrically dubious 'There She Goes Again'. Borrowing heavily from a riff in Marvin Gaye's 1962 hit 'Hitch Hike', the song seems to encourage violence against women as it goads a man who thinks his girlfriend is having sex with his friends. 'Well, you'd better hit her', sings Reed, who himself had a reputation for misogyny and violence towards women. The track was left off the demo – a surprising decision given that it is one of the most professional recordings produced during the Scepter sessions, with all the instruments in tune!

Nobody seemed very impressed with the demo, and it was turned down by a string of record companies before MGM/Verve took the plunge, signing The Velvet Underground with a $3,000 advance on 2 May in Los Angeles. The label put the band back into a studio to redo three of the songs – 'Heroin', 'Venus in Furs' and 'I'm Waiting for the Man' – but producer Tom Wilson was still unhappy, believing there was too little Nico on the album.

Film director Paul Morrissey, who worked with Warhol, claimed MGM only signed the Velvets because of Nico. Quoted in Howard Sounes' book *Notes from the Velvet Underground: The Life and Music of Lou Reed*, he said Wilson told Reed, 'You've got to get another song for Nico. And there's nothing here we can use on the radio, so why don't you get Nico to sing another song that would be right for the radio?'

In response, Reed and Cale came up with the deliberately commercial 'Sunday Morning' – indeed, it was written in the early hours of a Sunday morning. But when it was recorded in November, Reed decided it was too good for Nico and sang it himself, with Cale playing a tinkling celesta he spotted in the studio. It was released as a single just a month later, but despite being the most commercial and least offensive song on the subsequent album, it failed to chart anywhere.

It was another three months before the album appeared, in March 1967. The absence of any urgency to release it, coupled with the lacklustre promotion of the singles ('All Tomorrow's Parties' was an optimistic debut in July 1966), strongly suggested MGM were regretting their association with the band. But this was more than just an album – it was an artistic event, thanks to the one part of it that interested Andy Warhol a lot.

Credited to The Velvet Underground & Nico, it's also known as the Banana Album due to the striking, quintessentially Warholian (if there is such a word) cover, which was stark white and sported a large stick-on banana with the instruction 'Peel slowly and see'. If you followed the instruction, you discovered... the inside of the banana coloured a suggestive pink. To hammer home the fact that this was an Andy Warhol creation, only *his* name was on the front cover – the band was relegated to the back. Today, pristine copies of the album, with the banana *peel* intact, sell for around $650.

What about the music? Well, if you were one of the 30,000 people who bought it (actually, it's sold about 600,000 copies to date), you discovered an album that was so shambolic and disturbing it could only have been created on drugs, and pretty hard ones at that. The opening track 'Sunday Morning' lulled listeners into a false sense of security with its dreamy pop sound and relatively polished production. But even this had a dark centre – the song is about paranoia, about someone always watching you – and Reed's hesitant, wobbly, almost monotone vocal added to a sense of subsurface unease.

He fares better on 'I'm Waiting on the Man', probably because he's talking rather than singing to stabbing piano chords. Delve into the lyrics and you find a story about the purchase of an illegal substance – the narrator has $26 in his hand, waiting for 'a dear, dear friend of mine' who takes him up three flights of stairs in a brownstone building where the deal is done – 'He's got the works, gives you sweet taste / Ah then you gotta split because you got no time to waste.'

'Femme Fatale' features the first lead vocal from Nico. It's a pretty ballad in a dreamy major-seventh, sporting a chord progression that's quite sophisticated for the Velvets – let down by the fact that the instruments involved are only barely in tune and suffer from serious sound defects. The lyric could've been about Nico herself – she and Reed had a sexual relationship that ended just before the recording session, and Lou was scathing about her and her singing, on one occasion reducing her to tears in the studio. But in fact, the title came from Warhol describing actress Edie Sedgwick, who had appeared in some of his short films.

'Venus in Furs' is an astonishing song: a ponderous medieval dirge, part British folk music, part Middle Eastern drug den, with Cale's electric viola sounding like a droning hurdy-gurdy. What a shame that, again, the instruments are barely in tune. In the song, Reed's Venus wears 'shiny, shiny, shiny boots of leather / Whiplash girl child in the dark' and wields a 'Tongue of thongs, the belt that does await you'.

'Run Run Run' is a more orthodox pop song. You could imagine the likes of Jefferson Airplane coming up with this, although they wouldn't have dreamed of being so lyrically explicit about their drug use. Here, Reed sings about various New York characters getting fixes in Union Square. It also sports a series of chaotic lead guitar breaks that defy normal blues convention, offering instead elements of eastern scales.

Side one ends with the first single – 'All Tomorrow's Parties' – in which Reed has used his 'ostrich tuning', with every string on D, to once again create a drone effect. There's also a prepared piano in here: paper clips were used to change the sound of the instrument's strings. Nico is lead singer, sounding very much like Reed, with her vocal single or double-tracked depending on which album release you have. It's completed by some fumbling lead guitar that sometimes hits a few dodgy notes.

'All Tomorrow's Parties' was one of Reed's early songs, dating back to 1965, but must've had rewritten lyrics, as they reference the crazy people who hung around Warhol's Factory. Cale later told *Uncut* magazine, 'The song was about a girl called Darryl: a beautiful petite blonde with three kids, two of whom were taken away from her'. There's a great song here somewhere, as Japan proved when they released it on their 1979 album *Quiet Life*.

'Heroin' opens side two, a surprisingly upbeat song for the subject matter, as Reed talks rather than sings about putting 'a spike into my vein, and I'll tell ya, things aren't quite the same'. Other lines are clearly drawn from personal experience of using the drug: about blood shooting up the dropper's neck; about how heroin is his life and wife and will be the death of him.

Every now and then, the song speeds up, almost as if mimicking the rush of a heroin injection. And the whole thing is virtually performed in just two repetitive chords: D flat and G flat. Cale talks about all Reed's songs being in D or G, so it could well be that the guitar was detuned or the recording has been slowed down a little. Towards the end, Cale adds viola squeals and the song crashes to a close after more than seven disturbing and relentless minutes. There's no bass here, and Maureen's drumming was intermittent and fairly random, as she couldn't really hear what was going on.

After 'There She Goes Again', detailed above, it's time for another Nico song. She was definitely the inspiration for 'I'll Be Your Mirror': it was a comment she made to Reed not long after they first met. It was also the most difficult song to get right. Bassist Sterling Morrison explains in Victor Bockris' book *Uptight: The Velvet Underground Story*:

> She kept singing 'I'll Be Your Mirror' in her strident voice. Dissatisfied, we kept making her do it over and over again until she broke down and burst into tears. At that point we said, 'Oh, try it just one more time and then fuck it – if it doesn't work this time, we're not going to do the song'. Nico sat down and did it exactly right.

Finally, the album closes with the random one-chord squealing of 'The Black Angel's Death Song' and the cacophonous guitar improvisation of 'European Son', which also features some fine bass playing from bass-hating Morrison.

*The Velvet Underground & Nico* was an album of threatening and daring music – mixing wild instrumental genius and utter incompetence – that sounded like nothing else in the record shops. Consequently, it was a massive flop, staggering to number 165 in the US, and failing to make an appearance anywhere else. Yet today, it's regarded as one of the greatest albums of 1967. It frequently appears in everyone's 'best of' lists and is number 13 in *Rolling Stone*'s top 500 – and is hailed by critics as prophetic and ahead of its time.

Certainly, you can hear a punk attitude festering here, a whole decade before punk itself took off; and you can see why Eno claimed it inspired so many teenage garage bands, because it showed you didn't need any particular musical skill or ability to make a record, so long as you had raw honesty and self-belief. When the likes of the Sex Pistols snarled at the world over a three-chord thrash, they were direct descendants of The Velvet Underground's uncompromising debut.

By the end of 1967, Nico had been forced out of the band and manager Warhol was fired. The Velvets spent just two days recording their follow-up *White Light/White Heat*: regarded as an equally influential album with its distorted sound, squealing feedback and a seventeen-minute jam around just three chords. Once again, Reed made sure the disturbing lyrics stayed in, as he sang about drugs, debauchery and failed lobotomies.

This was a band that couldn't possibly last; splits and fall-outs, as well as commercial obscurity, brought things to an end by 1972. But in their brief and tumultuous lifespan, the Velvets created a version of psychedelic rock that was raw and dangerous and helped change the face of popular music.

# Andmoreagain

Psychedelic rock would not have been what it was without some other bands and artists who deserve at least a passing mention in this tome. Here are a few more who served with distinction in 1967...

## Buffalo Springfield

Fate brought them together – Neil Young and Bruce Palmer were driving along Sunset Boulevard in a hearse when they saw Stephen Stills and Richie Furay going in the opposite direction. When they pulled over on the side of the road, they formed a psychedelic folk-rock band that had a major number-7 US hit in 'For What It's Worth (Stop, Hey What's That Sound)', about a riot on Sunset Strip. But they were already breaking up when they released their second album *Buffalo Springfield Again*: notable for Young's psychedelic, three-part classic 'Broken Arrow'.

## Scott McKenzie

As we have seen, there were several *anthems of the Summer of Love* in 1967, but none was as successful and ubiquitous as McKenzie's single 'San Francisco (Be Sure To Wear Some Flowers In Your Hair)'. Penned by John Phillips of The Mamas & The Papas, to promote the Monterey International Pop Festival, it was an instant hit, reaching number 4 in the US and number 1 in the UK and several other countries. Scott was a boyhood friend of Phillips, and the pair were in bands together during the 1960s, although, by 1967, MacKenzie was trying for a solo career. Unfortunately, he failed to capitalise on the success, taking far too long to release his solo album *The Voice of Scott McKenzie*, which consequently sank virtually without trace. Chronic stage fright also impeded his ability to promote himself, and he remained pretty much a one-hit-wonder.

## The Small Faces

Named because all four members were fairly short in stature, The Small Faces were a mod band who had a psychedelic hit in 1967 with 'Itchycoo Park', one of the first music recordings to use flanging on the vocals, creating a swirling, other-worldly effect. The single reached number three in the UK, number 16 in the US and number one in Canada and New Zealand. But their psychedelic peak was in the following year, 1968, with the release of the concept album *Ogden's Nut Gone Flake*. Later, they turned into normal-sized Faces with Rod Stewart and future Rolling Stone Ronnie Wood.

## Vanilla Fudge

Hailing from Long Island, New York, Vanilla Fudge's schtick was to create slow, organ-heavy versions of other people's songs. *AllMusic* described the tracks on their self-titled debut as all having 'a disjointed warm-up jam, a Hammond-heavy dirge of harmonized vocals at the centre, and a final flat-out jam'. The single 'You Keep Me Hangin' On' hit number 6 in the US. Subsequent releases failed to match that early success.

## 13th Floor Elevators

Formed in Austin, Texas, they were allegedly the first band to refer to themselves as psychedelic, using the word on their business cards and as part of the title of their debut album, which included sleeve notes encouraging the taking of LSD. Their 1967 album *Easter Everywhere* was dogged by band splits and sold poorly. They are better remembered for their influence on later bands.

## The Incredible String Band

Multi-instrumentalists Robin Williamson and Mike Heron mixed British folk with Indian music to create structurally complicated psychedelic compositions that were unlike anything anyone else was doing at the time. Their 1967 album *The 5000 Spirits of the Layers of the Onion* reached number 25 in the UK, and Paul McCartney named it his favourite album. But the ISB were probably a little too challenging for their times. Their commercial and critical peak came in 1968 with their third album *The Hangman's Beautiful Daughter*, but despite their influence on later bands such as Led Zeppelin, the ISB remained outliers for most of their career.

## Pearls Before Swine

A psychedelic folk band formed by later solo artist Tom Rapp, their 1967 debut album *One Nation Underground* has become an, appropriately, underground classic. A mixture of Donovan-style acoustic sweetness and organ-led stompers – with Rapp channelling Bob Dylan – the album is notable for its cover art of Hell from Heironymus Bosch's *Garden of Earthly Delights*, and a song that spells out the word 'Fuck' in Morse code.

## The Electric Prunes

An L.A.-based band, better known for their singles than the two albums they released in 1967. 'I Had Too Much to Dream Last Night' utilised an accidental buzzing effect and backwards guitar to channel the Rolling Stones in a dark, driving song that hit number 11 in the US. The follow-up 'Get Me to the World on Time' combined electronic sonic experiments with a Bo Diddley beat to slightly less commercially successful effect. Their self-named debut album was too full of standard pop songs to make much of a dent on the charts. The follow-up *Underground* was better but failed to contain a hit single, and by this time the band was falling apart.

## The Bonzo Dog Doo-Dah Band

The Bonzos sat squarely at the British end of psychedelia, with their jazz, vaudeville and comedy leanings. Their 1967 album *Gorilla* parodied a wide variety of musical styles, from badly-played jazz to the bubblegum pop of 'Piggy Bank Love'. Admirers included Paul McCartney, who put them into the *Magical Mystery Tour* film, and Eric Clapton, who played ukulele on *Gorilla*. They also made regular appearances on the British TV comedy series *Do Not Adjust Your Set*. Brief commercial success had to wait until 1968, when 'I'm The Urban Spaceman' – penned by multi-instrumentalist Neil Innes and featuring Vivian Stanshall blowing through a hosepipe – was produced by Apollo C. Vermouth: a pseudonym for McCartney.

## Kaleidoscope

But which Kaleidoscope, I hear you cry, because there were two: a US and a UK version. The American band was formed in L.A. but included members from Idaho, South Dakota and Oklahoma. With instruments such as banjo, resonator guitar, mandolin and dulcimer, there was a country feel to their debut album *Side Trips*, mixed up with Arabic scales, blues standards and jazz classics such as 'Minnie the Moocher'.

The UK version was a more pastoral, poppy affair with a basic instrumental setup of acoustic and electric guitars. Debut album *Tangerine Dream* was a loose concept album about 'happy people, sad people, lovely people and a few confused people', but failed to do much in the charts. Later they turned into Fairfield Parlour and had a minor hit with 'Bordeaux Rose'.

## Nirvana

No, not that Nirvana. This one was British, formed in London but featuring a trio including an Irish musician and a Greek composer. Debut long-player *The Story of Simon Simopath* was a concept album about the life and death of the titular character, pre-dating The Pretty Things' *SF Sorrow* and The Who's *Tommy*. *The Story of Simon Simopath* is typical UK psychedelia – twee, childlike, but with a charming simplicity, rather like a mixture of Donovan and The Kinks.

Nirvana tasted brief commercial success in 1968 with the single 'Rainbow Chaser' but broke up not long after. That didn't stop them from suing the other Nirvana, reaching an out-of-court settlement that allowed the US grungers to continue using the name.

## Big Brother and the Holding Company

Fronted by the powerhouse that was Janis Joplin, the band came from the same San Fran psychedelic scene that gave us Grateful Dead and Jefferson Airplane. They were the surprise hit of the Monterey International Pop Festival but failed to capitalise on it, releasing a debut album that was as weak as dishwater in comparison to those other bands. They had to wait until 1968 before producing *Cheap Thrills*: the psychedelic classic they should've released a year earlier.

## The Strawberry Alarm Clock

A great name, and great debut single – 'Incense and Peppermints' – which hit number one in the US for a California band created from the morphing of two groups: Thee Sixpence and Waterfyrde Traene. But their first album, also title *Incense and Peppermints*, failed to live up to the promise of the hit, and declining commercial fortunes led to the band's demise a few years later. The single was given a new lease of life when it was featured in the 1997 film *Austin Powers: International Man of Mystery*.

## Eric Burdon & The Animals

The Animals were part of the British invasion of the early 1960s but had an earthier, bluesier edge, as typified by their 1964 smash hit 'The House of the Rising Sun': a dark, moody interpretation of a folk song possibly dating back to the 16th century. When they broke up two years later, vocalist Burdon relocated to California and formed a psychedelic version of The Animals that had hits with 'San Franciscan Nights' and 'Monterey' (about the Monterey International Pop Festival). Album *Winds of Change* included the first-named single, a cover of The Rolling Stones' 'Paint It Black' and a response to Jimi Hendrix's album question *Are You Experienced?* (to which Burdon replied, 'Yes I Am Experienced'). However, the album and two subsequent releases failed to chart.

## The West Coast Pop Art Experimental Band

A California-born band that came across as a darker, more twisted version of The Byrds, veering uncomfortably from jangly pop and acoustic prettiness to disturbing sonic assaults such as a cover of Frank Zappa's 'Help, I'm a Rock' and the equally Zappa-ish 'Leiyla'. Of the two WCPAEB albums released in 1967, the second is the least compromising, with a harder-edged sound, disturbing, gloomy chords, and anti-Vietnam songs such as 'Suppose They Give a War and Nobody Comes', which ends with a crying baby.

## The Chambers Brothers

More psychedelic soul than rock, the four brothers came from a Baptist church background in Mississippi before relocating to Los Angeles. What makes them psychedelic for us is their eleven-minute 1967 hit 'Time Has Come Today' – edited down for single release – that coupled spaced-out fuzz guitar with vocal effects and cowbell, making a strange and hypnotic epic that sounds out of place on their more straightforward debut album of the same name.

## The Seeds

A California garage band that had modest singles success before embarking on its psychedelic 1967 album *Future*. With dark nursery rhymes, eastern influences and liberal use of orchestral strings and brass (particularly a tuba, for some reason), the album was criticised for being too much like The Beatles'

*Sgt. Pepper*, despite being recorded before *Pepper* was released. *Future* marked The Seeds' commercial peak and it was all downhill from there. But the album is remembered as a minor psychedelic classic.

## House for Everyone

You could be forgiven for thinking psychedelic rock was the preserve of UK and American musicians and failed to get a foothold elsewhere. But in this, you'd be mistaken because a number of other countries embraced psychedelia at the same time. The fact that they failed to make as much of a global impact was more down to the language barrier and sheer geographical distance than musical quality.

Most followed either the hard-edged or folky US version or were inspired by The Beatles, depending on their cultural ties or their proximity to the nearest American radio broadcast. Australia – where there was no language barrier, but an awful lot of miles between Melbourne and San Francisco or London – took the fab four to its heart, embracing Beatlemania when the band toured down under in 1964 (playing two dates in Adelaide with fellow Englishman Jimmie Nicol on drums, as Ringo Starr had tonsillitis). Aussie psychedelia originally owed much to the UK variety because many of the bands included British and European immigrants whose families back home kept them up to date with fashions and music.

For example, The Twilights were formed as a cover band in Adelaide in 1964 by Manchester's Terry Britten and Kent-born Glenn Shorrock, whose family had emigrated to Australia where his father got a job at a weapons research establishment. Two years later, they won a pop music competition in Melbourne, and first prize was a trip to the UK on a cruise liner. While there, they grew moustaches, bought Carnaby Street clothes, played at Liverpool's Cavern Club and recorded three songs at Abbey Road, including one The Hollies wrote especially for them, which hit the top ten back home. After they returned, they'd transformed into a psychedelic band, embracing eastern mysticism and filling their final 1967 single 'Cathy Come Home' with the exotic sound of the sitar. They also brought with them an acetate of the new Beatles album, and were so accomplished at recreating it live, EMI asked them to stop in case they damaged sales.

By 1967, the West Coast sound was also permeating through young Australians' transistor radios, and they started agitating for their own Summer of Love, sending Jefferson Airplane's otherwise moderately successful 'The Ballad of You and Me and Pooneil' to the top of the charts. Homegrown bands that embraced the psychedelic style included The Masters' Apprentices: whose August release 'Living in a Child's Dream' is regarded as one of the first Australian psychedelic rock songs. They even had an acid casualty in guitarist Mick Bower, who suffered a nervous breakdown after spending a gig standing motionless on stage with his hands hanging limp. They also played a free concert for 50,000 people in Sydney that degenerated into a riot.

The Wild Cherries started life in 1964 playing R&B and jazz, then turned psychedelic following a personnel shake-up, releasing four singles across 1967 and 1968 – beginning with the intriguingly titled 'Krome Plated Yabby' – that have been described by rock historian Ian McFarlane as 'exciting, revolutionary excursions into a musical void with no concessions to commercial demands ... All remain classic examples of hard guitar psychedelia.'

James Taylor Move – not to be confused with any other James Taylor you may have come across – were a short-lived band featuring future Sky guitarist Kevin Peek. They released two singles in 1967: one of them – 'And I Heard the Fire Sing' – proving to be too Hendrix-y for local Oz radio.

Moving north-west from Australia, we come to Cambodia: an unlikely spot, you may think, for psychedelic music to flourish. Thank the US forces for that, as they broadcast the current hit songs from bases in Vietnam, inspiring artists such as Ros Serey Sothea, who sang traditional ballads backed by rock instruments, including electric guitars and organ. Imagine, if you will, a higher-pitched Grace Slick with a Jefferson Airplane-style backing. Sothea had a hugely successful career until 1977, when she disappeared during the Khmer Rouge genocide. Her remains have never been found.

In South Korea – now known for producing boy bands playing catchy pop – guitarist and singer Shin Joong-hyun started the country's first rock band in 1962 and shot to fame in 1967 by covering Jefferson Airplane's 'Somebody To Love' on TV. He became a successful producer and songwriter, despite being briefly blacklisted, locked up in a psychiatric hospital and tortured for refusing to write a song about then-President Park Chung-Hee. Some of Shin's recordings are available on *Beautiful Rivers and Mountains: The Psychedelic Rock Sound of South Korea's Shin Joong Hyun 1958-74*, released by Light in the Attic records in 2011.

Latin America also embraced psychedelia. In Brazil, the movement was known as Tropicalia: a musical reaction to the repressive military junta that had seized the country a few years earlier. Bands such as Os Mutantes were heavily influenced by The Beatles – their debut album, recorded in 1967 but released the following year, is on *Mojo* magazine's list of the 50 Most Out-There Albums of All Time. At the time of writing, the band is still active.

In Chile, Los Mac's 1967 release *Kaleidoscope Men* owed an awful lot to *Sgt. Pepper* and The Byrds but is nevertheless a most appealing psychedelic album that kick-started the genre there. Staying in Latin America, Argentina joined in the psychedelic fun with bands such as Los Gatos, who had a huge hit with 'La Balsa', which became an anthem for the hippie underground. Their self-titled 1967 debut album shows a heavy Beatles influence mixed with Latin rhythms.

Heading to cooler climes, Swedish band Tages embraced psychedelic rock in 1966 from their third album *Extra Extra.* 1967's *Contrast* mixed Beatles and Beach Boys influences into catchy little psychedelic pop songs, with an orchestral *freak-out* on the mind-boggling 'You're Too Incomprehensible'. Their fifth and final album *Studio*, released in the same year, added traditional Swedish instruments, while the single 'She's Having a Baby Now' was banned by the BBC.

In the Netherlands, The Outsiders were a popular band whose 1967 self-titled debut album was half studio-recorded and half live, and showed some interesting experimental approaches. The short-lived Mother's Love drenched their pop songs with fuzz and wah-wah on their sole album *Take One*, but had more success after changing their name to The Dream.

Denmark's Steppeulvene were notable for releasing the first psychedelic rock album in the Danish language – 1967's *Hip* – that showed heavy blues and Bob Dylan influences. In Germany, psychedelia didn't really take off until a few years later, but we can give a mention to Soul Caravan, whose 1967 release *Get It High* contains the seeds of future Krautrock experiments.

Finally, let us end our whistle-stop psychedelic tour of the world in Canada, where the normally staid and sensible Canucks also embraced the genre. Standouts include the work of Mott Garson, an electronic music pioneer who was one of the first to use Moog synthesizers. His 1967 album *The Zodiacs: Cosmic Sounds* features twelve tracks – one for each sign of the zodiac – combining surprisingly catchy little space-age tunes featuring synths, guitars, drums, bass, and spoken-word poetry.

Meanwhile, The Paupers from Ontario appeared at the Monterey Pop Festival and were signed by Bob Dylan's manager Albert Grossman. They had a minor 1967 hit with the folky 'If I Call You by Some Name', then released an album of catchy, jangling pop songs – *Magic People* – that showed a definite Byrds influence. They had a particularly talented drummer in Ronald 'Skip' Prokop, whose work on the album is worth a listen.

## Love Is All You Need?

In many ways, 1967 was the calm before the storm. Yes, there were protests and upheavals, wars and atrocities in many parts of the world. But social unrest, particularly in the west, seemed to kick up a gear in 1968. Flower power wilted, the Summer of Love turned to hate, and the hippie dream died under a welter of blows from increasingly violent police forces. In 1967, we thought love was all you need. In 1968, it turned out love simply wasn't enough.

Some of our psychedelic heroes produced great albums in 1968, including Jimi Hendrix (*Electric Ladyland*), The Byrds (*The Notorious Byrd Brothers*), The Velvet Underground (*White Light/White Heat*), Grateful Dead (*Anthem of the Sun*) and Frank Zappa and the Mothers Of Invention (*We're Only in It for the Money*).

The Moody Blues' *In Search of the Lost Chord* featured tributes to Timothy Leary and chants of 'Ommmm'. And Cream's *Wheels of Fire* is undoubtedly their best moment, exploring both their psychedelic and live heavy blues sides. Meanwhile, Jefferson Airplane managed to combine the commercial sensibility of *Surrealistic Pillow* with the out-there waywardness of *After Bathing at Baxter's* to produce the excellent *Crown of Creation*.

Others found their psychedelic muse in full bloom in 1968 after tentatively dipping their toes in the water. Small Faces followed up their hit 1967 single 'Itchycoo Park' with *Ogden's Nut Gone Flake*: a cheerful psychedelic romp featuring the word-mangling of Stanley Unwin on a side-long fairytale. The Pretty Things – whose 1967 offering *Emotions* failed to set the world alight – released the *Tommy*-like concept album *SF Sorrow* in 1968, beating *Tommy* itself by six months. Country Joe and the Fish followed up their disappointing second album with the more together *Together*.

New psychedelic bands popped up to entertain us. Chief of these were The Nice, whose *Thoughts of Emerlist Davjack* blended rock, jazz and classical music but retained a pop sensibility. The Move's debut included bona fide psychedelic classics such as 'Flowers in the Rain' and 'Fire Brigade', while recycling Moby Grape's 'Hey Grandma'. Family's *Music in a Doll's House* contained complex arrangements and song structures, and, in Roger Chapman, a singer who sounded half man, half sheep.

Fairport Convention's debut was a trippy experience, although they swiftly embraced folk-rock and got high on real ale rather than acid. Iron Butterfly released two albums, including the classic *In-A-Gadda-Da-Vida*, and The Soft Machine's debut (imaginatively titled *Volume 1* on reissue) unveiled the left-field jazz-influenced sounds of the Canterbury scene.

Other bands withdrew from psychedelia and went back to basics. The Rolling Stones threw away their multicoloured kaftans and returned to the blues-rock sound that had served them so well in the past – and would continue to do so in the future – with the hit single 'Jumpin' Jack Flash' and album *Beggars Banquet*. The Beatles began falling apart in earnest but released a double album that, while containing plenty of psychedelic moments, was the stripped-back sound of four individuals doing their own thing. Later, they would try to get back even more.

Some groups had great difficulty repeating their 1967 successes. You have to wait until 1971's *Surf's Up* for a Beach Boys album that, frankly, isn't an embarrassment, while Pink Floyd toiled away pretty fruitlessly before hitting the jackpot with 1973's *Dark Side of the Moon*. Love never produced anything remotely as good as *Forever Changes*, and the less said about Moby Grape, the better. Traffic's self-titled follow-up sold better but led to yet another breakup as the band members fell out over musical differences.

As for psychedelic rock itself, it gave birth to a genre that relied less on drugs and more on musical proficiency and ambition. In progressive rock, songs got longer and their jazz and classical influences grew stronger. Prog became psychedelia's more intellectual, serious and pretentious brother – psychedelia wore multicoloured clothes and got high, while prog sat at home writing four-part side-long symphonies that could be performed on ice. But the aim was the same – to break musical boundaries, to mix up genres, structures and lyrical content into something new and surprising: and in that respect, psychedelia and prog are linked at the hip.

As the musical focus shifted to singer-songwriters from America's West Coast, to glam rock and heavy rock in the early 1970s, and to prog (until punk upended it all in 1977), psychedelic rock seemed to wither away or be consumed by more successful genres. But there are some modern bands who today would probably be proud to wear the psychedelic label, including The Flaming Lips, Tame Impala, Knifeworld, and the delightfully named King Gizzard & the Lizard Wizard.

What has changed in most genres of modern music is the political content – big business and commercial pressures have sucked the social anger out of mainstream rock. In 1967, music embodied the frustrations of the young, vocalised opposition to the Vietnam war, and explored the outer reaches of conscious – and sometimes barely conscious – thought.

Today, protest songs are almost exclusively the preserve of black artists, and the charts tend to be dominated by safe, bland singer-songwriters. But look beyond the charts, the mainstream radio stations and the TV talent shows, and you will find many artists and bands trying to expand the boundaries of music, just as they did back in 1967. Psychedelic rock didn't die; it just went underground – dig a little deeper and you will find it, alive and kicking.

## On Track series

Tori Amos – Lisa Torem 978-1-78952-142-9

Asia – Peter Braidis 978-1-78952-099-6

Barclay James Harvest – Keith and Monica Domone 978-1-78952-067-5

The Beatles – Andrew Wild 978-1-78952-009-5

The Beatles Solo 1969-1980 – Andrew Wild 978-1-78952-030-9

Blue Oyster Cult – Jacob Holm-Lupo 978-1-78952-007-1

Marc Bolan and T.Rex – Peter Gallagher 978-1-78952-124-5

Kate Bush – Bill Thomas 978-1-78952-097-2

Camel – Hamish Kuzminski 978-1-78952-040-8

Caravan – Andy Boot 978-1-78952-127-6

Cardiacs – Eric Benac 978-1-78952-131-3

Eric Clapton Solo – Andrew Wild 978-1-78952-141-2

The Clash – Nick Assirati 978-1-78952-077-4

Crosby, Stills and Nash – Andrew Wild 978-1-78952-039-2

The Damned – Morgan Brown 978-1-78952-136-8

Deep Purple and Rainbow 1968-79 – Steve Pilkington 978-1-78952-002-6

Dire Straits – Andrew Wild 978-1-78952-044-6

The Doors – Tony Thompson 978-1-78952-137-5

Dream Theater – Jordan Blum 978-1-78952-050-7

Elvis Costello and The Attractions – Georg Purvis 978-1-78952-129-0

Emerson Lake and Palmer – Mike Goode 978-1-78952-000-2

Fairport Convention – Kevan Furbank 978-1-78952-051-4

Peter Gabriel – Graeme Scarfe 978-1-78952-138-2

Genesis – Stuart MacFarlane 978-1-78952-005-7

Gentle Giant – Gary Steel 978-1-78952-058-3

Gong – Kevan Furbank 978-1-78952-082-8

Hawkwind – Duncan Harris 978-1-78952-052-1

Roy Harper – Opher Goodwin 978-1-78952-130-6

Iron Maiden – Steve Pilkington 978-1-78952-061-3

Jefferson Airplane – Richard Butterworth 978-1-78952-143-6

Jethro Tull – Jordan Blum 978-1-78952-016-3

Elton John in the 1970s – Peter Kearns 978-1-78952-034-7

The Incredible String Band – Tim Moon 978-1-78952-107-8

Iron Maiden – Steve Pilkington 978-1-78952-061-3

Judas Priest – John Tucker 978-1-78952-018-7

Kansas – Kevin Cummings 978-1-78952-057-6

Led Zeppelin – Steve Pilkington 978-1-78952-151-1

Level 42 – Matt Philips 978-1-78952-102-3

Aimee Mann – Jez Rowden 978-1-78952-036-1

Joni Mitchell – Peter Kearns 978-1-78952-081-1

The Moody Blues – Geoffrey Feakes 978-1-78952-042-2
Mike Oldfield – Ryan Yard 978-1-78952-060-6
Tom Petty – Richard James 978-1-78952-128-3
Porcupine Tree – Nick Holmes 978-1-78952-144-3
Queen – Andrew Wild 978-1-78952-003-3
Radiohead – William Allen 978-1-78952-149-8
Renaissance – David Detmer 978-1-78952-062-0
The Rolling Stones 1963-80 – Steve Pilkington 978-1-78952-017-0
The Smiths and Morrissey – Tommy Gunnarsson 978-1-78952-140-5
Steely Dan – Jez Rowden 978-1-78952-043-9
Steve Hackett – Geoffrey Feakes 978-1-78952-098-9
Thin Lizzy – Graeme Stroud 978-1-78952-064-4
Toto – Jacob Holm-Lupo 978-1-78952-019-4
U2 – Eoghan Lyng 978-1-78952-078-1
UFO – Richard James 978-1-78952-073-6
The Who – Geoffrey Feakes 978-1-78952-076-7
Roy Wood and the Move – James R Turner 978-1-78952-008-8
Van Der Graaf Generator – Dan Coffey 978-1-78952-031-6
Yes – Stephen Lambe 978-1-78952-001-9
Frank Zappa 1966 to 1979 – Eric Benac 978-1-78952-033-0
10CC – Peter Kearns 978-1-78952-054-5

## Decades Series

The Bee Gees in the 1960s – Andrew Mon Hughes et al 978-1-78952-148-1
Alice Cooper in the 1970s – Chris Sutton 978-1-78952-104-7
Curved Air in the 1970s – Laura Shenton 978-1-78952-069-9
Fleetwood Mac in the 1970s – Andrew Wild 978-1-78952-105-4
Focus in the 1970s – Stephen Lambe 978-1-78952-079-8
Genesis in the 1970s – Bill Thomas 978178952-146-7
Marillion in the 1980s – Nathaniel Webb 978-1-78952-065-1
Pink Floyd In The 1970s – Georg Purvis 978-1-78952-072-9
The Sweet in the 1970s – Darren Johnson 978-1-78952-139-9
Uriah Heep in the 1970s – Steve Pilkington 978-1-78952-103-0
Yes in the 1980s – Stephen Lambe with David Watkinson 978-1-78952-125-2

### On Screen series

Carry On… – Stephen Lambe 978-1-78952-004-0
David Cronenberg – Patrick Chapman 978-1-78952-071-2
Doctor Who: The David Tennant Years – Jamie Hailstone 978-1-78952-066-8
Monty Python – Steve Pilkington 978-1-78952-047-7
Seinfeld Seasons 1 to 5 – Stephen Lambe 978-1-78952-012-5

**Would you like to write for Sonicbond Publishing?**

We are mainly a music publisher, but we also occasionally publish in other genres including film and television. At Sonicbond Publishing we are always on the look-out for authors, particularly for our two main series, On Track and Decades.

Mixing fact with in depth analysis, the On Track series examines the entire recorded work of a particular musical artist or group. All genres are considered from easy listening and jazz to 60s soul to 90s pop, via rock and metal.

The Decades series singles out a particular decade in an artist or group's history and focuses on that decade in more detail than may be allowed in the On Track series.

While professional writing experience would, of course, be an advantage, the most important qualification is to have real enthusiasm and knowledge of your subject. First-time authors are welcomed, but the ability to write well in English is essential.

Sonicbond Publishing has distribution throughout Europe and North America, and all our books are also published in E-book form. Authors will be paid a royalty based on sales of their book. Further details about our books are available from www.sonicbondpublishing.com. To contact us, complete the contact form there or email info@sonicbondpublishing.co.uk